G000270775

Eddie Had A Dream
Written by Peter Bell

Cherry Chimes blogger
www.afcbchimes.blogspot.co.uk

ISBN: 9781694976239
First printed edition 2019.

ABOUT THE AUTHOR

Peter Bell, 52, is the author of Cherry Chimes. He has been an AFC Bournemouth supporter since the management days of David Webb.

He currently watches AFC Bournemouth from the North Stand with his two sons, Robert and Stephen. As an exile, Peter, and his sons travel down to Dean Court from Redhill, in Surrey, for as many games as they can, while also often attending away games as well.

Peter has also written for many of sports sections in the national newspapers and has appeared on national radio, expressing his views on AFC Bournemouth. You may also have heard him talk on the Bournemouth podcasts of All Departments and Back of the Net.

Peter attended Portchester Boys School between 1978-84 and went to Bournemouth Grammar School, Sixth Form, between 1984-86. He has a 2:1 BA Hons History degree from Leicester University and a Postgraduate Diploma in Journalism Studies from the University of Wales, College of Cardiff. Peter works as a Production and Commissioning

Editor for International Cement Review in Dorking, Surrey.

CONTENTS

DEDICATION

Following AFC Bournemouth – Everywhere we go!

I first started to think about writing this book in 2013. It was a few months after Eddie Howe and Jason Tindall, or JT (as everyone likes to call him) had returned to the south coast in their second managerial spell at AFC

Bournemouth. I had become a season ticket holder in the Family Stand, along with a few friends, that regularly went to Dean Court. I saw matches with Michael Dunne, who recently authored 'Dean Court Days', Damien Hill and Tim Aston. They have been a great source of encouragement over the years and have come to know my two sons, Robert and Stephen, as I have come to know their families. Football brings families together and gives us all a means of escape come the end of the week.

In a way, travelling down to Bournemouth for home games was my escape. It started as a way to give my wife, Helen, a break from two young children and a means for me to keep in contact with the town I grew up in. My best friend, where I live now, is Colin Waite who is a Plymouth Argyle fan. He was instrumental in getting me to go and watch Bournemouth again in 2008, when Eddie Howe was just starting out as a manager. I didn't know Eddie would become a managerial great, but something compelled me to go back, game after game. AFC Bournemouth was just as I had remembered, when I used to run down from our house in Gloucester Road, at first to see David Webb's Cherries and then Harry Redknapp's team. I never thought that AFC Bournemouth would find greater success with any manager after Harry Redknapp's years at the club. But we weren't done with the Championship and newspaper headlining cup wins over Manchester United in the 1980s, and even better victories were to follow in the Eddie Howe era.

Writing a book is a huge undertaking for anyone. I'd been approached by a publisher to consider writing a history of AFC Bournemouth in 2015, and for various reasons I had declined the offer at the time. I didn't initially have a start or an end point exactly for this book. I just knew I wanted to say something about how Eddie Howe had brought back my love of the game. I had to express myself in some way. That is when I started writing the Cherry Chimes blog. Writing a daily football blog on a club that is 110 miles from where I live was supposed to be a little hobby. But being an exile in Redhill, in Surrey, does strange things to you. The passion for you club doesn't diminish with those extra miles.

My former boss was a huge Burnley fan and used to ask me why I didn't want to go down to see Dean Court in the first few years after it had been rebuilt? I knew that once I started going again, I would find it hard to stop. Like everyone, I'd seen years of the club going from one financial nightmare to the next. It was never ending and dominated anything that ever happened on the pitch. How could a team be successful when they couldn't even be sure of playing from one week to the next? Like many I suppose, I'd decided that AFC Bournemouth was not a good investment of my time.

But something was different about Eddie Howe. He spoke extremely well. His passion and drive for the club was being grasped not only by the players, but everyone around the club. Bournemouth might have been playing in League Two, but it was more like the Premier League in the patterns of play we were watching on the field. I had my focus now. It was the Eddie Howe years that I most wanted to write about. We all have heroes and yet, here was a reluctant hero. If he didn't try and save the club in his first managerial appointment, AFC Bournemouth could have ended up in non-league or disappeared altogether. With the help of others, Eddie would turn it around and make it into the successful club that we know today. We now know that, 'Together, anything is possible'.

If I had a hero when I was younger though it was my dad. He bought me my first football, an orange one with black lines, on my fifth birthday. I'd kick it with him on Sunday afternoons, when the family would all go out into the New Forest. Sadly, I lost my father when I was only nine and kicking a ball lost much of its fun. Still, my mum, brothers and sisters were a constant source of comfort. Being adopted can perhaps make you even closer as a family

A sense of belonging is something I think we all need. I have a bigger family now, as I traced my birth family after Helen and I had our first child, Robert. Now I have two families. They all think I am madly obsessed with my football team, and of course they are right. I didn't mean it to happen. What I do know is that I am grateful for them letting me enjoy my passion, especially my wife Helen. When the Cherries lose, which is thankfully not that often, she has to deal not only with my disappointment, but also with Robert and Stephen's frustrations.

Although I have enjoyed blogging and writing Cherry Chimes, I never fully shook-off the temptation to write a book. Having read the books that have so far been published on AFC Bournemouth's rise up the leagues, I was surprised very little had been written about Eddie Howe's early years when he played for the Cherries and the period when Eddie and Jason managed at Burnley. I hope this helps fill in some of the gaps for some avid AFC Bournemouth and Burnley fans.

We haven't all been lucky enough to watch every game from the stands at Dean Court, but I've tried to picture every game that has taken AFC Bournemouth to the Premier League and the first four seasons at the summit of English football.

I have tried to be factually correct, but I am not perfect, so please accept my apologies for any errors. Writing an error-free book, in the football world, is far harder than I ever imagined.

Thank you for buying this book. As everyone deserves a good start in life, I have decided that 15 per cent of the author's proceeds will be donated to the charity of which Eddie Howe is patron – Julia's House.

JULIA'S HOUSE
CHILDREN'S HOSPICE

Julia's House Children's Hospice should be well known to AFC Bournemouth fans. Eddie Howe is patron of the charity, so fans do see the club getting involved in some charity activities and some match days are devoted to highlighting the work and fund raising for this and other local charities. The hospice looks after very sick children in the Dorset and Wiltshire area. Approximately 65 per cent of the work occurs out in the community as some children are too ill to travel.

I would not have known about Julia's House unless the football club had brought it to my attention. While I no longer live in Bournemouth or the nearby area, I wanted to give something back to the local community and the link with Eddie Howe made it a simple decision.

I want people to read this book and know that they have done something worthwhile in rediscovering the AFC Bournemouth story, or perhaps reading about it for the first time. It's a scary time when your family has ill health and particularly worrying when it is the younger members of that family that need help.

I am sure that whatever funds are raised for the charity from this book it will be put to very good use.

FOREWARD

I hadn't intended to write the foreword myself. While AFC Bournemouth have become a Premier League club they have to protect their name and their public image in a way that they perhaps didn't even comprehend when they were a League Two club. Approaches to the club are therefore not as simple as they may have once been, and to even ask managers and captains or chairman to pen a few words perhaps takes a little more friendship than I have been able to achieve.

Still, I can't say that AFC Bournemouth don't know about this publication. Neil Vacher, AFC Bournemouth's club secretary was kind enough to give me some tips on the early drafts. I have spoken with various people at the club, and I acknowledge their willingness to allow an unofficial publication on what has been a remarkable time for all fans of AFC Bournemouth. I am just one of many thousands of fans that have been rubbing my eyes at just what has been achieved, especially in this millennium.

I have been very lucky as a writer of a blog in this period to be recognised as a fan that national media have called upon for comments about how fans feel about the club and its results or players. I have been fortunate to appear on *TalkSport*, *SkySports News* and *BBC 5 Live* as well as write match verdicts for the Daily Mail and half-season and season reports for the *Guardian*, *Observer*, the *Daily Telegraph* and *The Times*. I have to pinch myself when I am shaking the hands of stars like Dean Saunders, interviewing Ted MacDougall, rubbing shoulders with Jim White of *Sky News*, or saying hello to football pundit Jermain Jenas or giving research notes to comedian Lee Nelson to prepare for an AFC Bournemouth end of season evening. Never did I expect that people would be quite so intent on listening to what an observer of our football club had witnessed, when details on the actual players and managers were perhaps not quite enough to quell their insatiable thirst for information on how AFC Bournemouth had risen up the leagues.

People want insights on every aspect of the game and opinions matter, be they from former players, current staff or the supporter who remains enthusiastic about their side even in the worst of circumstances. I was also searching for more information or comment about AFC Bournemouth when I started to write Cherry Chimes. It's not that the club doesn't do a great job with its website to keep fans informed, but as an exile I don't often get the opportunity to meet in a pub with fans to talk about the last game. You have to do the miles on the road as an exile, so listening to post match views on *BBC Radio Solent* becomes a fabulous source of ideas for my weekly blog stories. A big thanks to Willo and Kris Temple! I loved appearing on the All Departments' podcast to have a chat about games, and yet writing has always been my preferred way of getting my feelings and thoughts out to people.

Cherry Chimes is much like a diary for me. I sometimes think what am I going to write about today, but I seem to always find something that has happened at the club that is perhaps not clear and has all fans thinking what might be going on. Exploring that side of the game is where I have found a niche with Cherry Chimes. People don't have to agree with me and it's often more entertaining when they don't. The important part is that it gets fans thinking and talking about who they believe has had a good game, who AFC Bournemouth should sign and what they love or dislike about a player or what should be done to change the club's form?

Time moves on very quickly. I can remember how nervous I was when going on to social media and launching Cherry Chimes. Not many people would know me then which was an advantage. But when they read the blog they would soon form an opinion good or bad about what I had to say and that was scary at first. I am not an extrovert or particularly noisy about expressing opinions, so for me to write a blog about AFC Bournemouth was more of an escape to get out some frustrations and to get other peoples' thoughts back on what they thought about the latest drama at AFC Bournemouth. During the chairmanship of Eddie Mitchell there were plenty of moments when the excitement just couldn't get any better. Controversy and strong characters are great hooks for all writers and journalists.

Now we have reached a point where AFC Bournemouth have become an established Premier League club and it is time to reflect on how the job was done. There will be another period when the next stage in the development takes over and the birth of the new training ground at the former Canford Magna Golf Club will probably be the start of that new chapter. Who knows what will follow, 'hopefully a new stadium,' I hear many of you cry, perhaps European football and cup success? For there are always targets to set and new objectives to strive for. But even if the future does not include Eddie Howe and Jason Tindall, it is important to state already that these men and their staff have put the Cherries on the path to a better future. As a football fan it has been amazing to see, and I feel extremely lucky that Eddie's dream happened in a period when I took my seat at Dean Court.

This is me with my favourite player - Junior Stanislas

My good friend and All Departments podcaster,
Michael Dunne and Ellis, one of his sons, in the Family Stand

Another of my friends, Damien Hill is triumphant having out-smarted Tranmere's inflatable security system as AFC Bournemouth win promotion to the Championship. Beach balls 1-0 Tranmere Rovers!

1. OUR SPECIAL ONE

Eddie signs autographs by the dugout at Dean Court

I have always been in awe of what men like Eddie Howe do. They not only have their own families and personal fears, but they put themselves on a platform to be judged every time their teams go out to play. Eddie Howe has not only touched the lives of people who love football on the south coast, but people all over the world. But how well do we really know the man? How close do we get to managers as fans? How much of his success is influenced by a manager's experiences as a player and the colleagues he has around him?

What Eddie has achieved in such a short period of time is simply amazing. But what has helped him along the way? Has he made mistakes, and if so, has he a natural talent for not making the same mistakes again? I wanted to know how Eddie Howe has won games and to trace his early football career. To look through the history and difficulties and experiences Eddie had as a player to see how it shaped his outlook on football. While asking Eddie Howe to explain all he could about the game would be the easy way to do things, he has a much bigger job to run a Premier League club and I have no wish to be another person who deflects him from the great job he is doing. So much of the words and Eddie's commentary have come from past newspaper reports and match programmes.

This book is more of a documentation of the Eddie Howe years than a face to face biography of his life. But I hope it throws up some discussion on why AFC Bournemouth has achieved what many football teams find so hard to do – how to win?

As a Bournemouth fan, I have lived through some of the highs and lows of the Cherries recent years. Harry Redknapp years as manager (1983-92) had been fantastic. To eclipse that has been incredible. There is a motto at the club which has now become enshrined in the Eddie Howe years that reads: 'Together, anything is possible.' It is a belief that reminds fans that there have been hard times, desperate times and even times when there seemed no hope of football having a future in Kings Park. Indeed, if Jeff Mostyn had decided to shake his head one morning in April 2008 and had not written another sizeable cheque, there would have been no football club to talk about – it came that close!

However, the worries of this perennial second and third tier professional English league football club were about to be not only saved, but transformed by one of their very own. It may seem corny to opposing fans when AFC Bournemouth fans cry - 'Eddie, Eddie give us a wave!' However, there is a genuine bond between the fans and the man who is undoubtedly the club's favourite son.

I want to try and tell you what it is like to be an AFC Bournemouth fan. You have to understand that it is the only football league club in Dorset. It has been dwarfed by the somewhat more successful Southampton FC, some 30 odd miles up the road. Something was needed to ignite this sleepy seaside town when it came to football. But how do we measure success? Is it surviving, when the odds are stacked against a club? That would have been good enough for those supporters that queued up with buckets at the Winter Gardens to save their club in its darkest days. Yet, even then some good would come out of the situation. Friendships were made, people dug deep for a shared goal. Fans refused to give in. AFC Bournemouth was the first community run club and, having been saved several times, we wondered – was there more to football than this? When something is saved, someone has to make the most of what is left.

The good work of many would not go to waste. With Eddie Howe you could say the club landed on its feet. He was a talented player who pushed himself to be the best he could. But when his knee injury cut-short his playing days at 29, it didn't prevent him from trying to achieve more as a coach. It may just have been fate that enabled AFC Bournemouth to bring him back to Dean Court, not once, but twice as a player and a manager. But nobody could have known that Eddie Howe would take the Cherries to the Premier League.

Eddie is the first to say that the events since 31 December 2008 have as much to do with other people, not always seen, who were there for him. It is true that a number of factors have conspired to bring unprecedented success to the red and black shirts. Players have come and gone, along with two other managers and a chairman or two, while wealthy foreign-ownership has steered the club to financial stability and provided a platform for growth.

The transformation has been remarkable in such a short space of time. Who would have thought that the likes of Real Madrid, Napoli, Olympic Marseilles and Valencia would ever grace Dean Court's silky green turf? As the club has risen through the divisions, there has been a lovely sense of the fans almost asking to be pinched, just to make sure it hasn't all just been a dream. The purpose-built training grounds, an enlarged club shop, a tarmacked car park, the Pavilion, and just having four stands around the ground, have demonstrated that hard fixtures and fittings have also flourished.

So why was there a new beginning at AFC Bournemouth? I'd like to say a bit of good fortune and a certain lad from Amersham, who rather fancied his hand at being a coach. But at 31, Eddie Howe wasn't even sure he wanted to be a manger. 'I didn't feel ready. I genuinely didn't think I was the right man,' said Eddie Howe.

But it would be Eddie Howe that would not only save the club but lead it to the Premier League in 2014-15, after more than 100 years of the club trying to climb the football pyramid. His right hand-man, Jason Tindall, AFC Bournemouth's assistant manager, has shared the experiences with Eddie. The two men were not the biggest of pals when they were playing, but as a management team they have broken all records. What's more they are continually passing on their knowledge to the new generation of players. Eddie Howe has also made sure Dean Court is not just a place of hard work, but also a place to have fun and build friendships. There is almost a conveyor belt of ex-players now that learn and teach the Bournemouth-way of playing. That is part of what a family club is all about. Bournemouth is family from the top to the bottom – a place to learn and improve.

There are some other important characters who perhaps jolted the club's uneasy existence by challenging the fans and the club to do things better. Some were outspoken, like ex-chairman Eddie Mitchell. Some had a good-humoured influence, like current chairman Jeff Mostyn, while we had players who would run through brick walls for the young Amersham manager, like club record appearance holder Steve Fletcher. Even the reclusive owner, Maxim Demin, came along at the right time to give the club the cash injection to steer it into the Championship and closer to the teams that had once dominated English football. Famous clubs like Leeds United, Nottingham Forests and Wolverhampton Wanderers, who were sitting waiting in the Championship and whose fans expected to stop clubs like AFC Bournemouth from going any higher. Yet in a period of about a decade, the Cherries went from relative hangers on of the 92 clubs to a ninth-placed finish in the top flight.

There is no doubt in my mind that the majority of AFC Bournemouth supporters are well aware success could not have been achieved without the extraordinary dedication of Eddie Howe and his love for the football club.

Around the world today, in living room, bars and family homes, there are far more than the 11,000 who regularly take a seat at Dean Court to see the Cherries play. Many wondered what the club was doing when they appointed a man with no first team managerial experience to be Bournemouth's manager on New Year's Eve in 2008. I was certainly one of those who were surprised. But AFC Bournemouth just got it right when they offered Eddie Howe the opportunity to teach the Cherries how to win.

2. EARLY PLAYING YEARS

Born on 29 November 1977, Edward John Frank Howe was one of five children. While Chesham was home for Eddie's early school years, he would be attracted to the playing style of nearby Watford as a school lad and the managerial inspiration of Graham Taylor, who would take Watford on a journey through the divisions, much like Eddie would do many years later at Bournemouth. Eddie has fond memories of watching games in the early period of his life. 'Watford is a special ground for me because it was the first professional stadium I went to as a child,' Howe said. 'I was brought up in Chesham and watched the great side of the 1980s, including players like John Barnes.'

Later on, it was Everton who Eddie felt a passion for, due mainly to the way they played against Watford in the FA Cup final of 1984. 'I was born and raised in Watford, so they were my local team until 10 or 11 when I moved. But Everton were the successful team,' remembers Howe. 'One of the very first games I remember watching was the Cup Final when Everton beat Watford in 1984 and it left a huge impression on me. From that moment on I was a real diehard Everton fan. I used to travel and watch the games in London and Southampton and turned into a big fan. I still look out for their results.'

While blue shirts registered more with Eddie than the red and black of the Cherries at that time, Eddie joined the school of excellence at Bournemouth from the age of 11 with his family having moved south. If Eddie wasn't playing sport he was listening to music. Growing up in the 1980s Eddie loved the Scandinavian sounds of pop group A-Ha. While A-Ha have a host of top hits, Eddie's favourite song is a less well-known album track called 'Summer's moved on', which was released much later in the year 2000, after the group had not released a single for six years. No doubt Eddie has fond memories of many holidays spent on the beaches in the summer months. Steve Fletcher believes Eddie is the missing member of the group: 'Eddie Howe, he loves A-Ha! Yeah, he went to see them in concert in Bournemouth the other year and he's obsessed with them, so there you go.'

Much has been written about Eddie's strong bond with his mother Annie, and his admiration for her in the time she gave up to ensure her children reached their aspirations. Eddie's younger brother, Steve Lovell, who also became a professional footballer, would practise with Eddie and their mum in the park and their upbringing in Verwood certainly gave Eddie a love for the New Forest area.

As a promising cricket player, and encouraged to play that game by his grandad, it wasn't certain that Eddie would work his way into football, but he certainly enjoyed playing sport – whether it was snooker, football or cricket. He considered himself an allrounder until football took over. While Dorset had called him up to play cricket, Eddie decided at around the age of 14 that football had to come first.

Eddie left school when he was 16. Most of his youth football was played at Rossgarth FC Youth, Phoenix Sports and Parley Sports from where he eventually signed for AFC Bournemouth in 1994. He was released by Bournemouth at 16 and had begun his A-levels when the club changed their minds and offered him their last Youth Training Scheme place. Eddie talked about his first pre-season training that year, under AFC Bournemouth's then manager Tony Pulis, as one of his steepest learning curves. 'I'd never experienced anything like that but it toughened me up,' said Eddie.

Indeed, hard work is something that Eddie is well known for. I have heard countless tales from players that the manager is usually the last off the training ground and the first into work and more often than not, the very last to leave.

Some of that pride in his work may well go back to his youth and his desire to please his mum who worked all hours in several jobs, including running a newspaper shop. Eddie certainly began to make sure he learned from his life experiences. Whether he was always as confident as he seems today is perhaps a bit more doubtful. Ex-AFC Bournemouth defender and *BBC Radio's Solent* match commentator for the Cherries, John Williams (Willo) commented on how he remembers Eddie's first day in the AFC Bournemouth academy and that he was 'as quiet as a mouse'. Not quite what you might expect from a future centre-half that today looks so at ease in front of a camera after a hard-fought Premier League match.

Asked about his thoughts by *TalkSport* on Dean Court Stadium as it was in 1994, Eddie Howe has fond memories. 'I loved it – it was run down, not a great place visually on the eye. Everywhere was broken, dirty, but I really loved it as a player. I loved playing here. The opponents didn't like coming here so you really got an advantage from the surroundings that they faced,' explained Howe.

Tony Pulis had taken over the manager's job at AFC Bournemouth in 1992, when Harry Redknapp had moved to join West Ham United. Eddie Howe was a trainee at the club from 1994, at the end of Pulis' two-year managerial spell that had seen the Cherries reach 17th in League Three. The ethic of hard work might have rubbed off on Eddie Howe, but Tony Pulis' style of play was not how AFC Bournemouth fans would see the club reborn under

Howe's successful period as manager many years later.

Tony Pulis saw something in Eddie Howe, because he took him on and gave him his chance to join the academy and start his AFC Bournemouth career. Later, Pulis even tried to sign Eddie when he became manager of Gillingham. Eddie Howe was to play more than 300 games in two spells as an AFC Bournemouth player. Dean Court really is his home and his managerial career would later etch his name in legendary status at BH7 7AF.

However, there were lots for this young footballer to enjoy before his coaching days. In Eddie's first playing spell at AFC Bournemouth, he would make 201 appearances between 1994-2002. His first team debut was handed to him by Mel Machin, who called on the 18-year-old defender in a home match against Hull City in League Two on 23 December 1995. To say that it came as a surprise to Eddie was an understatement. 'I could not believe it when the manager read out the team on Saturday and my name was in it – I was in total shock,' Howe said. 'I didn't even think I would be on the bench, so it came as a big surprise when I was in the starting line-up.'

Of course, Howe grabbed the headlines in the *Bournemouth Echo* with a splendid debut. 'Howe about that?' read the headline for the match report, as AFC Bournemouth secured a 2-0 victory. It must have been a pretty good Christmas present for the young man. Howe made three more consecutive starts that season, as well as appearing in the 1-1 draw against Hull City in the return match that March. It was the first of five first-team appearances Eddie made that season.

Reflecting on these playing years, Eddie Howe is modest about his own level of skill. 'I was 100 per cent all effort. I would say I was limited in terms of my physical attributes, I mean I was small for a centre-back at 5ft 11ins and that was always a challenge for me. I'd probably been suited at playing at a higher level more than at a lower level, playing against a target man. The lower leagues were difficult for me. I really survived on attitude and endeavour,' said Howe.

'I absolutely loved the challenge of going up against people and trying to become better than them, trying to win a contract and a place in the team when you are fighting against your peers – I loved that competitiveness of the sport,' remarked Howe. 'I felt defeat very, very hard. I really took the burden of defeat and it didn't matter that I was a new member of the team at 18 or 19, it would be tragedy in my life for that moment. If I made a mistake and it cost us a goal being a defender I didn't want to see anybody, I'd be embarrassed and would have felt like I let the team down,' Howe said.

'I was constantly working in training to avoid that feeling.'

The 1996-97 season brought a few more chances for Eddie to play in League Two. Having broken through to the first team, he managed to get up to 13 appearances. Early appearances came in October before he had a strong run in the team in the closing months of April and May. Bournemouth were to finish 16th in League Two which, by usual standards, was not a bad season. More importantly, the town still had a club. This was a truly worrying time. The funds had run out. Fans met up at the Winter Gardens to put their tenners, fivers or whatever they had in the way of change into the buckets to save the club. Over 2000 fans crammed into the Winter Gardens on 25 January 1997 to try and help rescue the club financially. The club was insolvent and yet the Football League allowed them to play on, having seen the support and efforts the club were making to pay off their debts of some £4.4m.

Trevor Watkins, former club chairman, was the man leading the calls to keep the club afloat. The outcome was the first ever community-owned club. The first signing that was made the following summer was for Jason Tindall, from Charlton Athletic.

Things changed dramatically in 1997-98 when Eddie
Howe became a regular fixture in the Cherries first
team line up as a centre-back making 40
appearances. He helped the team to a ninth-place
finish. Howe also won the Micky Cave/*Bournemouth
Echo* player of the year award and earned himself a
place in the England U21 squad for the Toulon
Tournament in France. Many future full England
international players featured in the squad, such as
Frank Lampard, Emile Heskey and Jamie Carragher
playing under the management of Peter Taylor.
Eddie was a sub and came on in the first match
against South Africa in a 3-1 win and started the
second game against Argentina, when the team lost
2-0. Eddie was subbed on 64 minutes in that game.

The league season began well with a 2-0 away
win over Northampton Town, Jamie Vincent and
Steve Fletcher had hit the ground running with a
couple of goals. Following a 1-0 deficit in the League
Cup to Torquay the Cherries went on to get their
second league win against Wigan Athletic 1-0.

The Cherries bowed out of the League Cup having
lost to Torquay on 2-1 aggregate, after a 1-1 draw in
the away leg. The home form continued well enough
with a 2-0 win against Blackpool, but fans had to
wait until October before the next home win against
Fulham.

On 25 October 1997, Bournemouth played

Burnley at Turf Moor and Eddie Howe scored his first professional goal. It was in front of a crowd of 9501 and helped achieve a 2-2 draw. Home wins against Southend and Carlisle United in November kept momentum going, as well as a 3-0 win over Heybridge Swifts in the FA Cup. Steve Jones who had joined from Charlton, on loan, gave Bournemouth more of a cutting edge up front, and he scored for three games in a row at the end of the year and in early January. The run started with a 4-0 win over Gillingham on Boxing Day, when Jones scored twice and he netted in a high-scoring 3-5 win at Bristol Rovers, before contributing another strike in the 3-0 win over Northampton on 10 January.

Bournemouth had also progressed in the FA Cup beating Bristol City 3-1 in early December. The third round brought them up against Huddersfield, who knocked the Cherries out 0-1. The Auto Windscreens Shield was another chance to experience cup games and Bournemouth put the FA Cup defeat behind them by beating Leyton Orient 2-0 to take on Bristol City in the next round. The league form similarly picked up with just one defeat in an away match to Blackpool in January 1998.

February's fixtures brought further wins against Bristol City and Chesterfield before another narrow 1-0 win over Luton in the Auto Windscreens Shield. Defeats began to hit the Cherries as the prospect of winning the shield grew. Beaten by Grimsby,

Preston, Brentford and Wrexham, before the Auto Windscreen Shield Southern Area Final with Walsall, the team needed some inspiration. Luckily, Bournemouth went 0-2 up in the first leg in March. They soon found themselves in difficulties though in the second leg at home, when Walsall pegged back the score in the second half to make it 2-2 overall. While an own-goal restored Bournemouth's advantage, Walsall scored again to make it 1-3 on the night (3-3 on aggregate), before Mark Stein's cross was met by Franck Rolling who put the Cherries into the final (4-3 on aggregate)!

1998 was certainly a special year for the club. Reaching the final of the Auto-Windscreens Shield Trophy Final at Wembley on 19 April. It was a game in which Eddie played alongside Ian Cox and was booked – he won't thank me for reminding you of that! On the way to the final the Cherries had beaten Leyton Orient, Bristol City, Luton and Walsall, but when they reached the final they had to take on a team that had already beaten them twice in the league. There were 62,432 fans attending the final which no doubt helped revenues at the time. John Bailey scored first on half-an-hour for the Cherries and everything seemed to be going well, but Jimmy Glass soon had rather too much to do in Bournemouth's goal. Kingsley Black and Wayne Burnett were instrumental in wrecking AFC Bournemouth fan's hearts when Grimsby ran out 2-1 winners, scoring an equaliser on 75 minutes and a golden goal winner in extra-time. Even then, the Cherries had problems in defending from corners!

The teams that day were as follows:

CHERRIES: Glass, Young, Vincent, Howe, Cox, Bailey, Beardsmore (O'Neil), Robinson, Stein, Fletcher, Warren (Brissett). Subs not used: Rolling

MARINERS: Davison, McDermott, Gallimore (Black), Handyside, Lever, Burnett, Donovan, Smith, Nogan (Jobling), Clare (Livingstone), Groves.

Some Bournemouth fans might recall that the Mariner's captain was Paul Groves who was to have a reunion with the Cherries a few years later as Development Squad coach and then first team manager, which did not go as well. AFC Bournemouth were to get their revenge before then though, when they faced Grimsby in probably the most famous match in the Cherries' history – on 25 April 2009. It is a date that will never be forgotten by Bournemouth fans. But more on that later.

Under Mel Machin, Eddie was also involved in the League Cup games that saw the Cherries reach the third round in both 1998 and 1999. Eddie scored against Colchester United in a 2-0 win at home in the League Cup in August 1998. The team went on to beat Wolves over two legs, before losing out to

Barnsley in the third round. In 1998, Bournemouth had to settle for a ninth-place finish in League Two. The Cherries had certainly got some value for money with Mark Stein though. He scored in the last two matches away at Watford and in the 2-1 win against Millwall to give hope for the following season.

League Two was an even more exciting affair in 1998-99. Bournemouth signed Mark Stein permanently from Chelsea on a free transfer. He netted 15 league goals in 43 appearances for the Cherries as well as seven cup goals. He was partnered by AFC Bournemouth legend, Steve Fletcher, who had a good season notching up eight league goals and three cup goals. Sorry, Fletch! It was fewer goals, but I bet there were one or two screamers! Another strong performer was Steve Robinson who powered his way to 13 league goals. In goal was Mark Ovendale, a £32,000 signing from Barry Town. Karl Broadhurst would also sign from Portsmouth to form a new centre-back pairing with Eddie Howe, while Richard Hughes was also brought in from Arsenal. Bournemouth even went continental in signing attacking midfielder Claus Beck Jörgensen from AC Horsens.

Eddie recalls what it was like starting out as a player in the early years. 'If you had a bad game you got shouted at. You got told how it was and that was a stereo type that you then expected. You made a mistake, you expected a reaction,' said Eddie. 'You would expect some repercussions and that was the way it as probably until I was working with Sean O'Driscoll (in 2000). So, he was the first coach who didn't necessarily shout and scream at you when you made a mistake. He looked at things totally differently and that was a real eye opener for me. That was the first time I thought, it doesn't have to be that way.'

The season began brightly with a 2-0 win over Lincoln City and a 1-2 away victory over Notts County. Bournemouth were just as successful in the League Cup, after a 2-0 away win in the first league against Colchester United, which included a goal from Eddie Howe. The second leg saw United win 3-2 at home, but Bournemouth had done enough to get through on aggregate.

A crowd of 6956 enjoyed a 3-0 thumping of Millwall in the August sunshine as the Cherries kept their winning start going in the league. Draws against Fulham and Blackpool were followed by a 2-0 loss to Stoke City and a 1-2 away loss to Man City. September's matches saw the Cherries consolidate their promotion position in the league with a 1-0 win over Wigan and a 0-2 away win over Wycombe Wanderers.

The second round of the League Cup had drawn

Bournemouth against Wolves and the two-legged affair started with a 1-1 draw at Dean Court, before Mark Steins' goals saw Bournemouth through to the third round after a 1-2 away win.

After a 2-0 home win over Oldham Athletic in September, the Cherries did not win a game in October and went out of the League Cup to Barnsley. Better fortunes followed in the FA Cup overcoming Basingstoke 2-1 in the first round and a 1-0 away win against Torquay in early December. This had followed a morale boosting 5-0 win over Burnley in the league in mid-November.

It set the club up for a much more productive December, when the Auto Windscreen Shield competition began again with Reading the visitors. Bournemouth progressed 2-0. But it was the league run that grabbed the attention. York City, Wrexham, Millwall and Luton all fell victim on the Cherries' unbeaten run. Eddie Howe's goal in the 1-0 home win over WBA, in the FA Cup, kept the momentum up, before a 2-1 loss to Lincoln City, at the start of the New Year, was soon rectified by a 2-0 victory over Notts County.

The FA Cup in January drew Bournemouth away at Barnsley, where Mel Machin had been a previous manager for three-and-a-half years. Bournemouth were behind after 14 minutes when John Bailey cleared a Don Goodman shot off the line, only for Sheridan to tuck the ball home after good work from

Craig Hignett. Eddie Howe got another FA Cup goal, when he capitalised on a corner routine with Neil Young's shot breaking to Howe to score from some 14-yards out on 51 minutes. Barnsley retook the lead when Jamie Vincent and Mark Overdale didn't deal with a cross and Hignett picked up the pieces to score. The game was wrapped up when Martin Bullock made it 3-1 two minutes from the end.

Preston North End were the next team to Dean Court. The Cherries put their FA Cup disappointments behind them and took all the points with a 3-1 home win, with Howe again on the score sheet. A 2-2 draw with Luton Town ended the month satisfactorily.

The Auto-Windscreens Shield success of the previous year could not be repeated with the Cherries losing out to Millwall, having been held 1-1 in the 90 minutes, before losing 3-4 on penalties.

A big 4-0 win over Stoke City, in early February, had fans hoping for a strong run in the league again. But a draw with Man City and 2-1 defeat at Wigan soon had it feeling like a long season.

Still, home form was holding up after wins against Wycombe Wanderers and Bristol Rovers, where Howe scored the only goal of the game. The 0-1 defeat to Reading in the middle of March was the first home defeat in the league. The away games in March had brought wins at Oldham and Preston

North End and a draw at Blackpool, but the season unravelled in April.

While home form had returned at the end of March with a 2-1 win over Colchester United and Macclesfield had fallen to a single Mark Stein goal in early April, the Cherries didn't win another home game. An away defeat at Gillingham provided no comfort and with another home defeat to Walsall the momentum had been lost.

The last five games of the season saw the Cherries pick up one win at York City 1-0 and three 0-0 draws, while the defeat came at Colchester United 2-1 on 27 April. Bournemouth finished in seventh. The 0-0 draw against Wrexham on the last day of the season confirmed AFC Bournemouth would not make the play-off places. In the end, 67 points was not quite enough. Bournemouth lost out on the top six by a goal difference of just five. The Cherries had accumulated 14 wins and seven draws, in League Two, as they pushed Wigan Athletic all the way for a promotion place.

In 1998-99 Eddie was again AFC Bournemouth's player of the year. He had played a big role in the team by appearing in all the league fixtures, bar the away game at Preston North End in March. Missing out on promotion though was not something that sat well with Eddie.

3. CAPTAIN FANTASTIC (1999-2002)

The summer signings in 1999 were primarily defensive. The big name was Irishman John O'Shea who signed on loan from Man United. Gareth Stewart joined from Blackburn and Nick Fenton joined on loan from Man City. The midfield was also bolstered with Scott Mean from West Ham and Kevin Betsy from Fulham, while striker Gordon Watson added experience up front.

The Cherries were expecting to go even better in 1999-2000, but they were not to win two-consecutive league games all season, even if they did get off to a great start winning three of their first four games. Eddie Howe recalls the first win against Cambridge United on the opening day of the season. It was memorable for what he claims was the best goal of his career. 'It was a diving header and the winning goal in a 2-1 match and I managed to get injured scoring the goal!' he recalled. 'It started off so well for me and I had a great start by scoring the winning game against Cambridge. Our early form was good and after the highlight of playing at West Ham, I got injured against Stoke and was out for four months, so I then had a great deal of frustration of not being able to play.'

The Cambridge game was not Eddie's best game though. He believed the Bournemouth match against Preston North End, the season before in January, was a better match for him when the team won 3-1 and Howe scored the team's second goal.

Eddie would play in the first 11 league games before getting injured against Stoke City in October. He wouldn't play again until Bournemouth beat Luton 2-1 at home on 5 February 2000, featuring 33 times in all competitions.

Sean O'Driscoll had given Eddie Howe the role of team captain in February, after Ian Cox departed for Burnley. Howe was more than a bit excited at being given such responsibility. 'It's something I've always wanted to do and when I was asked, it was a terrific privilege to captain the club I've always supported. I didn't expect it so soon, but I'm delighted and very proud to be doing the job.'

The League Cup again saw Eddie play his part in a 0-0 draw with Charlton in the second round before going on to win 3-1 in a penalty shoot-out. That led to a third-round tie against West Ham United which saw the Cherries defeated 2-0.

Still, it was injuries to Eddie Howe, Richard Hughes and Steve Fletcher that hindered the team from getting much above mid-table. Eddie was disappointed to miss much of the season and even more frustrated about what the fans had put up with in not seeing a winning side often enough. By May 2000, he laid out his opinion of the season. 'I can't put my finger on it. We have been inconsistent, we play one game like we did against Stoke very well, and then the next game against Chesterfield we don't perform. It's something we have to address although at the moment, we don't know what the problem is. We will find it and we will put it right and then come back a stronger side next season. We have definitely improved our character this season and we will want to get success after such a poor season.

'After last season, when we missed out on the play-offs, but played some brilliant football, especially at home, the supporters were quite rightly expecting a lot this season. We've blown hot and cold though and we can all understand the frustrations because I believe as a whole, we all have. The supporters who have stuck by us have all been terrific and we can only applaud those who have stuck with us throughout the season. What we need now is success on the field next season and the start of the new stadium and if we do that, then the future is bright,' he concluded.

With Howe unable to play for a large part of the season and with the goals starting to dry up for Mark

Stein, the Cherries limped to a 16th place finish in
League Two. The team had won 16 games and still
had one of the best scoring records at home, having
scored 37 goals at Dean Court.

The 2000-01 season was one of the most important
for Eddie Howe as he played a big part in the team
that got to the verge of the play-offs in the last
season at the old Dean Court Stadium. Eddie missed
the opening 14 games of the season and made his
first appearance in the away game against Notts
County on 24 October, which the Cherries won 0-1.

Transfers included the signing of Wade Elliot
from Bashley, who would become a crowd favourite
while Brian Stock progressed to the first team in
central midfield. Warren Cummings signed on loan
from Chelsea and Stephen Purches, who signed from
West Ham, would also soon become a regular starter
in his first period with the Cherries up to 2007. Still,
Bournemouth's odds to win promotion remained
rather high at 40-1. What Bournemouth really
needed was a top striker and they were to find a
young one at West Ham United.

In October, there was a major coup for Sean
O'Driscoll. West Ham's manager, Harry Redknapp
agreed for Jermain Defoe, 18, to join the Cherries for
a month on loan. Jermain found his feet straight

away. He started scoring at the rate of a goal a
game. Jermain soon won what could only be termed
as 'hero status' among the fans at Dean Court. At
first, West Ham United agreed to extend the loan
until Boxing Day. But if a season-long loan could be
arranged, he could stay.

Harry Redknapp didn't tell Jermain that Norwich
City were interested in taking him. He was doing well
as Bournemouth and Redknapp thought the
experience would be good for Jermain in League
Two. Defoe was clearly enjoying his football and he
decided he would like to stay at Dean Court for the
entire season.

Mel Machin, who had moved to the director of
football position at Bournemouth, explained that
Defoe was like the missing piece in the jigsaw. He
was Premier League quality and he fitted in
extremely well. He had started his scoring run
against Stoke City on 28 October and didn't look
back. The pieces were coming together well with a 2-
1 win over Peterborough. Then a 3-0 triumph over
Northampton Town in November was described by
Sean O'Driscoll as 'the most complete performance
since I took over as manager.'

There was good spirit in the team with a winning
mentality emerging. The leadership was not given to
Eddie Howe, having missed so many games, but to
Steve Fletcher who was made captain in December.
O'Driscoll scrapped the titles of team captain and

club captain and just gave Fletcher the honour of being responsible for both roles. Mel Machin had appointed Fletcher as club captain and Eddie Howe as team captain in the previous season, following the departure of Ian Cox to Burnley. Eddie Howe told *The Daily Echo* that he was 'disappointed' to lose the captain's armband and added that he had 'enjoyed' being skipper.

Eddie's personal enthusiasm to lead the team would come more through helping them to clean sheets. A 2-0 home win over Swansea City in December showed that Jermain Defoe fever was growing, as he grabbed the Cherries' second goal. But the game had only been seen by a crowd of 3738.

By Christmas time the Cherries had put a seven-game unbeaten record together since October. An eighth win in all competitions would be a new club record, if they beat Millwall. Howe was one of the players who had been involved in the previous record under Mel Machin's reign from 5 December 1998 to 5 January 1999. But Eddie was not really thinking about the record. 'It would be a fantastic achievement if we did equal the record, but it won't really act as an extra incentive to us. We have approached every game this season in the same way and we will do so again, whether it is Dover, Nuneaton or Millwall. There will be no difference tomorrow,' said Howe. 'Millwall's visit will be a good gauge of how far we have improved results-wise since October, because we have played some good teams in our current run. I believe we can win any game at the moment and we want them to come thick and fast, which they will over the Christmas and New Year period,' said a confident Howe. 'We are looking to continue our run and it would be a great scalp if we beat Millwall.'

Sadly, the Cherries lost to Millwall 1-2 even if Defoe kept his scoring run going. The incentive for Bournemouth was not only Defoe's appetite for goals, but that if they beat Nuneaton Borough in the FA Cup second round, having already beaten Swansea in November, Defoe would be able to play in the next round. In fact, the Cherries won 3-0 with Eddie Howe and Karl Broadhurst the only two players keeping their place after the LDV Vans Trophy win over Dover in midweek.

There was no stopping Jermain, who kept scoring. By the end of January 2001, he had set a new post-war league record by notching up his 12th consecutive goal in 10 league games, with another goal at Cambridge United in a 0-2 win. 'I saw big Fletch flick the ball on to Carl Fletcher and I knew he was going to knock it over the top to me,' said Defoe. 'Thankfully, I got on the end of it and I was going to chip the goalkeeper but because he was so close to me, I took it round him and hit it as firmly as I could. After I had scored, I was going to run over to our fans to celebrate but I was so knackered I didn't.'

O'Driscoll couldn't have been more pleased for his record-breaking on-loan striker. 'I am very pleased for Jermain because this (the consecutive scoring record) has been a bit of a noose around his neck,' said O'Driscoll.

The 2001 New Year started less well for Eddie Howe. He was injured and was a doubt to play in the LDV Vans Trophy second round match against Swansea City. He had picked up the knee injury in the game against Gillingham, in the FA Cup third round, when the Cherries had lost 2-3. Bournemouth had played at home and were 1-2 down by half-time. Chris Hope and Andy Hessenthaler scored the Gills' goals with Defoe splitting them with his goal on 21 minutes. Carl Fletcher had put Bournemouth level on 51 minutes, before Paul Shaw grabbed the winner on 71 minutes. The winning goal was hotly disputed for being offside, but referee Rob Harris let it stand. Howe had also been upset to see his effort ruled out when he thought he had made it 3-3.

Eddie Howe had played the full 90 minutes in a testing game that had seen four yellow cards for Gillingham players. But Howe had been caught on the inside of his right knee by Paul Shaw in the first-half. The problem was that the kick he received was right on the scar he had from the operation he had in the summer on his right knee. It was later diagnosed that he also had a bit of a calf strain.

Howe was back for the league game against Wrexham on 13 January, when the Cherries had a 2-2 draw. Defoe was on the score sheet of course, after just six minutes, and James Hayter made it 0-2 after 62 minutes. Kevin Russell cut the deficit for Wrexham, before Mark McGregor scored a 90th minute equaliser.

A 0-2 win over Cambridge United on 23 January, as we have seen, was a special match for Jermain Defoe as he re-wrote the record books. James Hayter's goal confirmed Bournemouth's fourth away win in their last five games. Eddie Howe had put the ball in the back of the net as well after 22 minutes from a free kick from Richard Hughes, but the goal was ruled out for offside.

Perhaps a bigger win for the team though came a few days later when Claus Jorgensen got the only goal in a 0-1 win over Millwall at the end of January, which took the Cherries to six points off a play-off place. The Cherries had now gone three months unbeaten and had collected 25 points from their last 10 games.

Howe was not understating the importance of the win at Millwall. 'This is the first major scalp we have got this season and they don't come any bigger than beating the league leaders on their own ground,' said Eddie. 'It was a superb result and a superb performance. The Den is such an intimidating place to play and everybody deserves a great deal of credit for this victory. The manager has told us we need to get 50 points to make sure we stay in this division and that must be our first target, but hopefully we will get to the stage when we can start looking further. There are a few teams putting good runs together and if we can keep the momentum going, there is no reason why we can't finish in the top half or even higher. Sean (O'Driscoll) keeps saying that somebody is going to come out of the pack and we want to make sure it's us. We know the squad is good enough and we must keep believing in ourselves.'

Even here you can start to see the managerial thought processes and analysis in Howe's mind as he thinks more and more like a student of the game.

The game against Millwall had been played on a pitch that the *Bournemouth Echo* described as, something that 'resembled a ploughed field in places'. Eddie had been in the thick of the action and had gone close to scoring when Bournemouth had a corner on 11 minutes. Richard Hughes had crossed the ball in for it to bobble around the six-yard box, before Howe seized on the loose ball and had a shot that was cleared off the line. The partnership between Howe and Tindall in defence proved to be as solid as ever to keep the clean sheet. In fact, the two central-defenders had only let in three goals in the last three months in their away games.

The manager of the month award was duly awarded to Sean O'Driscoll for January and the curse of getting the award struck fairly soon, with the Cherries drawing their next three games, before losing to Oldham and Bristol Rovers at the end of February.

Eddie Howe had scored in the 2-2 draw with Walsall at Dean Court on 17 February and Defoe had doubled the Cherries' lead, but the curse had seen Walsall come back with two penalties in the second half. The hoodoo seemed to lift as the team went into March, Sean O'Driscoll's side at last picking up three points against Brentford with a 2-0 home win. A 3-1 defeat at Rotherham United might have dented any hopes of making a real run on the play-off places, but the race was only just beginning.

Keeping hold of Eddie Howe became a bit of a preoccupation for Sean O'Driscoll as the season progressed. Sean was not keen on letting Eddie Howe go. Eddie was a young player that looked destined for big things. When the talk of Eddie moving came in February 2001, O'Driscoll made it clear that clubs would not get a cheap deal. In the programme notes against Walsall, Sean said: 'To clarify Eddie's situation, there have been numerous clubs watching games throughout the season. I was informed an offer from an unnamed club was imminent during the latter part of the week. To safeguard the interests of the player and the club, I decided to omit Eddie from the team.'

The writing was on the wall. Eddie would be sold it seemed. Speaking on all the speculation, Eddie Howe's agent, David Fordham told *the Dorset Echo*: 'With a player as good as Eddie, and remember, he is the best defender in the division, there is always going to be interest from other clubs. It's a matter of talent, not money. Eddie has never been money motivated.'

An unofficial bid of £600,000 was thought to have been sent to David Fordham a few days before the window shut, but Eddie Howe shrugged it off when he was named in the team to play Walsall. 'The game did me a favour and gave me something to concentrate on. In the build-up, I wasn't thinking about anything else and it will be the same for the match at Swindon tomorrow. I was pretty nervous before kick-off because I felt everyone would be looking at me to see how I played. I was tense during the week, but worked hard in training and was really looking forward to the game. I was a bit apprehensive about the reception I might get, but the supporters were absolutely fantastic and really helped me get through it all and I would like to thank them for that,' Howe told the *Dorset Echo*. Eddie even scored in the game which some may have felt was like a parting gift.

However, as the end of the window started to close in, Howe was still playing at Dean Court. In fact, he was being as vocal as ever in defence of his team which were not getting the rub of the green for big decisions. The league game against Bristol Rovers at the end of February had Howe fuming at referee Tony Bates, when Howe had been tripped up in the play that led to Rovers taking the lead. 'It was an unbelievable decision, I was just about to pass the ball back to Mickaël Menétrier and the lad came up behind me and tripped me,' said Howe. 'I was in no real danger at the time, so I was incensed when the referee allowed the goal to stand because everyone in the ground could see he tripped me!'

The defeat to Bristol Rovers was the fifth loss of the season for O'Driscoll's men, leaving them nine points above the relegation zone.

Things started to move faster on the transfer window as March unfolded. Burnley were expected to sign Howe for £700,000 but the transfer looked unlikely to go through in time before the 5pm deadline in 22 March. Burnley had been looking at a loan deal, but that didn't suit Eddie Howe or AFC Bournemouth. Mel Machin, director of football at AFC Bournemouth, eventually called Stan Ternent at Burnley to say the Clarets may renew their interest in the centre-back in the summer and Eddie didn't move. The Cherries were also well aware that other clubs like Middlesbrough, Cardiff and Fulham were also interested in the highly-rated centre-back.

A thumping 4-0 win over Bristol City soon had the team believing that this could be a promotion season. Richard Hughes had hit an absolute cracker of a free kick and was now being sought after by Portsmouth. Just keeping the team together would preoccupy O'Driscoll.

A 1-1 draw with Wigan brought up a new record for the Cherries of having scored in 21 consecutive league games and Eddie Howe scored the equalising goal.

Bournemouth had also brought in Warren Feeney, on loan from Leeds United, before the Bury game as they tried to enhance their promotion prospects. Eddie Howe had gone close to scoring in that game when a lob from Defoe set Howe up for a volley that he just put wide from 12-yards out. Bournemouth again had Jermain Defoe to thank though for the 1-0 win.

Keeping the squad together had given the team fresh impetus. They made short work of beating Swansea City 3-0 away on the last day of March. The win made the Cherries the leading goal scorers for away goals. A goal-hungry Cherries then won 4-3 at home to Oxford United, before slipping up 1-2 to Reading with Richard Hughes guilty of missing a penalty!

The Reading result fired up the Cherries as they hit April determined to regain points. They were to win all four league games in the month to leave them with an outside chance of the play-offs. The 2-0 home win over Northampton at the end of the month would have been celebrated more had it not been for other results not going Bournemouth's way. The Cherries' three rivals for the play-off places had also won. Walsall, Wigan and Stoke were battling just as hard.

The last game of the season would see the Cherries take on Reading away. With Wigan held by Bristol City, the Cherries were moments away from being in the play-offs, but an 88th minute equalising goal by Nicky Forster brought a pulsating game to a 3-3 draw and ruined the Cherries' hopes of taking sixth spot. Bournemouth had been 1-3 up at half-time. Eddie Howe gave away a free kick and was booked for a challenge on Martin Butler. Darren Caskey took the free kick and made it 2-3. Losing the lead in the last two minutes was a crushing way to finish the season in seventh. Jermain Defoe would end up scoring 18 goals for the Cherries in the season from 29 appearances, which would push the Cherries to the verge of the play-off, but again missing out to Wigan Athletic by just a couple of points.

The Cherries finished on 73 points. Bournemouth had been in League Two, or what us oldies still refer to as the old Third Division, for 22 years. Bournemouth were solid provincial stock that hardly

ever went up or down, and yet their tenure in
League Two was about to come to an abrupt-end.

The 2001-02 season was a historic one for other
reasons for the Cherries as well, as it marked the
move to the new Fitness First Stadium, which was
still Dean Court, under sponsorship for the first time.
The ground was also to be rebuilt and swung around
90 degrees. The problem was the club didn't have all
the finance in place to finish the stadium.

Three sides were as far as the new ground would
get for several years, until a temporary stand was
erected at the South End in 2011, before it was
removed and a new temporary 'Ted MacDougall'
Stand was erected in the summer of 2013, which
remains in place to this day. In the meantime,
Bournemouth had to play all their home games at
their temporary home at Dorchester Town, which
didn't help them forge a winning mentality.

Bournemouth picked almost as many loan
players as permanent transfers in the summer and
what transfers were made were mainly free. Derek
Holmes was signed to improve the goal scoring along
with Trésor Kandol a striker from Zaire. The left-back
was also a position where O'Driscoll wanted to
strengthen with Danny Thomas coming in from
Leicester City and Kieran McAnespie from Fulham.

Shaun Maher was also brought in on a free transfer to bolster the defence.

The season began poorly for the Cherries with defeats against Huddersfield and Blackpool, before defeat in the League Cup to Torquay. While Howe was playing with Maher, Broadhurst and Purches in defence, clean sheets were unobtainable. Draws with Cardiff City, Cambridge United and Swindon Town at least lifted the Cherries to 19th place in the league. It wasn't until 15 September and the game against Bury that Eddie Howe and his team mates could celebrate their first league win. Even then, Bournemouth had needed a 90th minute winner from Brian Stock to secure the points.

But if O'Driscoll thought that things would now get easier, he soon knew the depth of the team's slow start when they came up against mid-table Peterborough. It seemed Peterborough were always envious of Bournemouth. But they had no trouble on this occasion in putting six goals past Gareth Stewart.

The next game though was against Brighton and they were top. It was no surprise that Bournemouth lost the game, but Eddie Howe was very much the talk of the game having equalised with a superb diving header from James Ford's cross on 76 minutes, only to have the unwanted label of having netted an own goal just five minutes later to give Brighton the win. The seventh league goal of Eddie

Howe's career had been wiped out by a long throw from Kerry Mayo at the Withdean Stadium. Howe had inadvertently diverted it into Bournemouth's net, with the ball bouncing in off his shin and in off the post!

A much needed 1-0 win eventually came against Reading, at Dorchester's ground, in front of a crowd of 3691. Eddie Howe was keen to make this the turning point. 'A win like that over Reading is a massive boost for all the players and everyone in the camp, just to know we can compete with the top teams in the division. It's a result that also tells our fans that we are still a good team, that we haven't become a bad side overnight or from last season. Some good players have left the club, but some good ones have also arrived, so hopefully this win will help us start to move back up the table.

'A lot has been made of playing at Dorchester and if it has affected our confidence. But we have proved tonight we can play here. We want to make it a fortress during the remaining time we are here. If you win at home it boosts your confidence to go away and play well. A lot has also been made of Reading and how we wanted to get revenge for our 3-3 draw last season. I don't know if this result has put it to bed. Last season we only got one point off them, so to get three from this one is brilliant,' added Howe.

The Reading win was followed by a 2-0 defeat at Stoke City to end September in 20th place. Warren Feeney had seen his second half penalty saved at the Britannia Stadium, but the Cherries were already two down by that stage. A crowd of 14,803 had seen Eddie Howe go close to giving Bournemouth the perfect start. Stephen Purches had put in a good early free kick that had been headed back across goal by Derek Holmes and the fast-reacting Eddie Howe would have scored, but for Clive Clarke's clearance on his six-yard line.

Better results were just around the corner though. October began with a 3-2 win over Oldham Athletic, after Bournemouth had gone a goal behind in the first minute. Eddie Howe was looking after the captaincy, while Steve Fletcher recovered from a knee injury he had been carrying since pre-season. Howe was unhappy about the up and down form of the team, even if they had started to win games at their temporary Dorchester home.

'We don't want to get back to the situation of a couple of years ago when we kept winning one game and then losing the next. It has already happened twice this season and the biggest disappointment after the win over Reading was the performance we gave at Stoke.' said Howe. 'We need to build on this win against Oldham and hopefully we can do that against Wigan. It's no good taking one step forward and the one step back because you never get anywhere. The three wins at Dorchester have given us a lot of confidence and it's hard to believe now that we couldn't score a goal never mind get a win in our first two games there.'

James Hayter and Wade Elliot then bagged goals in a 2-0 win over Wigan Athletic. Another point gained away at Wycombe Wanderers saw the Cherries up to 15th, before they took on Barnet in the first round of the LDV Vans Trophy when Trésor Kandol was to score in his first game, only for the Cherries to go down 2-1 after extra-time.

Ahead of the match against Brentford, Eddie Howe went down with food poisoning. The defender still insisted that he could play though and was one of the better players on the day. While the league form faltered again with defeats in October to Brentford and Bristol City, the team ended October with a 4-2 win over Notts County. Eddie Howe was injured in the Notts County game and limped off on 63 minutes, but he was pleased with the result.

'I knew as soon as I went down that it was nothing serious. In fact, I tried to carry on until I realised it wasn't happening. I went up with my leg slightly bent and I couldn't straighten it before I came down so I just landed on it a bit awkwardly. I won't train again until Thursday, but if I am selected I will be more than ready to start the Colchester game,' said Howe.

'To win any game and score four goals always gives the boys a lift, but we also have to learn from that game. We can't keep giving teams a goal or two head starts. We virtually gifted Notts County a goal and we have to stop doing that. I have never known anything like it. You give any team a start like that and it is an uphill task from then on. We have got back deficits against Bury, Oldham and Notts County this season but we couldn't get it back against Brentford. If it was the other way around and us scoring early on it would be great, but it isn't. We have to make sure it doesn't happen again.'

The comments resonated with the team well enough as Bournemouth went 0-2 up in their next match against Colchester United with Eddie Howe adding to Warren Feeney's opening goal. Although Wrexham scored on 25 minutes, the Cherries took the points. It was Bournemouth's first away win of the season.

The next league match against Wrexham got the full build up with Eddie Howe deputising as captain for the injured Steve Fletcher. It was to be the first game that the Cherries played at their new stadium. It was Howe's 213th appearance for the Cherries and he was well aware of the historic moment.

'It's unfortunate for Steve that he's injured because I'm sure he would have loved to have led the team out in this game, but it's not to be for him. It is also disappointing that Neil Young won't be playing because both him and Steve have served the club through the tough times and it would be good if they could share in this special day,' said an emotional Howe.

'I started watching from the terraces when I was at school and it's incredible to think that I will be leading the team out on what will be a historic day. I will feel immensely proud. It's probably fair to say that I was one of those people who always said about us getting a new ground, I'll believe it when I see it and now I can see it with my own eyes. Everybody had heard the talk for so many years that I think people started to get a bit sceptical. But when the old ground was demolished, it really sunk in because there was no turning back then. It has actually happened now thanks to the fantastic efforts of the supporters and the directors and Saturday is going to be a memorable occasion for everyone connected with the club. But although it's going to be a big day for everybody, the most important thing is that we win, we have got a job to do and it's important the players don't get carried away with it all.'

The game saw a commemorative 68-page programme for the match with a pictorial development of Dean Court included. The game couldn't have gone much smoother with Brian Stock, James Hayter and Jason Tindall hitting three goals past the visitors. A crowd of 5220 enjoyed the special day of celebrations.

Bournemouth took on Worksop Town in the FA Cup first round in their second game at the new Dean Court. Some 4014 fans saw the 3-0 home win that saw the Cherries safely through to the next round.

Having secured a 0-0 draw with Port Vale, Bournemouth approached the end of November in 13th place. Eddie Howe had been booked in the Port Vale match for a fourth time in the season and was one booking away from a suspension.

The last game in November would see the Cherries go down 2-1 to Chesterfield. It was the start of a run of defeats that would see Bournemouth fall right back down the table. Tranmere Rovers inflicted a 0-2 defeat on the Cherries, before rivals Peterborough knocked O'Driscoll's team out of the FA Cup. Further league defeats to Northampton Town and QPR meant there was not much Christmas spirit among Bournemouth fans when they made the Boxing Day trip to Swindon Town. Bournemouth had dropped to 17th place and had to stop the rot, which they did with a 0-0 draw against the Robins, although Eddie Howe was distraught to be sent off for the first time in his career. A further 0-0 draw against Wigan concluded the year for the Cherries in a lowly 19th place.

The period had not been great for Eddie Howe as he had given the penalty away for the second goal in QPR's 1-2 win. Howe also received his fifth booking in the match against Wigan, which meant he would not play again until the return fixture against QPR – a 1-1 draw at Loftus Road on 22 January 2002. Luckily for Eddie, he was brought straight back into the side as the Cherries had conceded seven times in the games he had missed.

Playing Oldham in the next match was more entertaining 3-3 score line. While Oldham were 1-0 up at half-time, Eddie Howe scored an equaliser on 53 minutes. In a crazy period of just three minutes Bournemouth were to find themselves at 2-2, after Warren Feeney hit a penalty home and Karl Broadhurst scored an own goal. Oldham were back in control when David Eyre made the score 3-2, but Richard Hughes levelled the score again on 66 minutes. The point still left the Cherries in 19th place and their form read five points from a possible 33 in their last 11 games.

A 3-1 home win against Stoke City lifted the gloom at the start of February. Sean O'Driscoll was certainly pleased. 'We could have scored more really,' he suggested. It had been 12 weeks and 11 games since the young Bournemouth side had managed a win and the relief was enormous. Stoke had the second-best goals against record in the league behind Reading, but Steve Purches, Richard

Hughes and Warren Feeney gave Bournemouth a commanding 3-0 lead after 56 minutes. A Rikhardur Dadason penalty for Gareth Stewart's challenge, on a diving Andy Cook, couldn't claw all the deficit back for the visitors.

Play-off hunting Cardiff City were a far more difficult prospect when they came to Dean Court and they raced into a 0-2 lead in 21 minutes. Then Eddie Howe and Gareth Stewart had made a terrible mix up, which led to the third Cardiff goal. Stewart had handled the ball outside his box from Howe's back pass. From Rob Earnshaw's quickly taken free kick, Willie Boland made it 0-3. Derek Holmes had a consolation 73rd minute goal for the Cherries but O'Driscoll's men were well beaten.

The relegation battle was hotting up and Bournemouth were unable to get the results to lift them away from 19th place. An 84th minute goal for Brentford in the next encounter really opened the prospect of relegation up for the Cherries.

So, relegation was on everyone's mind when Wycombe Wanderers visited Dean Court and went into the lead on 67 minutes through a Sean Devine goal. Bournemouth would need to fight for every point and Eddie Howe's goal on 76 minutes looked to at least have given the home side something from the game. However, Jermaine McSporran hit a last gasp 90th minute winner to dash hopes of climbing up the league. On loan Danny Thomas from Leicester had provided the corner delivery for Howe's goal, but the Cherries left the pitch just two points above the relegation zone.

Worse luck was to befall the falling Cherries as they dropped into the relegation zone and 20th place, after a 2-1 defeat at Bury. Derek Holmes had given Bournemouth a 0-1 lead until Bury hit back with an equaliser on 45 minutes and a winner by Ian Lawson on 64 minutes. Bury themselves were facing a different type of challenge in that they had been given a winding up order in a week's time. Bournemouth's plight didn't seem quite as bad, but the Cherries were far from financially stable either. Warren Feeney and Derek Holmes were passed fit for the game against the team that was just one place above the Cherries. The half-time team talk could have been different, if Holmes' left-foot drive had hit the inside rather the outside of the post in the opening half hour. But Gareth Stewart had need to be at his best saving a fierce drive from Jon Newby and again from Martyn Forrester, before George Gregg scrambled the equaliser right on half-time. The *Bournemouth Echo* blamed the Cherries' 'statuesque defending' for Bury's winner, as the ball had hit the cross bar and dangled near the goal before Ian Lawson stabbed it home.

By now the rumours around Eddie Howe's possible departure began dominating the local paper's headlines. Bournemouth had lost again, to guess who? Yes, Peterborough United again. A 0-2 defeat on 2 March. By then, the gossip machine was in full flow. At first Harry Redknapp denied that Portsmouth were on the verge of making a bid for Eddie Howe. But Oldham Athletic had been trying to sign Howe and their deal had collapsed in the week before the Peterborough game. The door was now open for others to come in. The *Bournemouth Echo* highlighted that Eddie's brother Steve Lovell was already at Portsmouth and that Harry Redknapp was a big admirer of the centre-back.

'I read in the papers that Eddie was going to Oldham,' said Redknapp. 'We have had no contact whatsoever with the player and that is about the size of it. As for training with us, he is a Bournemouth player now and I think they might have something to say about that.'

The Cherries' chairman, Tony Swasiland, was keen to pour cold water on the matter stating, 'We have had no contact with Portsmouth regarding Eddie Howe.'

A bigger saga that was also developing during this period was Tony Swasiland's fight to keep the Cherries above water in terms of their finances. The club needed financial restructuring. Swasiland was keen that this would not mean the end of the club's community club status though. The Trust's 51 per cent voting share would remain but investment was needed.

With all these transfer rumours, and unsettling financial goings on in the background, all Howe could do was concentrate on his football. The next opportunity came on 5 March away at Reading. Bournemouth had to settle for a 2-2 draw after Wade Elliot had missed the chance to win the game from the penalty spot by smashing his shot against the bar! Sitting 22nd in the league before the game and with problems around every corner, the Cherries could at least take some comfort from drawn with the league leaders and having come within an inch of winning the game.

The result might not have been perfect against Reading, but it did move the Cherries up to 20th place and gave confidence going into the crucial relegation scrap with 21st placed Northampton Town. Bournemouth went in at half-time at 1-1, but then smashed four more goals past Keith Welsh in the Northampton goal to win handsomely 5-1.

Eddie Howe and Shaun Maher had to be giants in a 0-0 score line at Tranmere Rovers' Prenton Park to keep the points flowing. There were just seven games left to preserve the League Two status.

Bournemouth managed to get themselves just above the relegation zone on goal difference in the last minute against Cambridge United. Kieran McAnespie made a desperate goal line clearance to deny David Bridges a winner. Tom Cowan had put Cambridge in front with a scissor-kick goal from 12 yards, but Warren Feeney equalised just 12 minutes later from a Wade Elliot cross. The second half went perfectly at first when Adam Tann handballed and this time Wade Elliot made no mistake from the spot. However, Cambridge got a breakaway goal on 58 minutes. Although Howe headed away Danny Jackman's initial shot, Jackman finished at the second attempt.

The defeat against Bristol City would send Bournemouth back into the bottom four and reliant on the results of others for survival. Bournemouth were 0-2 down by half-time, and the Cherries luck didn't improve when Hayter was tripped by Louis Carey. The referee put the ball down on the 18-yard line for a free kick though and did not award a penalty. While Bournemouth would score in the 90th minute with a goal from Kieran McAnespie, Ian Thorpe made it 3-1 to City seconds before the final whistle.

What Bournemouth fans were not to know at the time was that this would be the last game for their captain before he was to be sold to Portsmouth. Time had run out on holding on to Eddie Howe and time looked to be running out on any hopes of the club's survival in League Two.

Bournemouth lost their next two games against Notts County and Colchester United, leaving them in 22nd place. Shaun Maher had even scored an own goal in the 62nd minute to give Colchester United their win. A 0-0 draw with Port Vale left the Cherries hoping for results to go their way. With two games left relegation appeared likely and yet a 3-1 win over Chesterfield moved the Cherries up to 21st place. The last game was against Wrexham, who were also in the relegation zone. Bournemouth went ahead with a Carl Fletcher goal, but late goals from Andy Morrell and Carlos Edwards saw the Cherries relegated to League Division Three.

In all, Eddie's Bournemouth 2001-02 season was made up of 38 games. He left the club on 28 March 2002 when he signed for Portsmouth for £400,000. Eddie made 208 league and cup appearances in his first playing spell at Bournemouth and scored 10 league goals, two FA Cup goals and one League Cup goal – not bad, for a centre-half!

4. PLAYERSHARE POWER AND FINANCIAL WORRIES (2002-07)

Portsmouth came calling for Eddie Howe, after Harry Redknapp became Pompey's manager. In March 2002 Eddie signed for Portsmouth on a three-year deal for £400,000. It should have been the making of the centre-back, but it turned out to be a frustrating period with Howe only making two appearances for Pompey, as he sustained a knee injury in his debut against Preston North End. Eddie was injured after 51 minutes of the game which Pompey lost 2-0. That would have been a crushing blow for any professional footballer, but Eddie is a man who considers and ponders his every move. For him, the period in rehabilitation gave him a chance to see how Harry Redknapp and Kevin Bond worked with players. Howe was once asked whether moving to Portsmouth had been a bad decision? It certainly wasn't for Eddie in terms of personal development. He viewed it as a chance to learn from others and to find something that would add to his own makeup.

Eddie made his comeback over a year later, on 10 August 2002, when Portsmouth played Nottingham Forest. The match was another devastating blow for Eddie, who lasted just nine minutes before his knee went again. It was only Eddie's second game for Portsmouth and he would not play for them again. He went to clear a ball and heard a click in his left knee. Eddie Howe spoke to *The Daily Telegraph* about the incident.

'I dislocated my knee cap and chipped a bit of bone under my knee, and then I had a micro-fracture and, basically, the joint was never the same,' explained Eddie. 'It was painful. I had lost all power. I couldn't squat, I couldn't run. I didn't actually know at the time what I had done. All I was thinking was that I had heard a click in the knee. The physio said, 'Just try and run over there'. I did try and I collapsed and then I knew there was something seriously wrong.

'The medical treatment I got was below the standard you would expect. The micro-fracture wasn't diagnosed for the first two operations. I had a lot of trouble explaining to Portsmouth that I was feeling a pain so I couldn't run.'

Not playing was becoming a habit for Eddie. Following two unsuccessful and wrongly diagnosed knee operations in England, Eddie had to have a career-saving operation in America to enable him to play again. Dr Richard Steadman operated on Eddie Howe in February 2003, in Colorado, USA. By January 2004, Eddie was running again.

He still had to get through another long rehabilitation period, before he was loaned out to Swindon Town in March 2004. Eddie didn't actually get to play a game for Swindon, because of an ankle injury. But he did have a full pre-season at Portsmouth and was delighted to get a call to try and restart his career back where it had all started. The season of 2004-05 was going to be a new adventure for Eddie, but it was a surprise to him as much as anyone else where he would end up playing.

Bournemouth had been relegated in 2002 to the fourth tier of English football – Division 3. Yet, in a historic 2002-03 season they had won promotion back to League Two, after a Cardiff play-off final against Lincoln City on 24 May 2003, in which they triumphed 5-2. While Eddie Howe had been working his way back into playing football in 2003-04, Bournemouth had completed their first season back in League Two and finished a well-placed ninth. Sean O'Driscoll was keen to improve on that, but with finances as always proving tight, the opportunity to sign an untested Eddie Howe he considered too good an opportunity resist.

So, in August 2004, Eddie came back to the Cherries, initially on a month-long loan. Eddie was all smiles, 'I'm just delighted to be back. Hopefully, I can get some games in after so long without playing. Two years is a crazy amount time in a football career not to be playing at a competitive level, especially after the run of games I had at Bournemouth,' said Howe. 'Sean has told me he can't guarantee me a starting place. It's up to me to prove I deserve one and I totally agree. I've got to prove myself in training and prove I'm fit enough to play games. My objective is to do as well as I can for Bournemouth and do my best for the club.

Asked about the decision on whether he was wise to come back, Eddie Howe gave an answer that he was going to have to repeat some eight years later. 'It was always in the back of my mind that people say you should never go back. But when I thought about how many friends I had at the club, the players, the respect I've got for Sean and the rapport with the supporters, it made my decision a lot easier. I had a great time at Bournemouth before and hopefully it can go as well again this time,' Eddie explained. 'I don't think I can look back and say I shouldn't have left. It was the best deal for the club at the time and they needed the money. It was a good move for me, a step up which I was looking for, so I don't think I can regret it – I think it was the right move. Unfortunately, circumstances meant I got a bad injury which really stifled my progress.'

AFC Bournemouth were equally as pleased to have their favourite son back at the club, especially as the finances would not usually have enabled such a conclusion. Chairman Peter Philips said, 'Eddie is a super player who the fans know well and it's a real boost to bring him back on loan. Obviously, in our current financial state, we can't afford to pay his wages and we've needed some help from Portsmouth, as well as some help from Playershare to enable this to happen. I'm delighted to see Eddie back, even if it only turns out to be for a month.'

Bournemouth played their first match against Hull City which they lost to a third minute penalty. Eddie Howe came on as a second half substitute for Marcus Browning. The Cherries had started the season by conceding a penalty after just one minute and 36 seconds! Karl Broadhurst having been struck on the arm by a shot from Danny Allsopp, and Stuart Green had no problem in beating Neil Moss from 12 yards. Neil Young was later sent off after 60 minutes to compound the Cherries' problems, pushing Allsopp to the ground, giving the home team a second penalty. Dani Rodrigues had made his debut for the Cherries but had not seen much sight of goal, although he did make Boaz Myhill have to make one save.

The Cherries could name Eddie in the starting line-up for the next home match against Walsall on

10 August 2004, which ended in a 2-2 draw. James Hayter and Wade Elliot got on the score sheet in the last 20 minutes to peg-back Walsall who had sped into a 0-2 lead. Keeping a clean sheet was proving beyond the Cherries, even with Howe. Carl Fletcher was on target against Bristol City in the next fixture, before Leroy Litter had kept the visitors in the game at 1-1. James Hayter's 88th minute looked to have won the game, but Jamie Smith equalised in the 90th minute. It left the Cherries without a win in 23rd place in the table after three games.

There was little panic though when three wins followed. A 1-3 away win at Milton Keynes included a brace from James Hayter. The Cherries managed the same 1-3 score against Leyton Orient in the Carling Cup on 24 August, with Hayter again among the goal scorers. But Howe was prevented from playing as he was still on loan from Portsmouth. He was back in the team for the Cherries' first home win of the season, a 1-0 victory over Wrexham. But it was a match where James Hayter broke his toe! A 1-0 reverse followed to Luton at the end of the month, when the Cherries had been nine minutes away from claiming a point, but the good run had edged the Cherries up to 14th in the table.

Defeats were starting to mount up again with Brentford and Colchester getting the better of the Cherries who had slipped back to 19th in the table by mid-September. With Hayter's return,

Bournemouth managed a 0-1 away win at Sheffield Wednesday, thanks to a goal from John Spicer.

Eddie was playing some of the best football in red and black shirt and he had one of his most memorable matches in September that year, when the Cherries eventually beat Blackburn Rovers away in the League Cup in a tie that ended 3-3 in normal time. It went on to finish 7-6 with Eddie Howe sealing the game with the final goal in a penalty shoot-out at Ewood park. While Eddie recalls that he was hoping it wouldn't come around to the seventh penalty taker, he never ducked a challenge.

The game certainly has special memories for Eddie: 'We were a very small club at the time and, to go to Blackburn and win, albeit on penalties, will live long in the memory for a lot of people. To be a part of it and to have played will always be special to me.'

Sadly, the club lost in the third round at Dean Court when Eddie again played and even though this game also finished 3-3, the penalty shoot-out saw Cardiff win through 5-4.

The cup heroics certainly gave the Cherries a boost and they had a super-charged 5-0 win against Doncaster Rovers at home in the next game. Bournemouth were 4-0 up in the first 25 minutes. Goals from a recalled Rodrigues, Hayter, Howe and Garreth O'Connor had ended Doncaster's resistance and the game was topped off by a fifth goal on 70 minutes by James Hayter. Bournemouth's league position had improved to ninth.

Shrewsbury Town were less charitable in the LDV Vans Trophy, going 3-0 up in 66 minutes helped by a Neil Young own goal for their second, but the Cherries fought back to 3-2 with a Brian Stock goal and an own goal from Stuart Whitehead in the 90th minute.

Bournemouth then had a seaside goal frenzy with Blackpool in an entertaining 3-3 draw, having been 2-0 down after 10 minutes. The *Bournemouth Echo* described the game as a 'rollercoaster'. James Hayter started the comeback heading in a Wade Elliot cross, before Dani Rodrigues deftly nodded past Lee Jones to make it 2-2 on 28 minutes. Paul Edwards then restored Blackpool's lead before half-time. But Dani Rodrigues merited his starting place with his second and Bournemouth's third on 64 minutes to prevent Blackpool from picking up their first home win of the season. Just as important for the Cherries, Steve Fletcher made a late cameo appearance after recovering from his knee injury.

Howe's loan period was renewed in September for another month. The loan would end after the 2-1 league win over Stockport on the 8 October, when he had to go back to train with Portsmouth to find out if a permanent deal could be done. Harry Redknapp at Portsmouth had concerns of his own over injuries to his other central defenders Arjan De

Zeeuw and Dejan Stefanovic. Redknapp would be reasonable but the charity had an end point.

'I will help Eddie all I can, he's a good lad,' Redknapp told *BBC Radio Solent*, 'but if Bournemouth want to take him they will have to pay his wages obviously. I am short of defenders and it is up to Eddie now he is back, let's see how he has come on in the last two months.'

As it was, Portsmouth agreed to loan Eddie Howe out to Bournemouth, in mid-October, for a third and final month. Stefanovic's return to fitness had enabled Howe to extend his stay at the Cherries and he played in the club's 4-0 home win over Port Vale on 16 October. Brian Stock was certainly enhancing his reputation as a match winner with a brace in the 4-0 rout and the Cherries were sitting very comfortably in fifth place.

The points had continued to flow in October as the Cherries won away at Torquay 2-1 and followed that up with another 1-2 away win at Oldham Athletic, after Hayter had netted two second half goals to turn the match around. Bournemouth were now in fourth place.

Bowing out of the League Cup at the end of October to Cardiff City brought the Cherries winning run to an end. In the league they fell at the next hurdle to Barnsley. Just before Howe was pondering over his future, Bournemouth picked up another three points with Hayter scoring away at Peterborough to move back into fourth.

Howe was not getting too stressed about whether he would get a chance to join the Cherries permanently. 'I have not had a chance to think about what happens beyond this final month. There have been so many games that I had not really thought about the future. But I've learned a lot over the past few years and one of those things is never to rule anything out. At the end of the month I just want to be 100 per cent fit and ready for whatever comes next,' said an excited Eddie Howe.

The Bournemouth fans wanted him back at the club permanently and the only problem was that there was no money to buy him back. Some money needed to be found though, to get him out of the time he still had remaining on his two-and-a-half - year deal with Pompey. Then a typical AFC Bournemouth initiative took over with a sponsored walk and an online 'EddieShare' scheme prompted by chairman Peter Phillips to raise money to buy him back. The Playershare scheme at the club had already been running for some two years as a way of raising money to buy players. This had helped Sean O'Driscoll to bring in players during some tough years for the club.

Sean O'Driscoll had no regrets on bringing Eddie Howe back to Bournemouth on loan, at the start of the season, and was prepared to take the risk to get him permanently. 'We took a chance on him as he hadn't played for 18 months. But we knew what he was capable of, we were prepared to nurse him through and he's just got better and better – he's repaid us 10-fold.'

While Reading were also keen to sign Eddie Howe, it was the Cherries that were in a mad rush to raise funds urgently to try and get their man and £13,500 was raised in just two days. In a short period, some £21,000 was raised, so that on 12 November 2004 Eddie was on his way back to Dean Court. Eddie signed a two-and-a-half year deal admitting that it was 'impossible to say no'. Bournemouth saw off interest from Bristol City and Reading to bring back their star defender. Howe had already made 19 appearances for Bournemouth on loan and he felt an integral part of the Cherries' season.

Speaking to the *Bournemouth Echo* Howe expressed his feelings at signing a new contract for Bournemouth, 'It's been a hectic few days, and I'm delighted to have pledged my future to Bournemouth again. I had such a fantastic time here on loan and it was a great experience to come back. Once it was put to me to come back permanently, it was impossible to say no. I could not have contemplated going anywhere else. I felt I owed the club something, because they stuck by me and showed tremendous loyalty and I felt I wanted to repay them for that.'

Bournemouth would now have Eddie Howe linking up with Karl Broadhurst again, at the heart of their defence, as they tried to mount a promotion push. Broadhurst believed Howe was just the player the club needed to make a serious challenge in the league, and he was just pleased that the speculation would now end and that Howe was ready to play his part.

'The situation has been going on for quite a while now so it's nice to get it done and dusted. I expect Eddie is relieved because he just wants to get on and play. Now it's all finalised, it's another string to our bow and another bonus squad wise...Eddie adds more, because he can play most positions at the back. He knows everyone here so it's good base for him to start again after the time at Portsmouth. He's always been a fans' favourite and the supporters have been putting their hands in their pockets now for the last few years here. Whenever we've needed help, they've always pulled through for us so it didn't surprise me they tried to help.'

The FA Cup drew Bournemouth an away tie against Forest Green Rovers but a Steve Fletcher goal was cancelled out by Jefferson Louis' 56th minute equaliser to force a replay 11 days later. In between the Cherries could only manage a goalless draw against Colchester United. With home support

well-behind Sean O'Driscoll's side, they put Forest
Green Rovers out of the FA Cup 3-1 in the replay.

League matters were the priority and a 3-2
defeat at Hartlepool was more difficult to take. Chris
Westwood had opened the scoring for Hartlepool,
but Bournemouth had been 1-2 up at half-time after
strikes from Derek Holmes and Brian Stock. Yet,
Bournemouth caved in late on with Michael Nelson
scoring in the 88th minute. Neil Moss then saved a
penalty from Adam Boyd, but Andy Appleby rounded
off a poor night for the Cherries to make it 3-2.

Bournemouth got back to winning ways by
beating Carlisle United 2-1 at Dean Court in the
second round of the FA Cup in early December. The
Cherries also got a 2-0 win over Bradford City with
Howe having to come off on a stretcher, at the start
of the second half with an ankle injury, after landing
awkwardly after an aerial battle with Michael Symes.
Brian Stock also picked up an ankle injury, which was
not helpful with another game fast approaching.

Eddie Howe would only miss the one game. He
was back for the 2-1 win over Swindon Town on 18
December which kept the Cherries in fourth place.
Howe didn't play again until he came on as a
substitute in a 3-2 defeat at Huddersfield on 22
January 2005. By then Bournemouth had drifted to
eighth in the table, but the 2-1 FA Cup win over
Chester City gave them an exciting fourth-round tie

with Burnley. Howe was not selected to play at Turf Moor and the team went down 2-0.

Shaun Maher was a player that Eddie Howe had to compete with to regain his place in the team. Over the Christmas period Maher was playing with Karl Broadhurst when Howe was injured, but come the New Year it was going to be hard to keep Howe out. Still Maher was just pleased he was at last avoiding injury himself and thought highly of Howe as it urged him on to better performances.

'Eddie was a good signing and he's a good player,' he said. 'We all like to see good signings coming in because it helps us all. Maybe it did galvanise me – increased competition is going to galvanise anybody. It gives it an edge. I don't want the be the odd man out and I'm sure nobody else does either so I'm no different to anybody else.'

The season was being hugely interrupted for Bournemouth with injuries and Howe was struggling, missing the 2-2 draw with Stockport, before featuring in the starting line up in the 2-1 loss at Port Vale that left the Cherries back in 10th place at the start of February.

A 4-0 drubbing of Oldham Athletic raised expectations again. Garreth O'Connor was the architect of Oldham's downfall with two goals, while Steve Fletcher had started the scoring and James Hayter had also got on the score sheet. A disappointing 3-1 defeat to lowly Colchester United did little to keep the pressure on the teams above them.

The Cherries had recovered to sixth in the table, beating Barnsley away 0-1 with a Garreth O'Connor goal in mid-February, but Howe was subbed 47 minutes into the game with a foot injury. It left Bournemouth with just one recognised defender before the next match with Torquay, but O'Driscoll was used to such a crisis.

'It depends how bad Eddie is. He'll have an X-ray and if it ends up being serious then maybe we'll have to get the begging bowls out to Playershare to see if we can do something,' said an ironic O'Driscoll.

But O'Driscoll was right in not worrying about the way the team was playing. Getting by with what he had was his great ability. Consequently, Bournemouth stuck three past Torquay without reply. Matt Mills came in to cover for the missing Eddie Howe. He helped the team to a 1-1 draw against Tranmere by scoring in the 43rd minute and he also scored in the 0-3 away win to Swindon Town. Replacing Eddie Howe wasn't proving such a hard job for once!

Still, Bournemouth were out-scored at home against Blackpool losing 3-2, and despite the 1-2 away win at Walsall, March was to be a crucial month in the promotion battle with the Cherries dropping points. Bournemouth lost to second placed Hull City 0-4 at Dean Court before the month was out and although Howe was back on 28 March, Easter Monday, to face a struggling Milton Keynes, who were in 20th place, the Cherries lost 0-1 at Dean Court. This was the third successive home defeat.

Everything was still to play for though, and a 1-2 win away at Wrexham was followed with a 0-2 win away at Bristol City to leave Bournemouth in fifth place at the start of April with five games to go. The run-in started badly though losing at home to an 84th minute goal from Enoch Showunmi, which kept Luton Town in top spot. The fans had witnessed Luton's Russ Perrett being shown the red card after taking down James Hayter with 22 minutes to go. But Luton going down to 10 men didn't make it any easier.

The importance of the Luton match was made clear by chairman Peter Phillips who was hoping there would be no trouble knowing that Luton's ticket allocation of 1300 had already been sold out. The worry was that Luton fans would seek to get home fan tickets.

'In principle, there's no reason why you can't enjoy the match just as much if you happen to be sitting next to a Luton supporter,' he said. 'It's a civilised world we live in and we are all football fans. We should just enjoy the game and make people welcome.'

I'm not so sure Bournemouth fans felt quite so welcoming having seen the visitors snatch a win in the last six minutes of the game. At least a crowd of 9058 set a new attendance record for the Fitness First Stadium.

Eddie Howe couldn't shed any light on how the home form was not nearly as good as the away results. 'We can't put our finger on what the difference is between home and away at the moment. I think we've performed quite well at home, but we just haven't had the breaks we had earlier in the season.

'The ball is not running our way in the penalty area, especially in the Luton game where we could have been a couple up before they scored. We've been playing really well away so it's difficult to know what the problem is. But all we can do is approach the game like we have all year, keep being professional and I'm sure it will turn around.'

Following Brentford's midweek win against Tranmere, the Cherries had slipped down to seventh. An away match against Chesterfield gave Bournemouth a chance to put the Luton defeat behind them and Steve Fletcher scored twice in a 2-3 win that put Bournemouth back in the play-off positions.

But a fifth home defeat in a row shattered fans' hopes. Losing to Peterborough 0-1 was a big blow. Peterborough were fighting for their lives in 22nd place and their need seemed more pressing. Even the exceptional away record fell apart with

Bournemouth's penultimate game when they lost 4-2 to Bradford City. Eddie Howe had a premonition about how the game might go and who would be the likely player who would cause them the most problems – Dean Windass. 'I haven't played against Windass before but he's obviously got quality. He played in the Premiership and scored goals so he's going to be one of our toughest opponents this season.' Unfortunately, Howe proved to be spot on as Dean Windass helped himself to a hat-trick.

Bournemouth would close the season with a home fixture against Hartlepool United. It was simply a winner takes all game. The promotion door was open but Bournemouth had to find some home form. Twice Bournemouth were to take the lead through goals from James Hayter. Jon Daly and Anthony Sweeney were the ones celebrating though at the final whistle, when their goals had secured a point for the visitors and a place in the play-offs. Bournemouth had missed out again, finishing eighth.

O'Driscoll didn't dwell on the disappointment too long. 'It's gone, it's finished,' he said. 'Now you've got to look forward. This club wallows in the past far too much so it's gone and now we're looking forward to pre-season and next season. That's what you've got to do. You've got to march on.' Arguably it was the failure to get more than nine home wins that had cost the Cherries their place in the play-offs by just a point. Eddie Howe had featured well in the

Cherries' campaign, having played in 35 games, but he still hadn't felt the thrill of a promotion and he'd have to try again just like the rest of the club in 2005-06. Pre-season games would be organised against the likes of Charlton Athletic, Brighton, Winchester City and Hamworthy Recreation.

AFC Bournemouth were not just fighting on the pitch for wins. Financial problems had reared their head again in April and May 2005. Peter Philipps had a couple of ideas concerning the future of the ground. Either it could be sold and leased back or a fan-driven idea to raise money for the ground through a pension scheme.

The club still owed Bournemouth council its £250,000 loan that it had taken out five years earlier to help build the new stadium. The *Bournemouth Echo* stated that at the time there was little chance of repayment as the club was some £4.3m in debt. The club had been given a £250,000 grant as well as the loan, but it was tax payers' money, even if it had been a community project. What chance then for new players at the club with mounting debts and repayments needed to keep the council onside?

Off the pitch things were changing fast with Dean Court with the Supporters Pension Scheme (SPS) designed to safeguard the new stadium. Dave Stone,

one of the directors, had suggested the scheme and things had started to turn to serious discussions by May 2005. The initial money would come from around 40 fans putting part of their pension funds into the SPS. A lump sum would be raised to clear the most pressing debts and enable the club to pay rent of around £360,000 a year to the investors for the Fitness First Stadium. But Peter Phillips didn't think the club was in a position to pay £30,000 a month on a leaseback deal.

Bournemouth somehow managed to bring in a few players on free transfers in the summer, such as Shaun Cooper from Portsmouth who was to play a pivotal part of the Cherries defence for the next few seasons. Other free transfers included Stephen Cooke from Aston Villa and Callum Hart from Bristol City to bolster the defence, as well as Josh Gowling a centre-back who had been playing in Denmark's first division with Olstykke FC. Steven Foley also signed from Aston Villa to play in midfield and loan signings included a young Andrew Surman from Southampton. A 17-year-old Brett Pitman would also step up to the first team.

By September, the hope was for around £2m to be raised from the fans and this would be enough to allow the SPS to borrow £3.5m to now buy the stadium, but it all depended on getting the right investors in place.

The first match of the season pitted

Bournemouth against Milton Keynes Dons on 6 August 2005, where Bournemouth quickly fell 2-0 behind before goals from James Hayter and a 90th minute equaliser from Andrew Surman helped the Cherries to their first point of the season. Dani Rodrigues scored Bournemouth's first home goal of the new campaign against Hartlepool in a 1-1 draw in the second match. A comfortable 2-0 win against Bristol City at home then gave the Cherries their first win.

Gillingham would be a harder game and the 1-0 defeat after a Marcus Browning own goal left the Cherries in 12th. Eddie Howe would not play again though until 17 December, by which time the Cherries had added a further 25 points from the 18 league games he missed.

A pressing problem was the financial situation that had arisen from debts from the previous season. Peter Philips was sure that the repayments for the new stadium would continue, whether it was sold to a Supporters' Pension Scheme or to property developers Londonewcastle.

The state of the financial liabilities was made very clear in *The Daily Echo*. 'It is obvious that we need a long-term solution,' said Peter Phillips. 'In the current season, many of our legacy costs are going up. Lloyds want an extra £270,000 a year starting this month, Northover and Gilbert want £1m by November, the Inland Revenue want the arrears paid off and so on. The club would have to be massively profitable to pay all these liabilities as well as meeting our day to day obligations – like paying the wages. Although replacing 'unfriendly' with 'friendly' debt has worked well up to now, it cannot continue indefinitely and it doesn't solve the underlying problem.'

The total club debt structure over the past year was then printed in the *Bournemouth Echo* to show the importance of how the club needed to restructure its debt after the money owed for the new stadium.

The situation had become grave enough that the chairman admitted in November that one man could send AFC Bournemouth to the receivers that very week. Stanley Cohen, the club president, had enabled his business – Northover and Gilbert – to loan the Cherries £1.445m to keep the club afloat. A longer-term restructuring of the debt was required and chairman Peter Philips could see a way out by selling the freehold of the Fitness First Stadium and leasing the ground back. Northover and Gilbert had been paid £192,000 in interest which was less than what the company was owed. An extraordinary meeting was held to get the creditors to agree to the sale of the freehold of Dean Court, so clearing the debts owed Lloyds, Bristol and West and Mr Cohen's company.

It was time to get back to the football. Eddie

Howe made his comeback as a sub in mid-December when the visitors to Dean Court were Gillingham. Bournemouth would win 2-1 and they were in a reasonable mid-table position of 12th just before Christmas. Eddie still didn't feel quite right and he next appeared in the 2-1 defeat at Southend, in the last game of the year, when he came on as an 84th minute sub for Marcus Browning.

Bournemouth started the New Year in 10th and picked up a 1-1 draw against Scunthorpe United with James Hayter getting the equaliser five minutes from time. A point against Tranmere Rovers and win against Rotherham took Bournemouth up to ninth, before a run of defeats against Swindon, Chesterfield and Swansea put the Cherries back in mid-table. Eddie didn't get a full 90 minutes until the Chesterfield match. The 4-2 away defeat to Swansea was particularly disappointing as the Welsh team were well down in 23rd place.

Draws against Oldham and Blackpool steadied the ship, but February also saw defeats to Rotherham United and Bristol City before a 0-1 home defeat in early-March from Bradford saw the Cherries drop to 16th place. Steve Fletcher scored a goal against Yeovil Town to at least get one win in March, but there were no more thoughts of putting a series of results together to challenge the top teams anymore.

There were more people turning up for Elton

John's concert at Dean Court than there would be
for the games. A crowd of some 20,000 would
attend the concert on 1 July 2006, numbers which
the Cherries could only dream about.

Bournemouth would draw their next three games
before beating Walsall 0-1 away on 11 April 2006,
but the 1-1 draw that followed against Huddersfield
would be the end of the season for Howe. The team
went on to finish in 17th place, drawing three of
their last four games, including a 2-2 draw against
Brentford in the last game, which drew a crowd of
9359.

Stanley Cohen, AFCB's Honorary President left
the club in May 2006, having sunk £500,000 of his
own money into the new stadium. Player departures
would include Steve Claridge, Stephen Cooke and
Jason Tindall.

There were many free transfers coming into the club
in the summer of 2006, but the big name that was a
real surprise was the arrival of Darren Anderton at
34, being a free agent having ended his time at
Wolves. Anderton watched the Cherries win 3-2
against Oldham, before discussing a possible pay-as-
you-play contract with the Cherries. He played a
behind-doors friendly against Salisbury Town in
September and scored the only goal of the game. He

hadn't played for six months and did well to get through 90 minutes. Eddie Howe didn't play in that game, but he'd thought he'd soon get some games with Anderton in the side. Sadly, it would only be a few games because Howe's playing career was to be cut-short prematurely.

Bournemouth had started the season slowly with a 0-3 home defeat to Chesterfield on the opening day and a draw at Yeovil, before losing to Leyton Orient 3-2 away. The opening win came against Cheltenham 2-1 on 19 August, which was followed by a 3-1 defeat against Southend United in the Carling Cup that Howe was rested for. Howe came back to help pick up a point against much fancied Doncaster Rovers – it would be Eddie Howe's 300th appearance for the Cherries. The game might have quickly got away from Bournemouth, when Howe was deemed by the home fans to have escaped with a handball in the 33rd minute. There was no VAR then and luckily Eddie didn't get pulled up on it by referee Mike Thorpe. 'It hit my forehand and I headed it away,' said Eddie. I didn't even think they were shouting for handball against me. I thought it must have been someone else!'

Bournemouth were less fortunate on the hour when Steve Roberts ran into the box and found Lewis Guy with a tap-in from a yard. It needed an 84th minute equaliser from James Hayter to get a point. It was the last occasion Bournemouth would play Doncaster at the Belle Vue ground, before Doncaster moved to their new £32m Keepmoat Stadium.

By the time Darren Anderton was looking on at the Oldham game, the Cherries had built up a bit of momentum and were 13th in the table. The Cherries kept the form going with a win against Crewe Alexander on 9 September 2006. It was a historic game as it proved to be the last for Sean O'Driscoll at the club. After being associated with the club for 23 years, he left to become Doncaster's new manager. It was to be five weeks later when AFC Bournemouth's chairman, Abdul Jaffer, finally found a replacement manager. Kevin Bond, son of former Bournemouth manager John Bond, would take up the position having been dismissed by Newcastle United in September 2006 as assistant manager.

Eddie Howe was confident the Cherries had picked a good new manager. 'He's a good man and a good coach. He brings a wealth of experience here and I think he'll do a great job. Hopefully he can take us to the next level as well. He used to take all the first-team coaching at Portsmouth when I was there so he's dealt with some great players. He used to put on some really good sessions for us and his coaching was a lot of fun and you could always learn from it as well. I think he brings the whole package and, of course, he's got strong links with the club, so I think it's the right appointment,' said Howe.

A 2-2 draw followed against Brighton with Eddie Howe scoring a 74th minute equaliser after Brighton had gone 2-1 ahead. After playing in the 0-0 draw against Brentford, Eddie had to visit a knee specialist and he didn't play again until the FA Cup second round match against Bristol Rovers on 2 December 2006. Howe only came on in the 83rd minute for Shaun Cooper and the match ended 1-1.

Eddie made the full 90 minutes in the next league match against the leaders Nottingham Forest, which the Cherries won 2-0. While beating the top side was seen as a bonus for Kevin Bond's side, it was the game against Port Vale which would be more significant match for Howe, as Port Vale in 12th were a catchable target for lowly AFC Bournemouth who were looking up at almost everyone from 21st place.

'I think we always knew that Port Vale was going to be a more important game. We weren't expected to get anything from Forest, but this game is totally different because we are probably expected to win. I think it's a bigger game and more important. These are the games we have to win and we'll be going all out to do that. Most of the experienced players know that these are the bigger ones for us because we need to beat the teams in and around us in the table,' he said.

While the importance of the game was not lost on the players, the result was a crushing 0-4 defeat to Port Vale. The win over Forest didn't mean as much now.

The appointment of Kevin Bond had also given Eddie Howe the chance to become a player-coach and he accepted the role in early December. Bond said Bournemouth could not afford to bring in more coaches, but by appointing Howe it was a win-win all around. 'Eddie will come in and help out with some of the fringe players and help if we need to concentrate on specific training,' added Bond. 'He fits the bill perfectly and this will give him an introduction into something he has always been keen to do.'

Eddie Howe was open-minded about where the new role might take him. His main thoughts were still on playing as much as he could despite his persistent knee problems. 'My first objective is to play and I want to play. Nothing will take away from that focus. It's no big secret that I've been struggling with my knee for a while. I have good and bad days and can't really predict what it's going to be like from day to day. I'm never going to be 100 per cent and it will always be a bit of a struggle, but the manager is fully aware of my situation. If he needs me to play, I will, providing I think I'm fit enough and will do the team justice.'

Eddie would only play one more match in the year against Scunthorpe away, which was a 3-2 defeat with Howe featuring as a second half sub.

Sadly, the New Year would see the end of Howe's playing career fairly quickly. He played three more times in January with the home fans just able to see him twice, against Brighton and Brentford – two games that Bournemouth won 1-0 – Pitman scoring the 90th minute winner against Brighton and Anderton on the score sheet against Brentford. Eddie had started the season well enough, playing in the first nine games of the campaign, but after the 0-0 draw at Brentford in September, he did not appear in the starting places for a league game again until the memorable home win over Nottingham Forest in December.

Eddie finally played 90 minutes with Darren Anderton in the Brentford match in January, when the Cherries hauled themselves up to 19th in the table. While Anderton would play with Howe in one more match against Crewe on 13 January 2007, this was to be the last time Eddie Howe would play for Bournemouth and his playing career was brought to an abrupt end. It wasn't clear at the time that this would be the outcome and Kevin Bond still hoped that Howe would be back.

'Eddie has played the past three-and-a-half games and done really well for us. But every week, his knee is a little sorer than it was the previous week. It catches up with you in the end and eventually you have to take a step back,' Bond said.

'Hopefully, it will only be for a short period of time and the we can use him again.'

The prognosis was perhaps more hopeful and supportive than realistic. Howe had been suffering for many months and his knee just wasn't up to the rigours of professional football anymore. 'At the end, I was a shadow of the player I had been and I was very keen to finish while people remembered me for the player I was rather than the player I had become,' said Howe. 'It was really tough, because the biggest challenge I found when I came back was that I wasn't as effective. I had lost a lot of my attributes that made me the player I was: my pace, my turning ability, my jump. I wasn't very big for a centre-half so I had to jump well and that was one of my strengths.

'When I came back I was jumping about two feet lower. I struggled with my identity and I lost what I was. Everyone forgets very quickly what you were and judges you on what you are – and I wasn't very good. I found that period of my career very, very difficult.'

It wasn't until June 2007 that Eddie Howe finally called it a day on his playing career. At 29, Howe certainly would have hoped for a few more years on the pitch, but he knew when he had to hang up his boots. 'It's a decision I've been battling with for a number of years but I've had a long time to think about it and have come to terms with it. It's a shame to miss out on the best years of my career, but now is the right time to do it,' said a reflective Howe. 'I will miss playing massively. I will miss getting up every morning and being able to run around and play football for a living but I won't miss getting up and having to hobble about and feeling pain every day. I first sustained the injury when I was 24 and always hoped I would fully recover. But I had another operation a couple of years ago and it's always been at the back of my mind because my knee has never felt the same.

'I played against Crewe and remember quite vividly thinking to myself that it would be my last game. I knew I couldn't go on and realised that with every game I played, I was coming closer to calling it a day. It was becoming a real battle to play. My movement was more limited and my knee was becoming more and more painful. It was just a case of trying to get through games rather than enjoy them and hoping to play well.'

Kevin Bond had been at Portsmouth on the coaching staff when Eddie Howe injured his knee against Nottingham Forest and he had no doubts that Howe would have played in the Premier League, but for the injury he had. But Eddie had to stop playing. 'I think it's a dreadful shame that he's had to pack in but that's football and I know he understands that,' said Bond. 'He would give himself problems in later life if he were to continue so he decided to call it a day.'

Eddie's second spell as a player lasted for 63 games before ending on 1 July 2007. Eddie ended his playing career at the age of 29. He made 313 appearances in two spells as a player for the Cherries until his knee injury finally caused him to end his playing career in 2007.

Bournemouth not only lost Howe as a player but only just avoided relegation, at the end of the season, after a 2-1 defeat at Port Vale to finish 19th.

5. A MODERN COACH (2006-19)

Eddie Howe is always looking to the future
to find new ways to win

Eddie Howe was a tremendous player and may well have reached the very top of the game, but his career was cut short. His misfortune in that respect propelled him into the role of coach much sooner than many like-minded professionals. It has enabled him to experience things that some managers will never have to deal with in their career – let alone in their first managerial job. Eddie was very much thrown in at the deep end when he was appointed manager for AFC Bournemouth in 2009, but before that he had found that his love for the game could be continued with his ability to coach players.

'I was a player when Sean O'Driscoll was in charge and I knew how hard he worked, I knew the job was his life. It has to be if you want to make a success of it,' Eddie said.

'Sean just got us all to question him really. To question his training – why is he putting these training sessions on? Why, when the goalkeeper gets the ball should we all run up the pitch and chase it in the corner? It was the first time I'd ever had anyone question the stereo types that I'd always believed to be right. And I just thought he was a great innovator,' said Howe. 'He was the first person who really went against the grain on everything. He just wanted to do everything differently and that was refreshing.'

In December 2006, Kevin Bond offered Eddie the chance to coach the reserves and he became player-coach at just 29, having already done some scouting for him. 'I didn't think it was something I wanted to do long-term. But once I tried it I got the bug. I suddenly found I was studying, doing my badges and falling in love with it,' said Howe. 'I owe a huge amount to Kevin,' Howe told *BBC South Today*. 'He showed faith in me when I was coming to the end of my career and I was going nowhere. I had no plans set out for me and I'm thankful to Kevin for giving me an opportunity on the coaching side. At that stage I did not know coaching was what I wanted to go into so he pushed me in that direction. I loved working with him and I've always been close to him and speak to him on a regular basis as he is someone I have huge respect for.'

Looking back, Howe can now say he considers himself a teacher but he didn't back in 2006. 'I just did what came naturally to me without analysing it too much. But in time, I realised that I really wanted to coach rather than manage. I wanted to improve players more than care about my profile or how I looked in the media – that had no interest to me whatsoever. It was just about the actual training, so that's where I get my buzz, where I enjoy myself the most, out on the training pitch,' said Howe.

Kevin Bond was clearly pleased with the way Eddie took to coaching, because in June 2007 he offered Eddie and Rob Newman new contracts. The one-year contract for Eddie made him reserve team manager. Eddie had only announced the end to his playing career a week earlier, but had been on the coaching staff for six months. Howe's calm manner with the younger players was just what the club needed. 'To get the best out of young players, they need to be given freedom to play, rather than expecting someone to snap at them for every mistake they make.' Howe said. 'That's what I try and do. The approach at reserve level is to say go out there to impress me and show me what you can do.'

Kevin Bond had every confidence in giving Howe the opportunity to see how good a coach he could become. 'Eddie is very conscientious and very eager to learn. He's just starting off on the bottom rung of the coaching ladder and we are pleased he's decided to start with us, Bond told *the Echo*.

Chairman Jeff Mostyn was just as enthusiastic about Eddie being the reserve team manager. 'It's fantastic to have Eddie on board as part of the coaching staff and he'll be a fantastic role model for the younger players at the club. Eddie has shown tremendous commitment to this football club throughout his career and it's nice for us to be in a position to put something back into the system.'

The job offer to Eddie Howe at the time might not have seemed that enlightened, but if the club had not managed to retain his services at this transitional period, the club would never have had the success that was to follow. Eddie Howe certainly wasn't thinking about the new contract leading to anything more long term. Asked if he thought he could one day become Bournemouth's manager he said, 'I honestly haven't thought about it. I'm doing this job to the best of my ability. You cannot worry about the future, you just have to wait and see what happens.'

Yet, Eddie wasn't ruling himself of rising to the

challenge one day. Eddie knew it would not be an easy job to do, but you can tell that he liked the prospect with the humour of his replies to any such suggestions. 'I've seen how Kevin works behind the scenes and so far, it hasn't put me off. I know what would be required, but it's another thing going out there and doing it... It's a big workload being a manager and it's a very hard job to do properly. But I'm told it's a lot better if you win on Saturday.'

Kevin Bond was also asked by the *Bournemouth Echo* whether he thought Howe had the right ingredients to become Bournemouth's manager one day. Bond said it would just depend on two things. 'Firstly, if and secondly, whether he would want to, he would need to be given the opportunity and quite often that means being in the right place at the right time. Neither Bond nor Howe though could foresee how events would move so quickly to that point. In September 2008 Eddie Howe lost his coaching job, as Kevin Bond along with assistant manager Rob Newman was sacked. Yet, it was only a short period of nine days when Eddie was not involved at the club and his return was something of a surprise even to him.

Reflecting on the decision of Sport-6 and board members Paul Baker and Alastair, some years later in 2018, Eddie Howe said. 'We had been put in a difficult situation with everything that was going on off the pitch and, with it being so early in the season, you think it is unfair. But that is the world of football and you know how volatile it can be. You know these things can happen at any time,' recalled Howe. 'Taking myself back to that day, I wouldn't have seen anything ahead of me in professional football because, at that moment, I probably saw my future away from the game at that level. I probably saw it more towards coaching at youth level and developing younger players. If I hadn't quickly got back in, that is where I would have gone. But I got back immediately with the centre of excellence, so it looked like that would be where I would stay for a period of time.

'Things like this, which are perceived as negative, are life-defining moments. How do you react to that moment and what do you do? I tried to stay very cool, calm and level and to not over-react to the situation. I just tried to figure out what I was going to do next,' said Howe.

Jimmy Quinn became AFC Bournemouth manager on 2 September 2008 and gave Eddie the job of youth team coach. It was perhaps destiny that Eddie stayed with the club in this role. When results did not come for Jimmy Quinn, Eddie Howe was in the right place to take over. It happened just as Bond had predicted. Eddie was around at the right time, during the club's greatest hour of need. But keeping Bournemouth in the football league was a huge job.

When the call came to take charge of the first

team on 31 December 2008, it was totally unexpected and Eddie would have been quite within his rights to say the job was too much for him to take on so soon. But Eddie likes a challenge. 'I have been here since I was 10-years old. I didn't think I'd ever hear anyone say, 'Can you take Bournemouth into the Premier League?' said Howe.

'I always remember the New Year's Eve situation. I was at a party [held at Richard Hughes' house], nothing too raucous, and took a phone call which rocked my world. I was enjoying my job in the centre of excellence and was quite happy with what I was doing.

'When I took the call and I went into a separate room, so that I could hear the conversation. It was close to midnight. Bournemouth were in a state of alarm really, because the situation for the club was grave. Someone was obviously working late at night to make sure the future of the club was okay and, yeah, I got the call offering the job. It was quite bizarre actually.'

'I immediately spoke to my wife – I think I may have sworn a few times – and said we had a decision to make. I told her that if I took the job, it would change our lives forever because she would never see me. I couldn't have been more accurate with that statement!

'That first six months in management, when we managed to stay up, felt like about five years,' he recalled. 'With players not getting paid, the bailiffs turning up, having no training pitch, trying to find ways to do things with no money, it was really difficult. Then add the next season on, when we had a year-long transfer embargo and couldn't sign any players – and we got promotion with that squad.'

The opinions that Eddie had gained to make his own philosophy on football were wide and varied. He was quick to take the opportunity to study how Swansea City managed to climb the leagues and was delighted to be invited by Brendan Rodgers to Wales to see how the club operated.

'I was lucky enough that when I asked, he [Brendan Rodgers] allowed me into Swansea to see how he worked there. He was so generous and I will never forget that.'

The aim has been to play football with bravery and from the back with wide men and pairs and trios of players working together to progress up the pitch and to become clinical when in front of goal. The plan has worked very well and has seen the club climb very quickly through the leagues, much to the envy of fans of other clubs, many of which have had bigger budgets to work with. Eddie only works one way though. He'd soon prove that he wouldn't change the football style of his team just because they faced a Liverpool, a WBA or an Aston Villa or another Premier League side at the time. 'I've never veered away from what our core aims are,' said

Eddie Howe. And this stayed with him when AFC Bournemouth's philosophy of playing open football was highly criticised in their first Premier League season in 2015-16.

Eddie was to meet up with Brendan Rodgers again in January 2014 when Bournemouth took on Liverpool in the FA Cup. The Liverpool manager was impressed by what Howe was building at Dean Court. 'It is coaches like Eddie Howe who will take the game forward in this country because they believe in a way of working and they have a philosophy. Bournemouth are a very good side and I give credit to them first of all,' said Rodgers. 'Eddie is similar to myself in terms of the philosophy of football. It is not easy when you're a young manager to stick your head out to get your teams to play and pass the ball but he certainly does that.'

Stuart Gray is another manager, then at Sheffield Wednesday, who knew Eddie Howe from first-hand experience of working on his coaching staff at Burnley during Eddie's time there. 'I worked with Eddie [Howe] for 12 months when he came in and took over the Burnley job; I have a lot of time for him,' he said. 'I learned a lot from Eddie and he will probably say he learned a lot from me. He's very articulate and hands on at the training ground. He puts a lot of hours in. He's a student of the game. He's very placid, calm and collective individual. He's a very good coach who puts on good sessions. What he has done with Bournemouth is fantastic.'

Russell Beardsmore worked at AFC Bournemouth for its Community scheme and has had another close up view of Howe's coaching skills. 'I used to play here with the [current] manager Eddie Howe and along with another former Bournemouth team-mate Steve Cotterill. They were the ones who I thought would become managers. They were deep thinkers who were already knowledgeable, but always wanted to learn more.'

It's the current AFC Bournemouth team that Russell has been able to see at close quarters and he has seen how Eddie coaches from the sidelines. 'They train at a high-tempo and include all the lads, even those not playing,' he says.

Eddie is at home more than ever when he is on the training pitch. This is when you see him at his best in the job he loves to do. Being around players that want to learn and to improve their skill is a tonic to him and that buzz he gets from it seems to translate to the players.

'Good football to me, is in part, making sure your players develop and I know that's not directly linked to the style, but how your players are going to develop every day. So, for me how many more touches you can give them with the ball, the more you can flood them with technical decisions, football-based decisions they are going to become better' said Eddie Howe. 'To do that you need to train in a certain way. You need to give them the ball as much as you can in tight situations.

'To do that then to get the benefit from training, you need to do the same in the game. So being expansive with the ball, being brave with the ball – not making 50/50 calls in playing balls up that are based on percentages – working the ball up with your team, from defence to attack.'

The aim was to make AFC Bournemouth a supply chain, improving every player at the club from youth teams to the U21 squad and first team. It is central to the Bournemouth and the Eddie Howe ethos.

'I believe we put a lot of work into improving players to make them and the team better. If you do that for six months with a loan player and they return to their parent club, you develop them but you do it for someone else,' said Eddie Howe in an interview with the *Bournemouth Echo*. 'I prefer to develop the players we have here for us so we reap the rewards of that hard work and not the parent club.'

What makes Howe stand out is his studious hunger for the game. Former AFC Bournemouth defender, John Williams said, 'The attention to the detail is the one. He is always looking for that different edge, that little angle. How your team plays, defends – he is always trying to pick up on something that is going to make a difference.'

The Bournemouth players also know that Howe gives them the extra-edge to win games and most of it is done on the training pitch. Simon Francis explained to Daniel Storey, of the *Set Pieces website*, the innovative approaches that Eddie can bring to a practice session. 'We work a lot on training on the stuff that Guardiola does, what he did at Barcelona and does at Bayern. Obviously, we're nowhere near what they are doing, but Eddie likes to look at them and how they are playing positionally. We have to prepare for every eventuality. He's the next level with this kind of thing, honestly. We do some sessions in training where we get split into two XIs. One team will go into one changing room and one into the other. One team is Barcelona and the other Bayern Munich. We pretend it's the second leg of a Champions League game and one team is 2-1 down and with 10-men, so they have to go for it. We'll go out onto the pitch and we'll play the last 15 minutes out with two different styles of play.'

Eddie Howe gave an in-depth interview with Guillem Balague in 2017, for *TalkSport*, which threw unprecedented light on how Eddie wanted to develop his attractive brand of football. From video preparations on the opposition to walk through tactical positioning for goal kicks and free kicks and corners, nothing is left to chance.

Charlie Daniels speaking on *TalkSport* to Matt Holland in August 2015 said about Eddie that no day is the same when training at AFC Bournemouth. 'He sets you targets and goals. It is all based on working up to the next game. I don't know any other coach that works like that,' said Daniels.

Darren Anderton also explained why Eddie's coaching was doing so well in AFC Bournemouth's first season back in the Championship in 2013-14. 'As a player, Eddie was always very organised, a thorough professional who trained brilliantly and did everything whole-heartedly. You can see he has clearly impressed those values on his players. You can see he always had a very good chance [in management] because of his mentality. He always wanted to do it and it was no surprise to see him do so well,' said Anderton. 'After I left, I stayed in touch with a lot of the boys and they spoke very highly of him. There was a buzz about them and Eddie's impact was instant.

Still, you can't forget either that there is someone close by Eddie Howe's side, assistant manager JT. Jason knows better than anyone how Eddie works and how he expects to get the best out of everyone. Eddie Howe is also very clear on making sure people know that Jason and him are very much a management team. Having returned to Bournemouth in 2012 Eddie Howe explained that success was always easier with JT working with him. 'We bounce off each other and I am very comfortable with his ideas on the game and my ideas on the game, and they mirror each other well. I think we bring out the best in each other in terms of always trying to push the boundaries to find new ideas, and trying to evolve our coaching style. If you are still doing the same drills you did two years ago, you have stood still. We are always trying to find an edge and a new way of doing things. I am very thankful to have him [Jason] by my side and I know we are better as a team than we are individually, so I think that is the important thing,' commented Howe.

'No one is going to give you the success or wins and you have to earn every one. You do that by working as hard as you can to be the best prepared as you can be. That is very much our motto and we both share that together,' explained Howe.

The next game is certainly the most important thing for Eddie and he was clear about this in the period of his managerial career when he returned to Bournemouth after leaving Burnley. 'From my perspective, I don't have a long-term view on things. I was very ambitious as a player where I wanted to try and reach the highest level that I could and I worked every day to try and make myself better. I'm the same as the manager. I try and learn and develop myself every day, but in terms of my ambitions I don't have a long-term goal to say this is what I must achieve. I think I have slightly changed in that respect. It's now that I must win the next game.'

he said. 'That's the only thing that I'm bothered about and I will work towards that.'

6. MINUS 17 (2008-09)

Cometh the hour, cometh the man

Kevin Bond lasted 22 months in the manager's job at
Bournemouth, having been appointed in October
2006 he was in charge when the club was relegated
to League Two in 2007-08. He had presided over the
club during some of its most troubled years with
Gerald Krasner of Begbies Traynor having overseen
the sale of the club, when it had fallen into
administration on 8 February 2008. Then, it was the
financial support of Jeff Mostyn and his £100,000

payment that would ultimately save the club from
complete financial collapse and liquidation in April
2008. That was only the tip of the iceberg in terms of
the funds Mostyn had already sunk into the club by
then.

Mostyn had become involved in the Cherries
having come down from Manchester to support
Kevin Bond and soon found himself investing in AFC
Bournemouth's black hole. It was a huge gamble by
Mostyn to keep funding the club. He has rightly been
adored by the Bournemouth fans for his vision and
support in the club's darkest hours. But I don't
believe Jeff ever thought then that the club would
be heading to the Premier League, only seven years
later. He stepped in to save an institution that had
given pleasure to the local community for
generations, and he was not prepared to see it fold
without a fight.

Administration had also meant a 10-point
deduction and Bournemouth would be relegated on
the last day of the season to League Two. The club
had been some £4 million in debt, according to a
report on the *BBC*. While a rival consortium headed
by Marc Jackson was at one stage the preferred
bidder for the club, it was Sport-6 that took
ownership in the summer of 2009. Abdul Jaffer and
Jeff Mostyn had been talking to Paul Baker and
Alastair Saverimutto, the men behind the Sport-6
bid. Their hard work had paid off, or so they thought,

when Sport-6 bought the club.

The rocky administrative landscape at Dean Court in the summer of 2008 did at least steady enough for the club to take part in the new season. The 2008-09 season that will be remembered by Bournemouth fans as one of the most traumatic and yet ultimately satisfying ever. The club had been relegated to League Two and was not even starting level on points with most of the other teams. 'We find ourselves as new owners with a new season and a huge deficit to claw back, minus 17 points. It's quite a significant penalty,' said Alastair Saverimutto, AFC Bournemouth's then chief executive.

Sport-6 had taken control of the club in July 2008 and Alastair Saverimutto and Paul Baker were the men handed the challenge to get the club back on its feet. Bournemouth would fight on with just 14 senior players.

The cards dealt to the club at the start of the season were tough, to say the least. As well as having a transfer embargo, the club had been saddled with the deduction, regarding its failure to comply with a Company Voluntary Agreement (CVA) on emergence from administration. The same fate had befallen Rotherham Utd, while Luton had found themselves starting the season on -30 points, following failure to satisfy the league's insolvency rules. The Cherries felt they had, at least, a fighting chance with only two clubs certain of being relegated to the conference come the end of the season. But the club had been also forced to sell its best players in James Hayter and Sam Vokes. Neither Kevin Bond, nor the chairman knew that the administrators had decided to accept a £400,000 bid from Wolves for Sam Vokes, but no one was really in a position to argue. As administrator, Gerard Krasner had to sell what he could to keep the club going.

Bournemouth's points deduction to the League Two campaign in 2008-09 was not something that would win back many fans. Things didn't start too badly with a 1-1 draw at home with Gillingham, but the Cherries had been hauled back, after Darren Anderton had given them the lead, with an injury-time equaliser from Gary Mulligan's first touch, having come on as a late substitute. A crowd of 5377 had seen the opening game of the season.

Any optimism, in August, of a new start was soon quelled. Kevin Bond's squad got off to an awful run of defeats, gaining just two points by the 1 September 2008, when Bond parted company at the club. Kevin Bond hadn't managed to improve performances following on from Sean O'Driscoll, but it wasn't through a lack of trying. At that time Eddie Howe, who had been reserve team boss under Bond, also lost his job. Sport-6 wanted their own man in, Jimmy Quinn. Luckily for Eddie, the new manager, was more than pleased to give Eddie the position of heading up the centre of excellence.

The first league win didn't come until a 1-3 away win at Bradford City on 20 September 2008. Surprisingly, it was followed be another 3-1 win against Darlington, at home, with Marvin Bartley and Brett Pitman on the score sheet as well as an own goal from Darlington's Neil Austin. Darren Anderton was the captain. Still a class act, Anderton got the winner a few weeks later against Milton Keynes Dons in the Johnstone's Paint Trophy second round.

Jimmy Quinn was still finding his feet in the manager's role by the time Rotherham United visited Dean Court on 11 October 2008. Rotherham had also been docked points at the start of the season and yet had made a much better start to the campaign, having already reached a positive-points total of one. 'Most of the talking points leading up to today's game is that it is a game between the two clubs who had 17 points deducted at the start of the season,' noted Quinn. 'I'm not looking at it in that way. I am looking at it and asking the question, are we 17 points better than other teams in our division? And I think we are and I believe it is only going to be a matter of time before we get into the black. We need to get out of the relegation zone, and I believe we will do that. We need to strengthen in one or two areas and that is something I am trying to do. I feel that if we get a couple of players in the right positions, we can be more than a match for anybody.'

Optimism aside, Bournemouth had only won two of their first 10 games and they were only to get a 0-0 draw against Rotherham United. Quinn, true to his word, signed Blair Sturrock on loan from Swindon. The Scottish striker made one league start, in the next game, against Shrewsbury Town when the team lost 4-1.

By early October the crowds had slumped quite dramatically for home games. Only 3554 fans saw the 2-1 win over Dagenham and Redbridge with AFC Bournemouth sitting in 23rd place in the league. That day a certain Matt Ritchie, a future AFC Bournemouth star player, came on as a sub for Dagenham and Redbridge.

The 1-0 FA Cup first round win over Bristol Rovers had a crowd of 3935. Bournemouth were at least showing a bit of form, but they crashed 0-3 against mid-table Accrington Stanley in the next league match. Before the away match with Grimsby, Quinn brought in striker Matt Tubbs on loan from Salisbury City. Tubbs had been at the school of excellence as a youth at Bournemouth, but had ended up in non-league football when he'd failed to get a contract with the Cherries. It was third time lucky for the striker to get to play for the club, but he was also to return under Lee Bradbury's management in January 2012, when he was to cost Bradbury £0.5 million and not the £0.8 million often quoted in the media.

Quinn later revealed that he thought his meeting,

with the board of directors, on New Year's Eve was to be about whether the club could afford to buy Matt Tubbs permanently. 'I already knew all about Matt before he arrived on loan,' said Quinn. 'He has always been a terrific goalscorer and he [Matt] wanted to know if there was any chance of him staying until the end of the season. I wanted to keep him but the club being in a bit of trouble and wages not being paid, I couldn't give him an answer. I had a meeting on New Year's Eve, which I thought would be about the possibility of money to spend in the new window, only to be told I was no longer required. Unfortunately, Matt was left in limbo.'

An early FA Cup exit to Blyth Spartans in a replay game at the start of December hardly helped the atmosphere, heaping more pressure on Jimmy Quinn. Coming in the 90th minute of the game, substitute Ged Dalton had scored a goal that would stay in the minds of Bournemouth fans for many years. It was one of the lowest points in the club's history. Brett Pitman will also have had better games than this one, when he was red carded after 59 minutes for a foul on Paul Watson. The forward would have to serve a lengthy suspension period.

It wasn't until the bottom-two game against Luton Town on 2 December 2008 and a thrilling 3-3 draw that saw the Cherries finally work off their pre-season 17-point deduction to reach zero points. Two Mark Molesley goals had kept Bournemouth in the

game, before new signing Matt Tubbs scored
Bournemouth's third goal against Luton. But Tubbs
was only to make eight appearances for the Cherries
in this season.

December was not a complete write-off. A 2-0
home win over second placed Bury gave home fans
something to be pleased about before Christmas.
Joe Partington also scored his first league goal for
the Cherries against Bury. But defeats to Bradford
City and Barnet still left the Cherries in 23rd place.
The axe finally fell on Jimmy Quinn as the club's
manager following the appointment of a new board
on 31 December 2008 that called on Eddie Howe to
become the youngest manager in the football
league. On a dramatic evening, Paul Baker stepped
down as chairman and his shares were sold to a
consortium headed by Adam Murry. When Eddie
was invited to take over the caretaker manager's
position the club was second-bottom and were
entering the New Year still seven points from safety.
Eddie's first task was to ask himself, did he really
want the position?

If Eddie was daunted by the task facing him, he
didn't show it. 'I was forced to work with the players
I had,' Howe recalls. 'What a great learning tool. It
made me realise, sometimes you don't have to look
for new players, you just have to make the ones you
have work better.' This was an opportunity to save
the club he loved. To establish himself as a young

manager who also had something to prove, having seen his playing career cut short. *The Guardian* wrote in March 2009 that the appointment of Eddie Howe was likely to have been seen by many as: 'a last throw of the dice'. All I can say is, that was some throw!

From a personal point of view, it was probably Eddie who was taking all the risks. He had not been a full-time manager before and the task he faced of keeping the team up was looking bleak, to say the least. Two managers had already been in place since the start of the season and they had both failed, so why should a young 31-year-old, with only youth and reserve team managerial experience be any better at the job?

'It was a crash course in management at its harshest level,' said Eddie. 'I'd had two years as a coach under Kevin Bond and experienced relegation. I'd been sacked from that job and had a lot of lows. That can only inspire you not to go through it again, but it could all have been over very quickly and I would never have been seen again.'

The one person that Eddie knew he could rely on for support was Jason Tindall. 'We were not great friends as team-mates. We didn't socialise. We had a mutual respect but we weren't close, we didn't really have a relationship. When I was offered this job, I said I wanted Jason [then the assistant manager] to stay. I didn't know whether we would work together well, but we instantly clicked and have not looked back.

Eddie was well aware of the people around him at the club and it was no surprise that he asked Jason Tindall to be his assistant as he had been number two to Jimmy Quinn. Continuity is something that the club has always believed in. Eddie would need support from someone he could trust to back him and help him make the difficult decisions that would surely have to be faced.

'I didn't go into the job with any set plan,' says Eddie Howe. 'Being in management came as quite a shock really, in terms of how I was offered the job and the position at the club. At that moment in time it was all about staying in League Two. Trying to get as many points as we could to stay out of the Conference.'

Eddie hadn't wasted any time in bringing players in either. On the Friday 16 January he had completed the loan signings of Jake Thomson from Southampton, Rhoys Wiggins from Crystal Palace and, keeper, David Button from Tottenham Hotspur.

The first match that Eddie took control of, as caretaker manager, was the match against Darlington which the Cherries lost 2-1 in front of a crowd of 2571. A 90th minute penalty by Rob Purdie spoiled Eddie Howe's big day. It didn't go much better in his second match, as Rotherham beat the Cherries at home 1-0 and Danny Hollands was sent off for two yellow card offences. Howe had given starts to three new loan signings, but Mark Hudson's 18th minute strike decided the day. The disappointment for Bournemouth was particularly felt as Alan Connell had a late goal disallowed for offside.

Speaking about the game, new signing Rhoys Wiggins was not sure Danny Hollands should have seen red. 'I thought the sending off was very harsh. I put in a far worst tackle about five minutes later and didn't get a booking. Danny got booked just prior to the sending off and I think he could have got away with a warning,' Wiggins said sympathetically.

After the match, Bournemouth remained only above Luton in the table in 23rd place, on seven points, chasing Grimsby who were 10 points ahead of them after 25 games. Despite losing his first two games in charge, on 19 January 2009, Eddie Howe was named the permanent manager of AFC Bournemouth.

One positive Howe had was to see striker Brett Pitman return for the games against Darlington and Rotherham, following his suspension from the Blythe Spartans FA Cup replay. Brett returned having every confidence that Howe was the right man to have on charge. 'A lot has happened to say the least!' said a bewildered Pitman. 'Eddie has come in along with Jason and Joe [Roach] and all the lads will work ever so hard for them and they have got a lot of respect

from everyone here. It is good that they can provide
continuity. Eddie is very tactically switched on along
with Jason and Joe, so we will have no problems
there. They will take each game on its merits and
this week we will be working on a game plan to
counter a good Wycombe side,' Pitman told *Match
Day programme*.

Eddie Howe's first thoughts as Bournemouth
manager were also fully explained in the programme
for the Wycombe Wanderers match on 24 January
2009. 'It is with a great deal of pride that I write my
first notes. I have really enjoyed being in charge and
delighted with the lads' attitude and commitment.
This has all happened very quickly and it's a brilliant
honour for me and I can't thank the board enough
for giving me this opportunity,' said an enthusiastic
Howe.

Why indeed wouldn't he be enthusiastic? He was
thrust into the top job in a pretty much impossible
position, trailing Grimsby Town, and possible safety,
by 10 points. But he didn't appear daunted by the
task, which was probably why we all now think
'anything is possible' at our club.

'My message to you all is to stick with us and we
will do our best. We know that we need to dig out
some results and we need all of you with us as we
strive to do that...' said Howe. 'It is a simple aim we
have, to keep this club in the Football League. I know
I have to get results and I am under no illusions

about the task ahead.'

Credit should go to Adam Murry, director of operations at the club, who with the other directors decided that Howe was the best option to lead the club to safety. Murry knew it was a big risk. 'The actions we took on New Year's Eve had to be made if we were to achieve our aim of maintaining our Football League status. I wholeheartedly believe we can. The performances at Darlington and Rotherham showed some of the confidence and self-belief that has been missing too often throughout the season,' he added.

But appointing Eddie Howe as manager was not perhaps the biggest concern of the club at that point. It was more a case of keeping the club going that would pre-occupy Murry. 'Part of my role as director of operations will be to work closely with Eddie and his team, offering all the support he needs, and to look at the structure of the club, particularly with regard to getting costs down. Work has already started on that, but please be patient with me. There's a lot to do and plenty of 'firefighting' to tackle on a day to day basis. But I promise you this. I will be honest and open about what we are doing and how things are,' Murry said.

Bournemouth captain, Shaun Cooper, expressed the atmosphere among the players in Eddie Howe's two first games in charge and before the match with Wycombe Wanderers in his programme notes. 'In the first game, we should have got a result against Darlington and were really unfortunate to come away empty handed. Even though we lost that game it was a step in the right direction and the lads probably gained a bit of confidence. We had a game plan and stuck to it and it showed how it can work for us. Obviously, it doesn't sound right because we lost, but performance wise it was good and there were a lot of positives,' said Cooper.

Direction is what the players needed and Eddie, as we now know, is quite a meticulous planner and worker and the new regime hit home with the players, once they put their trust in what Eddie was trying to get each of them to do.

'Eddie likes to go in to games with a plan and makes everyone aware of what they are doing. It nearly worked at Darlington, we were close at Rotherham at the end and the more games we play like that, then I'm pretty sure we'll start to get results,' Cooper added.

There was certainly an improvement in the mood around Dean Court following Howe's permanent appointment and things on the pitch were about to get a whole lot better. The signing that turned things around for Eddie Howe, and the Cherries, was the welcome return of Super Steve Fletcher from Crawley Town on 22 January 2009. It was a shock signing, but one that Eddie Howe will always look back on as the trigger for the club's amazing transformation into a team with belief. At 36, Steve Fletcher was not the youngest striker around in League Two, but he had the heart, desire and knowledge to win games. He was Mr Bournemouth, through and through, and just what Eddie and the team needed at that time.

'So, I think my first signing was Steve Fletcher. He was a 6ft 3in old fashion target man,' said Eddie Howe. 'Long ball?' said Jamie Carragher when interviewing Eddie on the subject. 'Yes, erm. At that time,' said Eddie. 'I'm not proud to admit that. And I've got to say Fletch was magnificent for the club and we were able to achieve our goals. It was not about style of play at that stage, it was about survival and of course we have adapted as we have gone on and learnt what we have wanted and what we don't,' said Eddie.

'In terms of the style of football, that definitely evolved after the first season. The first season was all about survival. It really hurt me at the time to play quite direct football but we did – we had no choice with the players that we had,' added Howe.

The first home game of Eddie's first spell as manager was against Wycombe Wanderers and Steve Fletcher recalls that it was the game that started the ball rolling as far as believing that they just might be able to stay up. 'We had nearly 6000 here that day, and all of a sudden the belief from the squad and the supporters was that 'we can stay up' -

just from that one victory,' said Fletcher.

Before the game against Wycombe on 24 January, the Cherries had 21 matches to go in the season and were 10 points from safety. The match went as well as could be expected from being a goal down in the ninth minute. A 3-1 win for the home side in front of a crowd of 5946. It gave the team a start. The players were still going to find it tough though, while co-owners Paul Baker and Alastair Saverimutto (Sport-6) were still looking for potential buyers for the club. It was a PFA loan in March that enabled the club to pay the player's wages for the month of February. A percentage of the back pay had already been paid though in cash. It was handed out to the players from a Marks and Spencer bag, along with money from gate receipts, in the dressing room by a member of staff before the Port Vale game. Unlike Fletcher, some of the squad players were youngsters and trainees. Jayden Stockley was still at school.

Bournemouth weren't the only club facing problems as Darlington were deducted 10 points having entered into administration in February 2009. Darlington wouldn't be in trouble in the table though as they had bagged over 50 points by then, whereas Bournemouth were down in 23rd place on 18 points, five points behind Grimsby Town.

At around this time, Bournemouth gave a trial to Charlie Austin. He was under contract at Poole Town and had scored 24 goals in 20 starts for the Dolphins. Austin had been playing in the Wessex league but had impressed Howe. Eddie couldn't commit to taking him and suggested he might look at him again in pre-season. While Charlie would train in the summer with the Cherries, it was ultimately the embargo on transfers for Bournemouth that stopped Howe from signing Austin. Therefore, Charlie was destined to join Swindon Town in the following October.

Howe had better luck in bringing in Liam Feeney, an expert winger from Salisbury Town on a two-and-a-half-year deal in February, along with Anton Robinson, who would be a key central midfielder.

By March, it was evident that Eddie Howe had taken to management like a duck to water. Asked whether he found it difficult asking things of players that were older than him, Eddie had commented: 'I haven't found any downside yet to being a young manager. We'll have to wait and see,' he says. 'Ring me back in about a year and I'll tell you.'

The team was digging in well. Going a goal behind against Exeter City and struggling to pass the ball well, Steve Fletcher said Eddie Howe didn't tear strips off them at half-time, but simply told them to relax and play the football they had shown in training all week. It did the trick – Bournemouth made a 1-3 comeback. They had climbed to 20th in the table, by 17 March 2009, and notched up another big win 4-1 against Bradford city with Steve Fletcher on the score sheet twice.

Things were still happening off the pitch that were causing huge concern. Adam Murry's consortium had gained control of the club by the Notts County game in March and, in his programme notes, Adam explained he had settled up the winding up petition the previous week, so the club could keep trading. The rent was paid, but HMRC remained a serious issue.

Bournemouth were now seven points clear of the bottom two and things were looking up on the pitch, until defeats to Notts County and Bury dropped the Cherries back down to 21st in the league. With six games to play the pressure was really on and Rochdale, in third place, came visiting after a couple of indifferent performances from the Cherries. But a 4-0 home win, with goals from Liam Feeney and Brett Pitman's first senior hat-trick, boosted the Cherries' chances of survival, although narrow defeats to Barnet and Brentford at the end of April opened up the trap door again.

It was not the time that Howe wanted to play league leaders Brentford. Bournemouth lost to a single goal by Billy Clarke, even though Brentford were reduced to 10-men, having had Darren Powell sent off after 49 minutes. The need to survive was very apparent though among the fans with a whopping crowd of 8168.

Eddie Howe's own position was not clear either. While he battled to keep the team in the league, there were no guarantees that his contract would be extended. Former Cherry, John Bailey, spoke about the situation in April. 'He's done a fantastic job and, if we stay up they've got to give him a five or 10-year contract,' Bailey suggested.

There were still big games to go though, against Chester and Grimsby especially, where the Cherries would need to points to stay up. Eddie Howe recalls: 'When I think back to the Grimsby and Chester games, it wasn't enjoyable and I didn't relish those moments. It was a case of just trying to get the job done and looking to the future. I thought about the dire consequences and I didn't want to be the guy who took the club into oblivion,' Howe said.

The culmination of the season, on 25 April 2009, was as dramatic as any in the club's history. It was winner takes all against Grimsby Town in battle for league survival. The importance of the game was not lost on a home crowd of 9008 who witnessed Steve Fletcher's greatest hour. Nathan Jarman had scored first for Grimsby in the 40th minute and Eddie Howe had to find the words required at half-time to help save the Cherries from tumbling into non-league football. It was going to be 45 minutes of jangling nerves and Liam Feeney gave the home crowd hope, when he equalised after 47 minutes. The game was not the best advert for beautiful football, but it was all about who would come out on top, and after 80 minutes Steve Fletcher repaid his signing in full. His now legendary chest down, turn and volleyed strike saw the ball rifle into the roof of the net. The home fans were able to watch Big'Un (as he is affectionately called) run over to the Main Stand and celebrate along the touchline, twirling his shirt up in the air, before stopping to show his muscle-man pose, before he was mobbed by his team-mates. It was mission accomplished.

At the end of the season the team had recorded 46 points and were safe in 21st pace. It was the home form that had kept the club up with 11 wins, while six away wins had also been managed – the last of these was a last day of the season 0-4 thumping of Morecambe.

The month of May not only brought the end of a remarkable season, it also left co-owner Paul Baker with a decision to make about selling the club. While Eddie Howe would also have a say in the new owners, Baker was making plans that Eddie Howe would remain as manager no matter what. 'All the interested parties have been asked whether Eddie is part of their plans going forward and, to a man, every one of them has given me a positive answer,' said Baker.

There were still some unanswered questions about Eddie Howe's contract, but the fans were aware that every effort would be made to keep

Eddie Howe as manager. Ryan Garry was also convinced Howe would stay, as he signed in June on a free. 'Eddie is a huge reason why I'm happy to stay. I like him as a person and, as a manager, he's spot-on. You always know where you stand and I like him as a coach and enjoy working under him,' said Garry.

Things quickly sorted themselves out. As part of the Adam Murry Consortium, Eddie Mitchell took over as the new chairman in June 2009 and quickly formed a strong partnership with Eddie Howe and Jason Tindall. In July 2009, Murry gave the Howe and Tindall management team three-year contracts at the club. Jeff Mostyn also returned along with goalkeeping coach Neil Moss, which meant Vince Bartram who had been at the club, since Kevin Bond was the manager, was let go.

Eddie Howe recalls the first time he met Eddie Mitchell there were a few words said. It was 'quite hilarious. We had a stand-up argument for about 10 minutes and were effing and blinding at each other, that was a good start!' said Howe.

The situation both men faced was incredibly difficult because of the transfer embargo being in place for the season. Eddie Howe had a clear objective now – to turn the club into a successful one – and he wanted close friends around him.

'Hopefully we can have some stability – which I think the club is crying out for – both at the boardroom and managerial level. We can try to be successful in the coming three years and really look forward to a brighter future,' he hoped.

There was no certainty that everything would go well. Eddie Howe was as cautious as ever about a lot of work still needing to be done. 'We don't want to be shouting from the rooftops saying we're going to do this, that and the other. There is a long way to go before the start of the season and a lot of hard work needs to be done. As a squad, we will be focused and prepared for the new season. We will also be fiercely determined to do as well as we can. This club has spent long periods battling against the odds and that has certainly been the case so far during the close season. But the club is still in existence and, at some stages, that seemed to be in the balance. There is a real optimism in the camp but we also have to be realistic. People just have to be sensible with what they expect because this is a tough league and it's going to be another hard season.' said Howe.

7. WE COME FROM LEAGUE TWO (2009-10)

Even at the start of the 2009-10 season, Eddie Howe was having to watch the pennies and try and build a side that could take the club away from the bottom of League Two. The players also wanted to help and Warren Cummings was, no doubt, not alone in making a considerable pay-cut to help the club when he signed in July. The club chairman made clear the position in August, stating that the club had to pay off its creditors before it would have the transfer embargo lifted. While the club had worked off the points deduction of the previous season, it had accumulated another £1m of debt. AFC Bournemouth had to start leaving within its means.

That meant Howe would have 20 players at the start of the season, two less than the season before. Eddie Mitchell was adamant that Howe was the right man to manage the team, but he would also need the financial means to keep the team doing well when injuries occurred. Shaun Cooper was already out for six months with a hip injury and Danny

Hollands had to have an operation on his knee in early August. As rumours of centre-back Jason Pearce being linked with Wolves and Plymouth surfaced, Eddie Mitchell was clear that Bournemouth did not have to sell their skipper. 'If Eddie [Howe] wanted to sell players, that would be his prerogative and his choice – not mine,' said Mitchell.

Another important deal was seeing Brett Pitman commit to a three-year deal at Dean Court. He admitted that Howe and JT were a massive part in why he decided to sign the deal and he knew what his job was. 'I'm in the side to score goals, but if I work hard for the team and the goals come that's a bonus,' he enthused.

Well the team and Brett Pitman could not have got off to a better start with a 0-3 away win over Bury. Brett, Anton Robinson and Mark Molesley scored the goals and optimism was instantly installed in the fans, although Eddie Howe was less convinced that the result would lead to a good season. 'It's a good start for us but we're not getting carried away,' he said. 'If anyone had offered me three-nil before the game I'd bitten their arm off. We've got a fantastic group of players and they've responded again with a really good performance.'

While the Cherries were thumped 4-0 by Millwall in the Carling Cup, there was no panic about the result as matters soon turned to the league again.

Even after the second league game win over Rotherham United there was no way Eddie was thinking any more than another three points safely tucked away. 'The lads gave everything today and we looked a threat going forward despite only scoring one goal,' he said.

Sometimes football is about momentum and the Cherries had found a taste for winning after going so close to being booted out of the league. This season would be different. After seven games and a 3-1 win over Lincoln City, on 12 September 2009, the Cherries sat proudly on top of League Two. It was six wins out of seven, and while the crowds were only just nudging over 5000, Howe believed the good football results would bring them back. Eddie was even in line to be the League Two manager of the month but lost out to Dagenham & Redbridge's John Still. Howe didn't want to be concerned with such matters though. 'Things like that don't bother me in the slightest. All I'm concerned with is trying to get results so awards like that, although they are nice, don't mean anything,' he added.

Howe had taken the Cherries from the depths of League Two and oblivion to one of the best teams in the division in just eight months. The 1-0 win against Burton Albion was completed with just 14 players available to the Cherries, so it was somewhat of a relief when the football league allowed Bournemouth to sign one player on a non-contract basis. It was more or less make do with what you have for Howe and he needed favours from the players like Marvin Bartley, who was used as a make-shift centre-back, for the Johnstone's paint Trophy match against Northampton Town in October. Bartley was far from wanting Howe to pick him there every week, even though the manager thought he was 'outstanding' in the match. 'I know a few players who have dropped back, but it's usually when they get older and slower,' Bartley jested. 'Eddie asked me if I could play centre-back and I said I hadn't for about 10 years. He said – that'll do!'

A player that did catch Eddie Howe and JT's eye was Marc Pugh. Pugh lined up for Hereford against the Cherries on 29 September and scored twice, as Bournemouth fell to their second defeat of the season. But Eddie Howe saw something special in Pugh that he would not forget. Eddie had also tried to bring Steve Lovell, his brother, in on loan in October. However, the football league blocked the move of the former Falkirk striker to Bournemouth. Max Gradel at Leicester City was also much desired, following his loan spell in 2007-8.

Still, a player that was doing well at Bournemouth was striker Alan Connell. He was told he'd keep his place in the team, after scoring in the 3-1 home win over Grimsby Town in October. That was his first league goal for the Cherries since October 2004, having had terrible knee injury problems. He'd also had to deal with the loss of his mother. Eddie Howe was pleased with Connell's performances and he needed him with numbers of the squad so low. 'He is a little unfortunate because he's got Brett Pitman and Steve Fletcher as competition and they have both been outstanding,' commented Howe. 'But competition can only benefit the team and, if Alan keeps playing well, he will keep his place.'

Meanwhile, Eddie Mitchell was trying to win more time to head off the HMRC's winding up order for the club, as well as unfreezing the current account to pay wages. A tough defeat also came at the end of October when Rochdale moved into second place with a thumping 0-4 away win at Dean Court. Rochdale's manager, Keith Hill had no sympathy for the Cherries financial position saying they overspent to the detriment of other teams in the league – he exacted his punishment on the pitch it seems. The Cherries were battered by Chris O'Grady's great strikes and yet Eddie still pointed out the positives in his players and the larger crowd of 6378 was something to be pleased about.

'We need to use this as a watershed game; move on from it, but learn from it and use it as motivation,' said Howe. 'We're still in a great position, so it's not all doom and gloom. The lads are very disappointed which is a good sign, it shows they care.'

The players had endured periods when they had not been paid and the transfer embargo on the club had severe consequences which were still resonating as late as November 2009, when the club went to an away game at Bradford. 'There were only 15 players on the coach travelling to the match, so we had a lot of room to stretch out,' said Eddie Howe in jest.

Amazingly Eddie Howe had carried the team to the top of the division having won nine out of their first 10 games. He had only signed one player, the versatile, Anthony Edgar, from West Ham on loan for a month and that was only allowed after it was clear that the team would be struggling to put out a side with their injuries. School boy, Jayden Stockley had to make up the numbers.

Succeeding in such difficult times meant that Eddie Howe's progress was being monitored closely by other clubs. When an offer came in from Peterborough United to manage their team in November 2009, it came as a shock to most Bournemouth fans. The approach was handled very diplomatically though by Eddie Mitchell. 'I met with Eddie and Jason this morning after letting them know of the interest late last night. Eddie, Jason and myself were all very flattered that somebody had taken the trouble to approach us,' said Mitchell. 'But the circumstances are that Eddie and Jason are keen to see us progress and want to stick with us.

The AFC Bournemouth team was probably not as talented as the players at Peterborough, but Bournemouth had menace in the tackling of Marvin Bartley and the calm distribution of Anton Robinson and Danny Hollands in midfield. Brett Pitman was scoring the goals, while Shwan Jalal, Stuart Pearce and Shaun Cooper were keeping goals out at the other end. The club now had momentum. They were used to being written off and had started to play some very attractive football that was bringing results.

I recall going to the second round FA Cup match against Notts County at the end of November with my mate Colin Waite and my two boys. It was kind of a grudge match as the Bournemouth fans viewed County as one of the big teams. County would prove to be a worthy foe over the course of the season. Just the sight of Lee Hughes would make me fear Bournemouth would be taken apart. He had that little celebration jig when he scored that used to infuriate me and many others I'm sure. It was the first time in 20 years that I had been back at Dean Court to see a game and I didn't bring much luck. Bournemouth only managed to put one goal past Kasper Schmeichel, who already looked too good for League One. Of course, Lee Hughes got on the score sheet and Craig Westcarr heaped on the agony with the winner nine minutes from time. But by that time, it was too late, Robert and Stephen and me had

*already got the AFC Bournemouth and Eddie Howe
bug. We'd come back again, for sure.*

So, the club had been knocked out of the FA Cup
in the second round 1-2 by the League Two
heavyweights of Notts County, who were managed
by Sven Göran-Eriksen. But the team remained in
second place throughout December, despite Eddie
Howe's biggest ever defeat – a 0-5 away pummeling
by Morecambe. It was a debut for goal keeper
Marek Stech he'd rather have forgotten. Stech was
brought in on an emergency seven-day loan by the
Cherries from West Ham for the game, as Shawn
Jalal was out with a calf problem and Danny Thomas
was suffering from a back problem. Eddie Howe
didn't just have goal keeping problems. Marvin
Bartley had been sent off during the Morecambe
game for a challenge on Stewart Drummond and he
had to miss three matches.

If the defeat wasn't bad enough, the club missed
out on a big TV payday of £50,000 a few days later,
when the Notts County match was called off because
of a frozen pitch, despite the best efforts of fans and
the chairman's Seven Developments company trying
the clear the pitch.

Jeff Mostyn was still doing his best to get the
football league's transfer embargo lifted, having
notified them that the HM Revenues & Customs
(HMRC) debt was cleared. The legacy debt though
from the previous owners was still not paid off and

the league would not lift the embargo for loan players until it was.

The Boxing Day message was a simple one for the supporters. 'My message to the fans would be to stick with us. You have peaks and troughs but the message is to stick with us because I can tell them we are doing absolutely everything we can to achieve success,' said Eddie Howe. 'Hopefully we can make amends for Morecambe and get back to winning ways. The lads have really responded well in training and we'll go there [Cheltenham Town] with confidence, looking to put on a display and get Morecambe out of our system.'

Sadly, a 1-0 away defeat at Cheltenham meant the Cherries would have to wait for their next game on 28 December against Torquay to close out the year with another win in front of a home crowd of 7626, the biggest of the season for the Cherries.

January would bring its own problems. Peterborough were rumoured to be keen on taking Brett Pitman to London Road. Other players like Liam Feeney, Ryan Garry and Jason Pearce were also going to be hard to keep hold of. It didn't seem to worry Howe though who said, 'when you're at the top of the league your players are going to attract interest.'

With all the speculation, the year 2010 didn't begin well. January saw three defeats and just the one win at the end of the month against Crewe

Alexander, when Rhoys Wiggins came back to Bournemouth, having played the season before on loan from Norwich City. Remaining in second position, all was not lost, especially when the highly-fancied Rotherham United were beaten 1-3 with Brett Pitman and a brace from Danny Hollands seeing the promotion-chasing challengers off in front of 124 away supporters. Eddie Howe felt it was the team's best performance of the season.

AFC Bournemouth had closed to just four points behind leaders Rochdale. The team now needed to start winning at home. A 0-0 draw with Cheltenham was the best Howe's men could do against the 22nd placed team. Notts County would fare less well, losing 2-1 to Bournemouth in a crunch match in February. Two goals from Danny Hollands did the damage in the first 35 minutes, even though Neal Bishop got a goal back in the second half. Bournemouth only managed one more home win in February – a 3-0 hammering of Barnet. Even a defeat by Shrewsbury hadn't dislodged Bournemouth from second place as we entered March.

The whiff of promotion excitement was certainly apparent when Eddie Howe managed a win and a draw against Morecambe and Notts County, respectively. But the Cherries let in a 90th minute goal against Grimsby Town to leave them with a bitter 3-2 defeat mid-month. Home wins over Accrington Stanley and Bradford kept the Cherries in

third, while the following game on 5 April 2010 was
the promotion battle everyone was looking forward
to. First played third at Spotland, and the crowd of
5037 had to be satisfied with a 0-0 draw. That was at
least better than the 2-1 away loss to Lincoln City,
who were fighting to stay in the league. The fixtures
suddenly helped at this stage with two home games
against Hereford and Darlington. Brett Pitman
delivered the goals to beat Hereford United 2-1
before Darlington, who were already relegated,
were beaten 2-0.

The coaches were jam-packed for the away game
then against Burton Albion on 24 April. A crowd of
3977 saw the game and 1647 of them were away
fans. Brett Pitman got the Cherries off to a great
start after 67 minutes, before Alan Connell clinched
the win and promotion with a second goal having
come on as a sub. So, the 24 April 2010 was the day
when Eddie Howe gained his first promotion as a
football manger. We did not know then that it would
be the start of a story that would see him take
Bournemouth to the Premier League. Howe was
quite able to play the celebrations down for the
moment. 'Jason [Tindall] and I were back to work on
Monday to prepare for tomorrow as though it is a
normal week. There was no change from us. For the
players, I don't know, it may have been difficult to
come down from such a high,' said Howe on having
secured promotion to League One. 'But we need to

prepare properly because we're still trying to go for second place. It was a great weekend, but now it is back to business as usual. We want to win the game tomorrow [against Port Vale], because it is going to be a full house and there will be a lot of expectation.'

The 0-2 win at Burton Albion secured the points to see the Cherries promoted, but they wanted to finish with a flourish. Alan Connell was hitting the back of the net regularly. A 4-0 battering of Port Vale saw the club finish off their home games with a rousing win. The fourth goal scored by Alan Connell was just majestic. He scooped the ball up and over the Port Vale keeper to huge cheers from the North stand.

Eddie Howe was understated as ever in his personal contribution to the promotion effort, but he lavished praise on the team despite having a few words at half-time with them. 'The players have been magnificent since the start of the season and they've set their standards. The scenes at the end will always stay in the memory banks. They're very rare and you have to make the most of them,' sad Eddie.

Only Notts County robbed the Cherries of the League Two title. It didn't spoil what had been a tremendous season though. Eddie Howe had his first promotion and a sell out for the final game. He seemed quite surprised at what the team had achieved.

'I didn't think we'd finish where we have,' Howe said. 'I think the expectation at the start of the season, from myself and everyone else, was to stay in the league, first and foremost. I just felt with the embargo and the restrictions placed upon us, it was just going to be too big an ask. But I'm obviously delighted to have been proved wrong. They [the players] have just surprised everyone with the amount of games they've won this season...I don't win the games, the players do,' he concluded.

This was more of a satisfied celebration than the wild survival scenes of the previous season, because it was something positive to win promotion, something that Bournemouth had only experienced five times in their history. Finishing off the season with a win at Chesterfield would have been great, but Howe's men had perhaps allowed the promotion to sink in and they were beaten 2-1 in the final match.

Eddie was still pleased to have finished ahead of one team in particular. "We've had a good battle with Rochdale all season, to finish above them is fantastic and second place means a lot to us. It's going to be tough for us [next season] but we'll have a real good go at being successful," said Howe.

Bournemouth finished second on 83 points from their 46 games and with a positive goal difference of

17, just a point above Rochdale and 10 points behind champions Notts County.

8. FAREWELL TO THE CHERRIES 2010-11

Eddie Howe says goodbye to the Cherries

Steve Lovell had wanted to play for the Cherries in the summer of 2009, but the transfer embargo prevented him from coming to the club. He still trained with the team for free. The Cherries were limited to having just a 20-man squad at the time and the football league stopped the deal from going through. However, a year later in June 2010, having been at Partick Thistle, Steve Lovell was able to sign along with the much sought-after Marc Pugh and Michael Symes. They all signed on the same day and were the club's first permanent signings in over 17 months. Marc Pugh's transfer still had to go to a tribunal though, as Hereford and Bournemouth could not agree fee for the player.

It must have been surreal to have his own brother playing for him. But if Eddie could manage Steve, he could train any player. It became clear later in the October 2009 that Lovell had held off bids from seven other clubs in the hope that he could team up with his older brother at AFC Bournemouth.

Eddie Howe was now building a side that would compete on a level-playing field with League One sides. That heralded more signings that summer, among them was Harry Arter from Woking for £4000 and Stephen Purches from Leyton Orient. Youth was not ignored either with Concord Ranger's striker Lyle Taylor, 20, signing a two-year deal in August.

Feelings were running high for a successful campaign, so when Swansea chairman Huw Jenkins spoke out that Eddie Howe was the type of young manager he would like to bring to the south Wales club, his advance was quickly swatted away by Eddie Mitchell, who claimed that he would handcuff Eddie Howe to Dean Court, as he was going nowhere.

Meanwhile, AFCB had released quite a few players, including the much-liked Sammy Igoe, Alan Connell and Scott Guyett who had all been influential in the Cherries rise from League Two. The

striker department had especially been depleted
with the transfer of Brett Pitman to Bristol City in
August 2010.

The aim for this season was certainly to establish
the team back in the division where the club had
spent most of its history. Early signs were that the
club could perhaps do better than that, achieving a
0-1 away win at Charlton and a massive 5-1 home
win over newly-relegated Peterborough Utd.
Tranmere though soon inflicted the first defeat on
the Cherries and neighbours Southampton were too
strong at St Marys for Eddie's men in the Carling
Cup.

The clubs were soon lining up for Howe one after
another. Southampton looked an obvious option, as
they had made a slow start in League One and
needed to catch up fast. They came forward with a
pitch for Eddie and AFC Bournemouth fans feared
the worst. Would Eddie Howe really walk away from
the success he had achieved at AFC Bournemouth?
Did the last 18 months mean nothing? Had AFC
Bournemouth's success come at a price? And would
that mean losing Eddie and JT to that lot, up the
road?

Life didn't seem fair. So, imagine our jubilation
when we heard the following news from AFC
Bournemouth chairman Eddie Mitchell: 'We are very
pleased that Eddie has decided to stay at
Bournemouth. He's made his mind up - he's staying,

whether they [Southampton] come back or not. It's a great achievement for the club to hold on to such a good manager.'

It was a big relief that Howe had stayed and by keeping him and Jason Tindall there was every reason to believe that they could continue their good work at Dean Court. Still, Eddie Mitchell didn't think that the club could make it all the way to the Premier League in those days with Howe. 'Whether we were debt-free and had a few million pounds kicking around, I don't think we would be able to compete in the Premier League, because we just haven't got the fan base or the stadium to take the capacity to keep earning the sort of money that is needed to stay there. Eddie would be foolish to turn down the sort of money he could earn in the Premier League and what he could achieve in his career by moving there. I don't think we could ever offer Eddie and Jason anywhere near what the Premier League cubs could and I think that's where they will end up,' said Mitchell.

The FA Cup did Bournemouth no favours in drawing Notts County again, who ran out 1-3 winners dumping Bournemouth out of the cup for another year in the second round. It may have seemed annoying at the time, but there were more important matches to win.

Heading well into the winter months AFC Bournemouth were well enough in contention and there was soon a real buzz that this could be a play-off year for the Cherries. Yet, the underlining worry was that Eddie Howe and Jason Tindall could be pinched at any moment, shattering any dreams that the fans had of further success. That moment came again in January 2011, after AFC Bournemouth had secured a 3-0 home win against Plymouth Argyle to take them second in the table.

Eddie Howe recalls that he wasn't sure whether it would be his last game as Bournemouth manager, 'I have had many emotional days here, … Looking back at the Plymouth game, it was a great performance and we were flying in the league. I was really happy with the way the game went at that stage. I didn't know it was going to be my last home game in charge – but I did have an idea.'

It wasn't just one but several teams came fishing for the Bournemouth duo now, and there was a race on for just who would get them to leave. Eddie Mitchell had already given a statement to *The Daily Echo* to confirm that he had received 'no approaches' for his management team, after Brian Laws had parted company with Burnley. But Eddie Howe was made the bookies favourite to take the Burnley job. Preston North End had also parted company with Darren Ferguson. The options were there for Eddie Howe and Jason Tindall and Eddie Mitchell knew it.

'I'm sure they would be high on a few club's lists but they are contracted to us and I would be reluctant to see them go. I would wish them all the best in the future, but not the immediate future,' said Eddie Mitchell. 'We've got the best management team in the division and one of the best squads. Having achieved so much in such a short space of time, I'm sure there are going to be clubs thinking Eddie and Jason could be the solution. But I don't think they would have any desire to leave at the moment. If they did and if the offer was too great, I would do everything to stand in their way,' he said defiantly.

Charlton might have been a smaller club than Southampton, but they were a family club that had been in the Premier League and were a reasonable step up, too. Then there was Crystal Palace who also seemed a good fit with plenty of quality in their team and a division higher. Yet, standing in the wings too were Burnley who had fallen from the Premier League, but were looking for a quick return and had money to spend as well as players to off load. Who would Eddie Howe and JT choose and when would they decide what was best for their careers?

This was a week when supporters went through all the emotions that bring them closer to their club. There was the tantalising news that approaches had been made. Charlton and Crystal Palace would both make a move for Eddie having vacant management positions in the first week of January 2011.

On 7 January, the *Bournemouth Echo* was already reporting that AFC Bournemouth had 'reluctantly' given permission for Crystal Palace to talk to Howe. The wait during the week was agonising, but Eddie and Jason were offered a pay rise to stay at Dean Court, and with the club in second place in the league it was hoped that the matter would quickly be concluded in favour of AFC Bournemouth. That seemed to be the case at first. 'This club, the supporters and players mean so much to me - it's not going to be easy,' said Eddie Howe. I've got to battle with myself and come to a decision which is right for everybody,' he told *BBC Radio Solent*. 'Out of respect to everybody, I've got to get a move on. I don't want to be playing anyone along, that's not my intention at all. But it's got to be the correct decision, not a snap judgement. It may well be that my dog may be getting some exercise!'

Eddie went on to add: 'I'm never going to leave this club on a whim, or just because I've had an offer somewhere else, that's not how I work. I've had a terrific time here. I've loved every minute of doing the job, and when you're somewhere where you're liked and respected, it counts for a lot in my book.

I'm anguished as people say this is a nice position to be in, but it doesn't feel like that. I'm very torn, and when you see the players perform like that, it makes it even harder. To see their commitment and attitude to everything we've asked them to do, I can't fault them. They've never let me down, not once. They're a great group to work for, and I'm proud to be their manager, Howe said. 'They feel more than just a group of players to me, they feel like family.'

Eddie Mitchell knew that this was a fight that he would not keep winning. 'He loves the club and if he decides to move on it will be heart wrenching, but I'll give him a glowing reference,' said Eddie Mitchell when talking to *BBC Radio Solent*. 'Eddie's always up for the challenge and believes in himself and that's what's propelled him to where he is now,' added Mitchell. 'Money has to be a consideration as money gives you security, he's got to digest everybody's opinions and his own thoughts and make a difficult decision.'

Eddie Mitchell was pleased to bring Eddie Howe out in front of the media cameras on a Tuesday night at Dean Court and to proclaim: 'Eddie is staying!' With the sound of huge cheers from supporters this was an amazing outcome for the fans that had awaited the decision at the ground. Yet, no sooner had Eddie Mitchell looked so pleased with his prize, and relieved with being able to head off another two attempts to pull Eddie and Jason away than Burnley came in with an offer. It looked like Eddie Howe had made up his mind to embark on a new challenge. Did he feel that the turbulence of the previous week had unsettled things at AFC Bournemouth? And was it better for all if he moved on now? Eddie Howe had told his players on the Friday morning, before the Colchester United game, that it would be his last as the Bournemouth manager.

Eddie claims that it was purely for his need to prove himself at another club that he made the move and to show that he could be a success elsewhere. He needed to be ambitious and that he could not keep turning clubs down who wanted his services. 'I'll be travelling up to Burnley tomorrow to hopefully finalise things. I've been loyal to Bournemouth and it's extremely difficult to leave a club that's been close to my heart. We've had two years of unbelievable success here and I hope the lads continue that and go on to get what they deserve. I leave with great sadness.'

They were the words that no AFC Bournemouth fans ever wanted to hear. After the celebratory scenes of the last few days in keeping hold of their manager, this suddenly felt like a betrayal. It wasn't that the fans blamed Eddie Howe for furthering his and Jason's career, it was the drop in the emotion having heard that the duo were staying and believing that promotion could be secured with the team already sitting in second place in League One. A new manager would now have to come in. It was not sure how the recent events would affect the team or the club in general. Grown men were crying at Eddie Howe's decision, but the sadness would eventually pass.

As it happened, Lee Bradbury was to step up to become the manager and end his playing career at the Cherries, while Steve Fletcher would be his assistant. Continuity had been maintained and the leadership of Bradbury and the popularity of Super Fletch was what Eddie Mitchell felt was right for the club in its attempt to continue the dream.

The loan signing of Laurie Dalla Valle was designed to give more forward power to the team in March 2011 to see if it could kick on and grab a play-off place. While the young striker from Fulham did well and scored against the Saints at home, the Cherries found that Southampton would punish them in front of a bumper 10,008 Dean Court crowd, with a 1-3 defeat, and the pressure was on as the race for the top places picked-up. The team was further strengthened by the loan move of Donal McDermott in midfield, until the end of the season, as well as Mathieu Baudry from Troyes and Ben Williamson, who would eventually move on to Port Vale.

Early in January, AFC Bournemouth had seen an in-form Josh McQuoid snapped up by Millwall and Bournemouth brought young Danny Ings into the side, as it pushed for a top-six place. As if AFC Bournemouth weren't already feeling wounded,

Eddie Howe came in for Marvin Bartley as well at the end of January, and he moved for a reported £350,000 to join his former boss up at Burnley.

It was down to Lee Bradbury and Steve Fletcher to get AFC Bournemouth motivated to cling on to a play-off place at worse. Everyone knew that teams were chasing, especially Southampton who would finish runners-up in the automatic promotion places. I lose count of the familiar post-match interviews when Bradbury would comment that the Cherries had been 'different class at times', but the results showed that it was a case of hanging on rather than trying to win the league now.

Yet, a finish of sixth was good enough to put the Cherries in the play-offs and that was the highest finish the club had earned since the glory days of Harry Redknapp's era in the 1980s. Yes, AFC Bournemouth fans had lost a great manager, but they had a side that was still playing with tremendous spirit and still keen to give it their best to see the club get to the Championship.

The play-offs would now begin and the Cherries faced third placed Huddersfield Town over two legs with the first being played at Dean Court. The game was played on a sunny Saturday in May 2011. I remember it well, as my sons and myself were stationed in the East Stand and the blazing sun was as relentless as the football. The atmosphere was incredibly intense as Lee Bradbury's side tried to

*make a bit of history. The game didn't exactly go as
planned with Kevin Kilbane scoring first with a
header from a Gary Robert's cross. To make matters
worse, the Cherries should have had a goal back
before half-time, when the referee pointed to the
penalty spot, after Rhoys Wiggins was brought down
in the box. Danny Ings hadn't played more than a
handful of games for the Cherries' first team, but he
wanted to take the kick and Bennett guessed
correctly to keep the shot out.*

*Bournemouth had to take an advantage up to
Huddersfield's Galpharm Stadium and hopes were
raised on the hour, when Donal McDermott struck a
fantastic 25-yard shot that sped past Ian Bennett to
make it 1-1. Huddersfield were unbeaten in 25
games and they were going to be tested in the last
half hour. There would be a chance, and it fell to
midfielder Anton Robinson, who headed wide from
12 yards out!*

The second leg would be no less intense. I didn't
make it up to Huddersfield but Eddie Howe and JT
certainly did. They wanted to try and give the
Bournemouth players and extra boost and a few
words of good luck as they attempted to get one
step closer to the Championship.

If the first game was edge of your seat viewing,
the second-leg saw fireworks. It was like two
heavyweight boxers looking for the knockout blow.
Bournemouth again fell behind, this time to a Lee

Peltier goal and needed a penalty scored by Steve Lovell to get them back in the game. But by half-time the Cherries were again looking the less likely to progress, when Danny Ward made it 2-1 to the Terriers. Steve Lovell clearly wanted to repay Bournemouth fans for not having had much of a season and he scored a terrific 63rd minute equaliser to push the game into extra-time.

By this time, I was screaming at the TV in my local pub in Redhill as I lived every kick. Danny Ings soon had me falling off my bar stool as he headed the Cherries in front for the first time in the game. I had hardly got over the shock when Huddersfield had a corner and Antony Kay made it all level again at 3-3 and we were into a penalty shoot-out.

Misses from Liam Feeney and Anton Robinson ended the Cherries' brave fight and Huddersfield Town went through to the play-off final. Lee Clark had got the better of the Cherries and we wondered how many faces would disappear ahead of the new season?

9. DRESSED IN CLARET
2011-12

Eddie Howe was 33 when decided to leave AFC Bournemouth, after a dramatic few days in January 2011. Just when the fans had thought they had managed to hold on to their much-admired manager, Eddie Howe and JT headed up north to manage in the Championship.

Brendan Flood, Burnley's operations director believed he had a man that would bring a winning mentality to the Lancashire club: 'He's got something different, new ideas, different relationships to what we've had before for player recruitment and bringing in different coaching ideas.

When Eddie Howe was asked whether it had been hard to leave the south coast club, he replied: 'Extremely difficult. I've had a fantastic time here. The majority of my career has been spent here and you know I love the club deeply, but I just feel this is too good an opportunity to turn down,' saidEddie...'I leave with real sadness. I don't lack drive or ambition,' he added.

He had turned down two clubs on the Tuesday, but by the Thursday he was sure that Burnley was a club where he and Jason could develop. They would take over from Brian Laws, who had been sacked on 29 December 2010 after a 0-2 home defeat to 22nd placed Scunthorpe United. Everything was set-up to have a tilt at promotion with Burnley, lying in 10th place and just six points off the play-off positions.

Yet, Howe had inherited a team that had been relegated from the Premier League. It was a rebuilding job that meant stripping out the big wage earners and starting again. Howe was intrigued by the project. It was a club with heritage and in a small town, many miles from the south coast. Howe knew his credentials would be tested in a league where he hadn't managed before. He would sign a three-and-a-half year contract.

Burnley would change Eddie Howe but perhaps not in the way he expected. There was to be no instant success. The hard grind of the Championship was something Howe had to tackle in unfamiliar surroundings. His first job, as manager in waiting, was to watch Burnley play out a 0-0 draw at Turf Moor against QPR on 15 January 2011. He knew he had some experienced players in Graham Alexander, Jack Cork, Chris Eagles and former Cherry Wade Elliot. Making them an attacking force though was going to be a challenge.

The next match against Scunthorpe should have been a great way to ease into the manager's chair with Scunthorpe lying in 23rd place. But a draw was the best Burnley could do after Chris Eagles fired over from 12 yards and Chris Iwelumo's header hit the post!

One player Eddie Howe decided he must strengthen the team with was Bournemouth's Marvin Bartley, a defensive central-midfielder. Bartley was signed up just two weeks after Howe joined Burnley. Eddie Mitchell had said that no Bournemouth player would be leaving in the January window, but Bartley said he didn't know if he could play for the Dorset club again if the bid from Burnley was turned down. Burnley had come in late with their bids, some five hours before the end of the window. Four bids were made, one of which was withdrawn. The whole episode infuriated Bournemouth's then chairman.

'We are disappointed the player seems to have played such a big part in the negotiations. I've had three people on the telephone all claiming to be his agent. The Burnley chairman offered something and then changed his mind...' said Mitchell. '...It didn't come through the correct channels either and the person I believe to be his agent had to hear it from me first. Obviously personal terms had already been agreed, otherwise the deal wouldn't have been done. That's not how I like to do business.'

Howe's first Burnley win came in the next match. A 2-1 win over Portsmouth with goals from Jay Rodriguez and Dean Marney took Burnley up to ninth. Progression in the FA Cup followed with a fourth round 3-1 win over Burton Albion. Howe's first taste of defeat came away at Doncaster Rovers, losing 0-1 to a team that had lost their last four games. Howe was still finding out what he had, but it was a case of one step forward and two back as he looked for more consistency.

February started better with wins over Norwich and Watford. The big match that month came against West Ham United in the FA Cup. The match included a howitzer of a goal from Thomas Hitzlsperger when Burnley were given a finishing lesson. The Hammers ran out 5-1 winners. Burnley had started the better, but missed their chance when Jay Rodriguez shot over early on and Ross Wallace went even closer with a long-range drive. But Winston Reid, Carlton Cole and Freddie Sears swept Howe's Burnley aside.

Concentrating back on the league, Howe's side put three back-to-back wins together lifting them to seventh – just three points off the play-off places! Nathan Delfouneso had been signed on loan from Aston Villa and had scored the only goal against promotion hunters Hull City in early March. Shane Duffy had also joined on loan from Everton, but didn't feature until a 1-2 defeat at home to Ipswich on 2 April.

Burnley's season collapsed from mid-March, taking one point from six matches. The Clarets had slipped to 12th and were seven points off sixth placed Leeds United. Marvin Bartley was then sent off in the 2-0 defeat to Nottingham Forest on 12 April. Burnley couldn't make any more mistakes. They won their next three games, including a huge 2-4 away win at Derby – that pushed them back up to eighth, level on 66 points with Nottingham Forest and Leeds United. Chris McCann had returned to the side after a knee injury and scored the last goal in the win over Derby.

With just three games to go, Howe was in with a slim chance of getting Burnley to the play-offs. But a point at home to Portsmouth and a 0-1 defeat to Leeds United pretty much ended all hopes. With Cardiff a point off automatic promotion, the Bluebirds held out for a 1-1 draw in Burnley's last game. That put Cardiff in the play-offs, while Burnley had to be satisfied with finishing eighth.

With the end of the 2010-11 season, Eddie Howe went about making changes on and off the pitch. Striker Stephen Thompson and Kevin McDonald were released. Burnley's training facility at Gawthorpe was modernised with a new changing room, canteen, shower area and office. July and August saw more player changes, Graham Alexander was released, while Chris Iwelumo was sold to Watford leaving Howe depleted of strikers. Clarke Carlisle went on a season-long loan to Preston, but the less popular movers were Chris Eagles and

Tyrone Mears, who went to join former Burnley manager Owen Coyle at Bolton Wanderers!

Howe brought in Kieran Trippier and Ben Mee on loan from Man City for the new 2011-12 season. Keith Treacy was also signed from Preston North End. Further signings in August included Bournemouth players – Danny Ings and keeper Jon Stewart, while Zavron Hines of West Ham United also headed to Lancashire. The outgoings continued as well with Danny Fox and Wade Elliott moving on to Southampton and Birmingham City, respectively.

Burnley kicked off the season against Sean Dyche's Watford at home. Unfortunately, Ings had a set-back injuring his thigh on the first day of the season. Martin Paterson and Jay Rodriguez would lead the strike force, but it was Charlie Austin, who came on as a sub, that started the Burnley comeback with 13 minutes to go. It was another sub, Keith Treacy, who scored in the 84th minute to earn Burnley a 2-2 draw, having been 0-2 down on 70 minutes.

Chris McCann was Burnley's newly appointed skipper for the season with Graham Alexander having left the club in the summer. He had been at Burnley for eight years, but was still only 24. Howe needed a long-server, who knew everything about the club, to be his skipper and his eyes and ears.

A 6-3 thumping of Burton Albion in the League Cup saw Jay Rodriguez at his best netting four times, but Burnley had needed extra-time having been at 3-3 after 90 minutes. The stress of having to go to extra-time was not lost on Eddie Howe. 'These are hard games, people will look at them on paper and think well you should cruise it but football is never like that,' he said. 'We are thankful we are not on the end of a shock result and we progress to the next round which is the aim.'

A 2-0 away defeat to Crystal Palace gave Howe more reason to be anxious about how easy it would be to have a successful season. Marvin Bartley hardly endeared himself to Burnley fans coming on as a substitute, only to be sent off after clashing with Jonathan Parr in the last minute. Parr had opened the scoring in the 10th minute and Palace doubled their lead in the second half, when Ben Mee fouled Sean Scannell in the box. Owen Garvan put the penalty away, while both Jay Rodriguez and Chris McCann squandered great chances to score for Burnley.

Charlie Austin ensured the Clarets got off to a much better start in their next encounter with Cardiff City by scoring in the second minute, but Robert Earnshaw struck back on 40 minutes and neither side went on to find a winner.

Progress in the League Cup was earned with a 3-2 home win over Barnet, but again Burnley needed extra-time to get the win, after Ricky Holmes grabbed a 90th minute equaliser to make it 2-2 and Chris McCann grabbed the winner in extra-time. The winning feeling was just what Howe needed and they carried it through to the league match with Derby to get their first win in the Championship. Charlie Austin was starting to make the headlines with a brace of goals to sink the Rams 1-2, after Theo Robinson had clawed one goal back for the home team.

Speaking to *The Lancashire Telegraph* Howe was overjoyed with the result, 'I thought the game was there for the taking at half-time. We got our noses in front and looked quite comfortable, but then Derby got going and put us on the back foot a bit. They equalised and you feared for us for what has happened this season, but thankfully the lads dug in and showed great resilience. They showed team spirit and all the hallmarks of a good side.

'You have to win ugly sometimes and for the last 20 minutes we battened down the hatches and saw it out. It's that toughness we need to get as a side, and we still need to improve and do it better. But we put our bodies on the line and won our headers, all the things you need to do to win the game. We need to show that side of our game more consistently but it's a definite step in the right direction for us.'

As for Charlie Austin, Howe was beaming about his qualities. 'He has the knack of being in the right place and he's a fantastic finisher. He's still young and will get better and better so there are really positive signs from him,' Howe said.

Eddie was still looking to bring more talent in and he signed Junior Stanislas on a three-year deal from West Ham United ahead of the fixture with Middlesbrough at Turf Moor. The Boro were unbeaten and proved too strong for Burnley, scoring two goals from Nick Bailey and Joe Bennett. It still meant Burnley had not won at home after six games.

Junior Stanislas, 21, played in the Middlesbrough defeat as a sub, and this was the start of a long relationship he would have with Eddie Howe. When Bournemouth enticed Eddie Howe back for his second managerial spell at the club, he decided to re-sign Stanislas in the summer of 2014, after Junior had turned down Premier League football with Burnley. But when Junior joined Burnley, he had an added distraction. Within four days of his arrival, he and his partner celebrated the arrival of twin boys – Alex and Jacob. But despite the family time Junior obviously needed, it did not stop him from finding his feet quickly at Burnley, as he told *The Lancashire Telegraph*.

'The lads have made me feel welcome, and obviously I've got my friend Zav [Zavon Hines] holding my hand. It's been quite easy settling in... He

said the manager's terrific and the assistant, and all
the boys are really good as well so you can't ask for
more than that. It's been exciting times with the
move up here and becoming a father over the
weekend with twin boys, Alex and Jacob. It will be
good I'm sure. The boys were born in London and
my girlfriend's taken them home now, but hopefully
they will be here in the next few days.'

While Junior Stanislas got his family settled,
Burnley set about climbing the league from 19th
place. The trip to Peterborough though wouldn't
improve their situation, succumbing to a 2-1 away
loss. Burnley had now gone without a clean sheet in
their last 20 games. Matters weren't helped for
Howe when goalkeeper Brian Jensen had slipped
and suffered a groin strain after just 14 minutes.

The League Cup third round would be a far more
pleasing affair with Kieran Trippier and André Bikey-
Amougou scoring the goals for a 2-1 comeback
against Milton Keynes. Burnley even managed to win
without needing extra-time for once, thanks to
André Bikey's 89th minute winner!

Burnley's poor home form continued with a 1-1
draw with table-topping Southampton at the end of
September. Charlie Austin had given the Clarets the
lead in the 53rd minute, but Morgan Schneiderlin
scored 10 minutes from time to share the points. It
meant that Burnley had slipped to 21st in the table

with only goal difference keeping the out of the relegation zone.

A much-needed home win finally came against Nottingham Forest on 27 September and it was some win. Burnley turned on the style with a 5-1 thumping of Forest moving them up to 16th. Burnley were 4-0 up by half-time. Chris McCann and Ross Wallace added to Jay Rodriguez's brace with Stanislas bagging an assist for the second goal. And while Ishmael Miller beat Lee Grant to find the net for Forest, Charlie Austin still had time to score Burnley's fifth.

Following up this emphatic victory with a 0-1 win away at Millwall, after a Jay Rodriguez winner, Howe may have felt that he had finally got his side to turn the corner. Burnley were now up to 14th and just five points off the promotion places with a game in hand.

But confidence was soon hit again, after the international break, courtesy of Reading. The Berkshire club basically robbed Eddie Howe's team with a 90th minute winner from Jem Karacan. Lingering injuries to Danny Ings (knee), Bryan Jensen (groin), Martin Paterson (thigh) and Michael Duffy (knee) gave Howe even more reason to be frustrated with how the season was going.

Burnley were having little luck and slipped to 17th in the table after a 2-0 away defeat to Barnsley. Nothing was going well in front of goal with Ross

Wallace's goal-bound effort cleared off the line, before Jay Rodriguez's shot bounced off the bar! Even sharp-shooting Charlie Austin spurned two good chances.

A 1-2 away win at Coventry was pleasurable for the Burnley fans – not only for the result – but the way in which the game was won. Was Howe's luck turning? Cody McDonald had put the home side in front just before the hour, but Ross Wallace equalised on 73 minutes and Charlie Austin grabbed a sensational late winner on 90 minutes!

But Burnley still didn't have any consistency. The League Cup run came to an end when Cardiff City edged a 1-0 win at the end of October. Joe Mason scored the only goal with a left-foot strike from just inside the box on 40 minutes. The defeat was frustrating for Howe. 'It's disappointing to lose the game. We started the game really well and tested their goalkeeper early on. It was a positive start and, on another day, we could have scored a couple of goals. We also finished the game well and applied a lot of pressure with good possession, but we didn't work their keeper enough or hurt them in the second half.'

A 3-1 win against Blackpool in the league eased the disappointment from going out of the cup. Austin, Wallace and Bartley got on the score sheet, before Jonjo Shelvey got a 90th minute consolation goal for Blackpool. Austin had now scored nine goals by the end of October. Howe was pleased that his side had not suffered long term disappointment from exiting the League Cup. 'It was just what we needed. We are moving in the right direction, but we need to get more ruthless in defence,' he said.

Sadly, for Eddie, Burnley were to lose their next four games as November started disastrously. Home defeats to Leicester and Leeds were sandwiched by a 3-1 defeat at Bristol City and the month ended with a 2-1 defeat at Birmingham. So, Burnley travelled to Hull City in desperate need of points. It turned out to be an eventful game with Burnley winning out 2-3, having gone 2-0 down in the first 55 minutes. The Clarets showed their character with two goals from David Egar and a 90th minute winner from Jay Rodriguez. The dark clouds that were starting to gather over Howe's reign lifted, as Burnley climbed to 16th place.

An emphatic 4-0 win over Ipswich finally built some confidence. Goals from Sam Vokes, Jay Rodriguez and a brace from Chris McCann put similes back on faces and Howe was quick to praise his team's performance. 'The second half was enjoyable. I don't think I've had many second halves here at Turf Moor in my short reign that have been as enjoyable as that. I thought we were excellent. It was a strange game in the fact that we created so many chances. I think we could have probably scored double the four that we did,' Howe told the

BBC. 'Jay Rodriguez had chance after chance and to be fair to him he kept going and got the reward for an excellent individual performance. But what pleases me more is the team effort,' he added.

With performances much improved, Burnley reached the top 10 in early December – after a 1-2 away win over West Ham United. Chris McCann and Sam Vokes, on loan from Wolves, scored the Burnley goals in front of a crowd of 26,274, at Upton Park. Eddie Howe knew what qualities Vokes had from his playing days at Bournemouth and the striker gave Burnley a powerful front man until the end of January. But Burnley couldn't keep their unbeaten record going. Portsmouth inflicted a 0-1 defeat on 10 December with David Norris scoring in the 91st minute. For Howe, the pressure for results was mounting.

'I thought we had got over the late goal drama against us. We have had it already this season against Reading and Leeds and it is another lesson we have to learn. I didn't see the goal coming because I thought we were on top in the half. It was a slow and scrappy game but you have to give credit to Portsmouth, because they defended well and nullified our attacking threat. It looked like we were heading for a 0-0 and we would have taken that, even though it wasn't the result we were looking for. There is only anxiety when we don't play well. The atmosphere does get across to the players and it was quite quiet. That isn't a criticism of the fans, because they want to be entertained and we did not do that,' he bemoaned.

A trio of wins for Burnley would follow with the first coming against Brighton 1-0. Doncaster Rovers were beaten more comfortably 3-0. Martin Paterson had recovered from injury with his first start since August. In this Boxing Day match Paterson scored again, four minutes from time, after Rodriguez had given the home side the lead from a first half penalty. An own goal from Sam Hird completed a great afternoon for Burnley.

The third win came against Hull City – the 1-0 win would lift Burnley to seventh in the table, just three points behind Hull City in sixth. Paterson had given Howe every reason to keep picking him, and the striker netted again when there was indecision in Hull's defence.

Optimism grew then for the New Year with Burnley well placed to make a push for promotion. Yet, if Burnley had a bogey team it was Leeds United. The first match of 2012 was expected to be a hard one, and it was made even harder when Kieran Trippier received a second yellow card after 29 minutes having fouled Andros Townsend twice! Still, Charlie Austin gave Burnley the lead, with a volley after 69 minutes, and Burnley looked well set to win the game. However, the Clarets succumbed to two late goals. An own goal from Brian Easton was bad enough to concede in the 88th minute, but then Ross McCormack stunned the away fans with a 97th minute winner! Much of the defeat was of Burnley's own making – not just because of the own goal – but Lee Grant had spilled a 25-yard regulation shot from Andros Townsend leading up to McCormack's goal. But Eddie Howe's venom was not aimed at his players.

'I'm proud of the players and I thought we deserved all three points for the defensive display. It was heart breaking to concede but we can take great heart. At 11 v 11, I thought we were the better team. The ref changed the game with a really poor decision that made it a difficult afternoon for everyone. The second booking isn't even a foul and it was a big decision to make – a disgraceful one,' he suggested.

Eddie Howe decided to be more adventurous against Premier League side Norwich City, in the FA Cup fourth-round away tie, playing three forwards. The plan didn't really give the team any more ammunition, as Grant Holt and Simeon Jackson swiftly put the Canaries into a 2-0 lead before Jay Rodriguez pulled one goal back, heading in a Ross Wallace free kick. While Grant Holt missed a penalty, goals from Andrew Surman and Steve Morison made it a comfortable 4-1 win for the East Anglian side. The business side of trying to win promotion was back in full swing after an impressive 0-2 away win at

Middlesbrough. Burnley closed the gap to just three points on the promotion places after goals from Jay Rodriguez and Kieran Trippier saw off Boro. Howe was suitably pleased. 'We could have had more goals if truth be told. We've won seven out of nine now. There's no reason if this squad can keep it up that we can't compete with the very best in this league.'

Burnley were certainly on the up. Relying on past players he knew well, Howe also moved for another former Bournemouth payer, Josh McQuoid, who signed on loan from Millwall in January 2012. The player had been getting ready to re-join the Cherries, but with Millwall missing out on Barnsley striker Danny Haynes, McQuoid was kept by Millwall until Burnley offered McQuoid a chance to join up again with Howe at Burnley.

A 0-0 draw with hard to beat Derby County slowed Burnley's pursuit of the play-off places. Jay Rodriguez pushed Burnley closer in the next game against Nottingham Forest, on a cold night at Turf Moor. The striker scored a brace despite missing a spot kick, and had scored 16 times in all competitions by the end of the evening.

Meanwhile, Josh McQuoid had been given his full debut for Burnley, seeing Ross Wallace switched to the bench. Howe was pleased with his latest signing and felt that he was getting closer to finding what he needed to make a challenge for promotion. 'It's a group of players who have a mentality that they want to achieve things this season. We have a young, hungry team, said Howe. We haven't really spoken of targets this season and we've won't start now. I'm just delighted with what direction we are moving in.'

Jay Rodriguez was becoming the goal machine that was propelling the team up the table. While Peterborough had an early lead, through a Paul Taylor goal in the next fixture, Rodriguez found the net again with three minutes to go.

Adam Lallana and Billy Sharp soon put another dent in Burnley's hopes though with a 2-0 home win for second-placed Southampton at St Marys, which pushed Burnley down to 11th. Home advantage counted against Barnsley, with Rodriguez and Austin on target with a 2-0 win in mid-February, but it was to be the last win for seven more games.

Defeats came thick and fast with a narrow 1-0 away defeat to Reading, followed by a 1-3 loss against Millwall and a closer 3-2 defeat away to Watford. Jay Rodriguez had netted 20 goals as he came off the pitch at Vicarage Road, but Burnley were slipping ever further down the table and were eight points off the promotion places. They had been 0-2 up and had seen Watford come back from what looked like certain defeat, and Howe knew it would be hard to pick his side up after that.

'How we lost that game, I really don't know. At 2-0 the game's over. We've played excellently, executed our game plan perfectly, but once we conceded the first goal we just rocked. We looked unsteady, unsure of ourselves and for set plays we didn't do our jobs in the second half and it's a tough one to take. We shouldn't have even got near to losing that game. We have to learn from this big time, we've got to really step up to the plate and show a little bit more leadership during games. We are a young side but that's no excuse. There's enough people out there who've played enough games to react better to setbacks,' said a disgruntled post-match Eddie Howe.

Then Eddie suffered devastating news. His mother, Annie, had passed away. His relationship with Annie was of utmost importance to him and it was a blow that shattered his world. He may well have felt that he should have been nearby at this time, but he was trying to build his career a long way from home. Football didn't matter to him at this point. Jason Tindall took charge for the following game – a game of penalties with one scored each by Burnley and Crystal Palace at Turf Moor. Rodriguez was still putting the goals away, but Darren Ambrose, for Palace, was also capable of doing the same from 12 yards. This was the debut game for Danny Ings, who had been signed from Bournemouth in August 2011. His knee injury had kept him waiting to make his debut for eight months!

A goalless draw at Cardiff City followed. That left Burnley 10 points off the play-off positions with 10 games to go. Defeat at Ipswich was followed by a 2-2 draw with West Ham Utd. Burnley had been 2-0 up against the Hammers, but they saw their lead disappear in the second half and Sam Baldock could have even won the game for the Londoners in the last minute. Howe had more or less realised that the game was up for this season. 'We're kicking ourselves because I believe we had the capability of being good enough this year. We've surrendered some leads and that's something we need to focus on,' he stressed. 'We've competed really well against the top sides and given good accounts of ourselves in the big games. It's perhaps more the games against the teams down the lower end when we've struggled and dropped points when we should not have done so. It's such small margins as we could easily have been knocking on the door. We will have to learn that quickly for next year and keep the group together and have a good push for promotion,' Howe said.

With the pressure of promotion virtually gone, Burnley stuck five past Portsmouth in their next match. Charlie Austin ran riot with a hat-trick in the last 16 minutes, with Kieran Trippier and Danny Ings having already put Pompey behind in the first half, with only David Norris getting Portsmouth on the score board. Howe was still keen to highlight his strikers as being the best, even though the team had not mustered a strong promotion challenge. 'I think we have the best strikers in the Championship. We have Charlie [Austin], Jay [Rodriguez], Danny [Ings] who are all top-quality forwards. They are all very clinical and they showed that,' praised Howe.

But in the Championship, as in any league, teams have to be consistent to get to the top. So, the disappointment of a 1-3 reverse in the following game against Birmingham City summed up just how Burnley couldn't string wins together. Danny Ings was on the score sheet in the 74th minute to equalise Marlon King's opener, but two late Birmingham goals condemned Howe's men crashing to another home defeat.

The last six games in April included two back-to-back wins against Brighton and away at Doncaster Rovers. Charlie Austin got the winner in both games. Any thoughts of a strong finish fell away with three draws and one defeat in the last four games. The defeat came away at Blackpool – a 4-0 drubbing on the Tangerine's way to the play-offs.

Howe was not feeling charitable about Blackpool's win. 'We had enough chances to score three or four ourselves. We conceded some poor goals today, which has been unlike us of late where we have been quite tight and I think the score line is extremely flattering to them... I think it shows there are small margins between the top and the bottom sides in this league,' summed up Howe. We need a few more quality bodies to what we have and we'll have a good chance [next season],' he added.

The final game of the season saw Burnley end the campaign 1-1 with Bristol City with the visitors again snatching a late equaliser to match Danny Ing's earlier 30-yard strike. Burnley had let another game slip when they had been in a winning position and Howe couldn't hide his disappointment at the end of a season that had promised so much. 'We wanted to finish with a win and a performance to send the supporters off in good spirits with an idea of the kind of football we want to play next season, but we didn't dominate or dictate the game well enough from the middle of the pitch and that was disappointing,' Howe said.

Eddie had to cope with the emotion of his personal loss, along with feeling disappointed about his young team not quite clicking. He set about making amends bringing in seven players between June and August. Sam Vokes was signed permanently, but it was defenders that were seen as a priority. Luke O'Neil joined from Mansfield, Jason Shackell joined from Derby County and Joseph Mills signed a season-long loan from Reading. Midfield additions included George Porter from Leyton Orient, ex-Bournemouth player Brian Stock from Doncaster Rovers and Cameron Stewart on loan from Hull City.

More striking was the long list of eight players being released as Howe balanced the books. Zavron Hinds was one of those who left. More annoying for the supporters was the loss of striker Jay Rodriguez to Southampton. The fee was undisclosed but the *BBC* quoted it as £7m and the *Guardian* at £6m – either would have been a transfer record for Southampton at the time. Southampton had seen the value in the England U21's Championship goals and believed Rodriguez could do as well in the top flight.

So, Eddie Howe had to start the 2012-13 season without his leading goal scorer of the previous season. What he did have was continuity bringing Vokes in on a permanent deal, the menace of Charlie Austin and experience of Martin Paterson, as well as a fast-developing Danny Ings to spearhead his attack. The first game of the season began with the League Cup tie against Port Vale. It saw Austin chosen to play up front on his own and he grabbed the second goal in Burnley's 1-3 comeback win.

While the new season had got off to the best possible start, the club's financial accounts showed that for the 2011-12 season Burnley had been heading for a loss of £4.4m before the sale of Jay Rodriguez, which helped towards a profit of £3.16m.

Burnley followed up the good start with a 2-0

home win over Bolton Wanderers. Paterson and
Austin made starts and got the goals either side of
half-time. Howe was just a little pleased in spoiling
former Burnley manager Owen Coyle's return to Turf
Moor. 'The lads were outstanding from start to
finish. I thought there were some gigantic
performances from individuals – some great debuts
– and I thought we looked like a good side. It's only
one game so we can't get carried away, but it's
certainly a good performance and hopefully it will
give the lads a lot of confidence. I think everyone
looks back to last year and could see at times we
would wobble but I didn't think we did that in this
game,' beamed Howe.

Burnley were next on the wrong end of a 3-2
thriller against Tony Mowbray's Middlesbrough at
the Riverside Stadium. It was clear that Charlie
Austin was going to be Burnley's main man for the
campaign ahead, as he put the Clarets in the lead on
41 minutes. But within a minute Nick Bailey had
levelled. Adam Reach then put a curling shot in, to
put Boro ahead, before Junior Stanislas scrambled an
equaliser with four minutes to go. The late goal
problems of the previous season reappeared when
Luke Williams hit a stunning goal just two minutes
later.

Howe knew Middlesbrough were a strong side
who had finished seventh in the previous season and
such a narrow defeat in this game was not that

damaging so early in the season. 'They're goals that you won't see every week, especially in the same game. They were two great strikes. I can't be too critical of my team. I thought we battled back brilliantly from 2-1 down. Although we've lost the game, we fought right to the end and we can take credit from that,' said a thoughtful Howe.

For consecutive games Burnley had an away fixture to contend with in the relentless Championship. Huddersfield had gained promotion through the play-offs in 2012 after beating Sheffield United on penalties in the final and they were eager to get off to a good start as Burnley found to their cost. Huddersfield were to pick up the first win of their campaign with Joel Lynch and Jordan Rhodes giving the Terriers a comfortable win – Huddersfield's first over Burnley for 56 years!

Charlie Austin was back on target for the League Cup win against Plymouth Argyle, but a Robbie Williams penalty on 90 minutes took the game into extra-time with Burnley winning out 3-2 after a penalty shoot-out. Burnley had Brian Jensen to thank in goal for saving three spot kicks to see the Lancashire side through. New signing, Brian Stock secured the win with his penalty kick in his first appearance. Howe was not pleased that Burnley hadn't made a better job of seeing off the League Two side. 'I didn't want anything like that,' commented Howe, post-match. 'We were a goal up and in the second half we had the mode that we wanted to see the game out at 1-0. But, on the bench, we wanted them to go on and get two or three. It wasn't ideal. There were some good performances, but there were some ones which probably weren't so good. But hopefully that's a learning curve for the players.'

Further evidence that Burnley were not hitting top form came with Brighton's visit to Turf Moor on the 1 September 2012. Brighton had just beaten Barnsley 5-1 to pick up their first win of the season and Burnley would provide them with their second win. Craig Mackail-Smith tore into Burnley scoring twice and while Gordon Greer scored an own goal in between, he made up for that with Brighton's third goal two minutes from time. The defeat left Burnley in the bottom three – their worst ever start to a season!

Howe needed a reaction and he had to wait until after the international break. Fortunately, he got the response. Charlie Austin was proving inspirational as he hit his first hat-trick of the season in a 5-2 win over Peterborough United. Junior Stanislas and Chris McCann's strikes sandwiched the forward's goals to lift Burnley to 19th in the table. It hadn't all been plain sailing though. Burnley had gone 1-2 down after conceding a penalty scored by Lee Tomlin and a Nathaniel Mendez-Liang goal.

'We found ourselves 2-1 down, when we had

been the dominant side after 20 minutes and it was scratch the head time really as we had to show real character,' said Howe. 'For some reason, we conceded two goals and it was really then up to the players to show immense character because it's been a difficult few weeks for us and it would have been easy to go the other way, but they dug in and in the end, it was a comfortable victory. But we've done it the hard way,' said Howe.

Charlie Austin of course took the plaudits. His second goal was the class finish. 'It was a good little spot by Chris McCann and to find him, a little reverse pass and Charlie's had a touch and rifled it in the net. It's the hallmark of him that he shows us in training every day and I'm pleased he's got another three today.'

Charlie's third goal came from the penalty spot and he may not have been the penalty taker had Paterson still been on the pitch, but it was Paterson's first game back from injury and Howe had made some substitutions to ease him back into things. So, it was easy for Austin to ask for the ball and get his hat-trick.

New signing Cameron Stewart was especially marked out for praise from Howe when he had come on. 'He's a real talent, technically very good and he's quick and direct. It's great to see him and Junior at the end, because we had two players there who were frightening defenders by running at them. I know all Burnley fans love a good winger and they were good in tandem today,' Howe added. 'We've had a tough two weeks. Faced a lot of criticism. But even when you win now today we're looking at things we need to work on.

 'I'd say defensively we were not as solid as we want to be and that's not just the back four, but it's the midfield runners as well. We let a couple go, and there's plenty to work on. But the pleasing thing is I thought we were better defensively second half than we were first and it's a new partnership in Michael [Michael Duff] and Shack [Jason Shackell] so that's going to take time to develop.'

Eddie Howe was in deep thought in this period in trying to work out how the team could gel quicker, but he still had players only slowly returning to fitness like Paterson, while Danny Ings was expected to be out for three months with his knee injury. Taking his team to pre-season favourites Leicester City would be another difficult game. Leicester themselves had got off to a poor start winning just one of their last five games under Nigel Pearson. While Dean Marney gave Burnley a 10th minute lead, goals from David Nugent and Jamie Vardy condemned Howe's men to another league defeat.

Rumours that Eddie Howe may be in jeopardy of losing his job at Burnley surfaced in September 2012 when training was cancelled. The reason given was that there had been a power cut at the training ground, but the Burnley faithful interpreted that as Howe has been sacked, suggesting he had walked out of a board meeting. This came on the back of the midweek defeat at Leicester City. Howe couldn't say he hadn't been given the funds to rebuild, as seven of the players on the pitch who lost to Leicester were his signings, even if money was tight.

It was a delicate period when Burnley were seeing some signs of potential but were also making far too many mistakes. Howe was certainly under pressure and he needed to get a few wins. One did come against Derby County. Jamie Ward scored first for Derby on 20 minutes, but Austin had netted before half-time to go in at 1-1 at the break and he scored an 89th minute winner.

Austin would be on target again in the League Cup second round match against Swindon Town, even though Burnley would go down 3-1 to the Robins suffering an early cup exit. Austin was closer to getting a winner against Millwall, after Ben Mee had scored to cancel out Lee Trotter's third minute strike for the Lions. But Austin's goal just before half-time was levelled by Darius Henderson in the third minute of added-time. The late conceded goals were again becoming a feature. Just as gruelling was to see Junior Stanislas' strike controversially ruled out, before Henderson's equaliser. Burnley had been almost ready to even kick off again, so confident were their players that Stanislas had scored. But referee Craig Pawson and assistant referee William Smallwood took their time to discuss an offside in the lead up to the goal and ruled the goal out, causing uproar in the terraces. 'It was a killer blow for us,' Howe complained. 'I thought we were 3-1 up for a good period of time, certainly the players felt the same way and the crowd did as well. I've never seen a decision like it in football in all my life. It was cruel on us because mentally you think you're 3-1 up with a two-goal cushion, the game is potentially over. So, to then have to play the game out knowing there was only one goal in it was a psychological blow for us.'

Eddie Howe was vulnerable to criticism. The result and his new signings' performances weren't good enough, but he needed a change of fortune. The gods were not on his side. Another Charlie Austin hat-trick against Sheffield United on 2 October should have earned Burnley three more points, despite two goals from Chris O'Grady for the visitors. However, with Austin having completed his hat-trick in the 84th minute, less than a minute past before Michail Antonio salvaged a point for United. For Howe it was an all too familiar story. 'I'm hugely frustrated and hugely disappointed. I thought we were excellent first half. You can't need to score four to win a game, but it's been the same story this season. The beauty of it is in football you always get a chance to put it right and there is a lot of defensive work for the lads to do. Charlie Austin scored a great third goal and you think we have wrapped it up, but it wasn't to be and we have a lot of work to do. The goals were poor goals. We talked about the first goal, but what we didn't talk about is conceding so soon after,' lamented Howe.

Just to cap off a disappointing night, Howe had also seen captain Jason Shackell pull up in the warm up. A recurring theme had set in at Burnley. They were competitive but couldn't get over the line. Burnley were languishing just above the relegation zone, but Howe felt that he was tantalisingly close to getting it right.

On 6 October Howe took his team to play Crystal Palace in what would turn out to be his last match in charge for the Lancashire outfit. It was another thriller with Burnley coming out on the wrong side of the seven-goal feast of entertainment at Selhurst Park. Chris McCann and Martin Paterson had put the Clarets 2-0 up after half-an-hour, and it should have been a matter of containing the home side to take the three points, but Wilfred Zaha had other ideas. He was to score either side of half-time. Damien Delaney and Glenn Murray would then see Palace into a 4-2 lead, before Charlie Austin pulled a goal back nine minutes from time. This left Burnley in 16th place.

Eddie Howe's final post-match interviews as a Burnley manager were filled with expression about how frustrated he was that things were just not going their way. 'It is hugely disappointing to lose the game today. You score the amount of goals that we are at the moment and are not getting the points that that reflects, it's hugely frustrating. We feel pretty, well, very low tonight. I think at two-nil up, we were very in control of the game. The first goal was a frustrating goal to concede. They hit us on the counter-attack. The manner of the second goal we conceded when we get broken on three or four versus two is really suicidal defending away from home. You can't commit that many bodies forward and we set up with a system not to do that with the pace they have in their side and they are a threat with Zaha, he's got real quality, but we didn't deal with that threat well enough. We changed system today to be tighter, play three in midfield and defend a little deeper and I thought for the main in the first half, as I say, we defended really well. The plan was working perfectly, but at the moment we are just making individual errors and it's costing us and we're making too many of them,' said a frustrated Howe.

Told by a *BBC reporter* that Burnley were now the top scorers in the division, Howe replied 'It's a positive to take, but it doesn't mean anything at the moment. All that matters is your points tally and our points tally isn't good enough. We have two-weeks now to go away and work with the players. We said

Tuesday that when you are playing Saturday/Tuesday you have no time to do anything other than recover the players and get them going again.' said Howe. 'Now I think we have a period of time where we've got to work them and we have got to have a better mentality to defend all the way through the team... The lads are a great bunch and they're hurting at the moment and we've got to put it right.'

While things had been going far from smoothly, what Eddie Howe had not expected was that in such a disappointing start to a new season he would suddenly become the subject of a head-hunting exercise by his former club on the south coast. In truth he wasn't going to have time to work with the players at Burnley as he had planned, because the international break came at a very good time for Bournemouth to ask the question – will you come back and help us?

The *Lancashire Telegraph* was alarmed at the uncertainty regarding AFC Bournemouth's managerial vacancy and it was right that Howe was still topping the Cherries' wanted list. On 9 October 2012, the paper said: 'He [Eddie] could be leading a two-horse race, with Bournemouth believed to be eyeing up Karl Robinson as an option in case their hopes of Howe fall down.

While Eddie Mitchell had been declaring it was unlikely that Bournemouth could attract a manager from a higher division, the Lancashire paper was not confident that things weren't happening behind the scenes. In their pages, they stated that Howe had 'scrapped plans' for an extended break in the aftermath of Saturday's 4-3 defeat at Crystal Palace.

By 11 October, the paper's headline read 'No permission granted for Bournemouth talks with Howe'. Burnley's chief executive Lee Hoos had responded to Eddie Mitchell's confident boast that Bournemouth were close to sealing a deal to bring Howe back to the south coast after making an approach to Burnley.

'Bournemouth have made an unsolicited and unwanted approach for Eddie Howe. Burnley football club would like to stress that no agreement has been reached and Eddie Howe is still Burnley manager. No permission has been granted for Bournemouth to speak to Eddie.'

A day later the paper was printing a headline of a very different tone – 'Howe: I'm leaving Burnley for personal reasons.' Eddie and Jason lasted 21 months at Burnley in what Eddie himself described as 'good and bad times'.

10. THE HOMECOMING (2012-13)

Jason Tindall has always been at Eddie Howe's side.
Here Stephen and Robert wished Jason all the best,
in front of Dean Court in October 2012

AFC Bournemouth's team had virtually been ripped
apart in the summer of 2011, having failed to win
promotion through the play-offs, under Lee
Bradbury. Huddersfield Town had put an early end
to the Cherries' Wembley dream. It had been a
pulsating match and a penalty shoot-out, after the
teams had drawn 1-1 at Dean Court and 3-3 at the
John Smith's Stadium.

Pre-season had seen the Cherries take on a continental challenge by playing in the EC Group Cup with Glenn Hoddle's Academy, Lokomotiv Moscow and FC Saarbrücken for the prize money of £80,000. Dean Court was also under new sponsorship as the Seward Stadium.

Lee Bradbury and Steve Fletcher had rebuilt some of the team. Scott Malone was signed on loan in July 2011 from Norwich City, on a six-month loan before signing permanently in December. Adam Barratt signed from Crystal Palace to stiffen the defence further and would become the new captain. Welsh midfielder Shaun MacDonald was brought in as the legs in the middle, along with Steven Gregory from Wimbledon. The loan signing of Wes Thomas was also hoped to bring goals. Darryl Flahavan would compete with Shawn Jalal for the keeper's position. They were soon to be joined by ex-England keeper, David James in September. However, fans had to endure the departures of Danny Hollands and Rhoys Wiggins to Charlton Athletic, Danny Ings to Eddie Howe's Burnley and the retirement of Steve Lovell.

This was a period in AFC Bournemouth's history when one man really ran the show. The expressive and often explosive character of chairman Eddie Mitchell meant that these were times when the fans and the property developer rarely saw eye to eye. Eddie Mitchell and Eddie Howe had been a good combination that had steered the Cherries to a rare promotion. But it seemed that all that could be put in jeopardy in 2011-12 when the impact of losing Eddie Howe and JT was hugely felt around Dean Court.

By September 2011, the gloves were off for Eddie Mitchell. In the fan's forum the chairman had told the fans that if they don't like it at Dean Court, then they should go and support the lot down the road – Southampton. The fans were already rattled by this and their frustrations were about to be played out all over the national papers.

Eddie Mitchell was never a man to hide and he was well aware that he was seen by many as the instigator of all that was wrong at the club. Every word was under scrutiny and when Eddie Mitchell saw the fans not leaving the ground for a match in September, he lost his cool. His intentions may have been to imitate Delia Smith's famous Norwich rallying cry, but some fans saw it more of as ugly invitation to come and have a brawl.

The scene was set when Bournemouth had lost 0-3 to Chesterfield at home on 10 September 2011, leaving them second from bottom of League One. Eddie Mitchell had taken it upon himself to take to the pitch after the game, when a large crowd of supporters had decided to stay behind, and criticise the board for the dismal start to the season. Mitchell was having none of it, and he proceeded to grab the stadium announcer's microphone and talk it out with the supporters.

However, the stewards were lining up in front of Eddie Mitchell which was annoying him. 'To fans that are frustrated because we have lost today, you must remember that for the last two seasons... Well, let's put it this way, you obviously don't want to listen to me,' Mitchell gasped, as cries of 'You don't know what you're doing,' came from the crowd.

The stewards were by now trying to hold Mr Mitchell from getting any closer to the North stand. They simply wanted to try and calm the situation down. Every time Mitchell inched forward, one of the stewards stood in front of him and held on to him, trying to dissuade him from confrontation. They just didn't want Mitchell to incite the fans.

Eddie Mitchell singled out one fan in particular in a leather jacket, who he described as 'a lad whose eyes were just about to pop out of his head'. The chairman invited him down – 'why don't you jump over the fence and come and have a chat about it? Come on then.' The fans responded with chants of 'You don't know what you're doing,' and 'Come back when you're sober, tra, la, la!'

Eddie Mitchell tried to carry on to get his point across. 'Are you frustrated with the team that we've got?' he asked. 'Are you frustrated because we lost today?' Eddie Mitchell added. 'Would you be there if we won 4-1 today? Is football guaranteed? Are results guaranteed? This time four months ago you all invaded the pitch because we had a side...' He was stopped at this point.

'We want Mitchell out, we want Mitchell out!' came back the chants.

It became a bit of a dance, until Mr Mitchell retreated to the halfway line and then grabbed the microphone for a second time. 'Who do you want in then, have you got somebody? Let's have a name then,' he taunted angrily.

For most fans though, this was about as low as the club could go. The bond between the club and the fans had broken down. Eddie Mitchell is made of stern stuff and he wasn't going to be shifted easily. It wouldn't be the last time though that he would approach the fans and try and speak to them when things weren't going well. Some fans were willing to listen, but others would never be won over.

Arguably, Eddie Mitchell could have stepped away. In fact, it was Steve Sly and Jeff Mostyn who decided in November to sell their 50 per cent share in the club to allow Russian businessmen Max Demin to invest in new infrastructure and yet more players, having been persuaded by Eddie Mitchell to invest in the south coast club. Mitchell was already looking to buy back the stadium from London property developers Structadene. He had submitted plans for two full-sized and five five-a-side pitches for training in Kings Park.

It's in these circumstances that Bournemouth would make one of their best signings. A Brighton convert, Steve Cook would become an influential player in Bournemouth's rise up the leagues, before becoming a regular Premier League starter. He joined on loan in October 2011, and managed to survive the tumultuous year before Eddie Howe and Jason Tindall would return. Simon Francis would be just as important in Bournemouth's rise up the league. Francis signed from Charlton Athletic on loan, at first, before making a permanent signing in January 2012. Charlie Daniels also signed from Leyton Orient in November as a new side took shape.

Some of Bradbury's other signings did not fare as well. Stephane Zubar was an attacking defender who did well until Eddie Howe's return. Charlie Sheringham, Teddy Sheringham's son, was another signing that October who didn't manage more than six games for the Cherries. Wes Fogden was also signed in this period from non-league Havant & Waterlooville as a nimble and popular right winger.

Lee Bradbury fought hard in his first managerial job and was given the funds to have a real crack at promotion. He did get the team up to eighth place in League One by the end of January 2012. He gambled further on bringing back a former favourite Matt Tubbs.

The club paid in the region of £500,000 for Matt's striking services (at the time the *Bournemouth Echo* reported £800,000), which was a massive amount of money for the club at the time. Tubbs scored some goals, but was injured by April. The difficulty was fans expected the team to challenge for promotion. Instead successive 0-1 home defeats to Milton Keynes Dons and Charlton Athletic greeted the fans as February was left behind. By March the club had slipped to 12th place. The club was becoming a laughing stock to many when reports emerged of the Irena Demin, the wife of co-owner Maxim Demin, went into the player's dressing room at half-time when 1-0 down against Milton Keynes. Irena had been allowed to express her disappointment with the team. It seemed that things were out of control. It was a picture that was only made worse by Eddie Mitchell explaining his reasons for allowing Irena and Maxim into the dressing room on Mark Chapman's 606 show on *BBC Five Live*, which saw Mitchell cut-off air for repeatedly using foul language.

Matters had got so bad with relations between the local *Bournemouth Echo* and the club that the paper's reporters were banned from attending press conferences and were no longer welcome at the ground. The reporting of the 3-0 defeat at Sheffield Wednesday had triggered the club's decision, which Lee Bradbury took particular offence to over the 'immature' headline.

Still, Lee Bradbury was not able to turn results around and eventually departed in March 2012, having been at the club since 2007. He had brought in some key signings though like Charlie Daniels and Simon Francis from Charlton in November 2011, as well as Steve Cook. Cook, like Francis signed a permanent deal in January 2012, but it hadn't bought Lee Bradbury enough time.

A run of six defeats in eight games saw Lee Bradbury removed from his position by chairman Eddie Mitchell on 25 March 2012. Bournemouth were 13th in the table and Bradbury had lasted just 14 months in charge. With Bradbury failing to deliver, Eddie Mitchell acted swiftly.

The defeat at Oldham was Bradbury's last game in charge, but the way in which he left the club was not publicly explained at the time. Mitchell refused to say if Bradbury had been sacked or had left by mutual consent. His only comment was 'It was disappointing to see Lee leave the club.' A couple of weeks later, Bradbury explained in a statement for the League Manager's Association that he had not resigned or left by mutual consent and that the chairman had indeed sacked him. He said: 'I would like to clarify the fact that I did not resign or leave by mutual consent, the chairman decided he wanted a change and I was dismissed. I am naturally very disappointed that I have not been given time to see the fruition of all the hard work that has gone in to developing the current squad of players. I felt that we would be in a position to make a positive challenge for promotion next season, but it was not to be.'

It was left open for Paul Groves, youth team manager, to fill Bradbury's shoes and Shaun Brooks, head of youth, was made his assistant manager. Their first game was against Stevenage, but Groves and Brooks already had their excuses. 'We have tried to get our message across to the players in a very short period of time before Tuesday's game at Stevenage. We have had more time with them leading up to today's game and I have been delighted with the attitude of the squad,' said Groves in his programmes notes for the Yeovil match. 'We have seven games and we are working hard to ensure that this is a successful spell.'

The Cherries continued to stumble to the end of that season under Paul Groves, but simply did not inspire the fans or manage to create a bond like the club had seen under Eddie Howe and Lee Bradbury. It appeared Groves was the cheap option, because he was there. Before long the results would show that perhaps it would be too big a job for Groves and Brooks. One signing they did make that summer was the deal with Rotherham United for Lewis Grabban, and they also took a punt on a young Torquay United midfielder called Eunan O'Kane.

So, the Cherries still started the 2012-13 season
under Paul Groves despite the run of draws he had
started to specialise in by the end of May 2012. The
team was being captained by Miles Addison, who
Bradbury had signed on loan, at first. Miles had the
experience of playing Championship football with
Derby County, but he was slow and ponderous.
turning slower than a cruise liner, we used to think.
Frank Demouge gave the team a continental feel
with the Dutch forward joining in June 2012 from
Utrecht, along with Lorenzo Davids who signed from
FC Augsburg. A more important signing from
Brighton was the man who would become the
captain and was so influential in the change of
fortunes of the team - Tommy Elphick. Bournemouth
were also relying on the experience of ex-
Southampton forward, Lee Barnard to get the goals,
alongside the tall Michael Symes. Josh McQuoid had
also returned to Bournemouth in a swap deal with
Scott Malone going in the other direction to Millwall.

The managerial questions surfaced more
vehemently in September 2012, and where writ
large by a 4-0 defeat at Swindon with the promising
Matt Ritchie grabbing a brace of goals, as the
Cherries were torn apart and only managed two
shots on target themselves all game.

Paul Groves tried to find a way of plugging the goals going in and the former Liverpool shot stopper David James was signed at the end of September. James made his debut against Walsall on 29 September. A 1-1 draw looked to be earned with Charlie Daniels firing home an equaliser to Andy Butler's earlier goal, with nine minutes to go. But George Bowerman scrambled in a late winner for Walsall to leave Groves smarting at another defeat.

Tommy Elphick goes through his pre-match ritual

Groves was on very shaky ground having still not won at home and he acknowledged the crowd's discontent. 'People have had opportunities and it's not quite gone our way. The crowd voiced their opinion, which they are entitled to do. They tried to get behind us from the off, and obviously once things go against us, then the crowd show their opinion. That is natural,' said an impassioned Groves. 'My job is to try and continue to work with the players and address the issues that we might have in terms of trying to win some football matches.'

With Bournemouth nine games into the new season and defeat at home to Walsall, Eddie Mitchell bravely or perhaps foolishly stepped out in front of the home fans again. This time it was in front of the reception at Dean Court, to understand their frustrations and to plead with them that he wanted the same as them – a successful side. He was asked by one fan, after a home defeat, what he made of the current situation? And what was he going to do about it? While admitting that the situation was awful, in slightly more colourful language, Mitchell said: 'It's all very well saying change it, change it but we keep changing, changing it and we've got to find a way of winning.'

Eddie Mitchell did not have a microphone and so when he was asked to speak up, he took his time to try and hear the questions and to be heard. But this was an unhappy Dean Court and Mitchell was probably wondering what he could do to placate the fans. 'We're all on the same side.' said Mitchell. 'I could have employed Glenn Hoddle but we'd still be in the same situation. You know it's football. The balls round. We try our best.'

The chorus of, 'We want Grovesey out!' grew

louder and louder before fans started to sing 'Oh Eddie Howe!, Eddie, Eddie, Eddie, Eddie Howe!'

The fans had given their view on matters, however unlikely the possibility of getting their favourite son back to Dean Court. 'Sort it out!' was one shout. Eddie Mitchell then got more animated. 'Okay, sort it out, he says. I sack Groves tomorrow, yeah. I sack him, it costs the club a lot of money, but I sack him tomorrow. And we get, I don't know Glenn Hoddle, Eddie Howe and we carry on as we are. What do we do sack him?' said Eddie Mitchell.

It may not have been a ringing endorsement for Glenn Hoddle from Eddie Mitchell, but the crowd would have accepted anyone other than Paul Groves and Shaun Brooks. It just wasn't working and Mitchell knew it as well as those baying for blood. It was a noise that was ever more demanding of change. The end of the saga came on 3 October 2012.

The midweek game at Crawley Town on 2 October would be the last of Paul Groves' tenure. The game was a typical League One scrap. The rain was pouring down on Groves' last chance to get it right. Standing in the away stand was hardly glamourous, Bournemouth's fans were huddled together to keep their spirits up. I was in the middle of it, with my friend Colin, wondering what we were doing watching this miserable shower on the pitch? It was far from inspiring. Striker Frank Demouge had to be subbed for a nose injury after just 11 minutes, before Hope Akpan gave Crawley Town the lead, scoring from around the penalty spot. By half-time, Joe Walsh doubled the home team's advantage. In the away stand we wondered how much worse it could get before Groves was shown the door? There was a little glimmer of hope in the second half when loan striker Lee Barnard headed in from close range, but the optimism was short lived. Nicky Adams was fed through by Nicky Ajose's through ball and he easily out-paced David James in Bournemouth's goal to make it a night of misery for the travelling fans.

Even Groves had a hint of inevitability that the axe had to fall on him sooner or later. 'Before every single game we do set-plays, and you do every little bit of detail. But you've conceded four goals in the last two games from set-plays. People are responsible for doing their jobs. It's very difficult to accept,' he said. 'The team of late have been chopped and changed because of injuries. Twelve injuries make a difference to any squad. In football you don't quit. Never quit on the pitch, never quit off the pitch.'

Groves might not have quit, but the results sealed his fate. Bournemouth were left needing a new manager, their third in eight months. Bournemouth had always been a club that had found success far from easy. When they had found it, with Eddie Howe, it had been snatched away from them again, just when things were great. Now the mood was angry, not just at the results and the instalment of Paul Groves, but also the way Eddie Howe had left in the first place. To the fans it was no surprise that Lee Bradbury had not taken the club forward – he didn't have the 'wow factor' to lift the club to the heights that Eddie Howe could. Groves had been even less successful. He'd used 24 different players as starters in the first 10 games of the 2012-13 season. It was just too many changes. But who would bring the right balance to the team?

The answer seemed the impossible solution. Why would Eddie Howe want to drop back down a division to a club that he had left less than two years earlier? Was Eddie Howe's love for Bournemouth as strong as the fans' love for him? Eddie Mitchell didn't encourage any thoughts of Bournemouth attracting a manager from the Championship or the Premier League simply because of the wages. Bournemouth had to live within their means and so an approach for Eddie Howe looked out of the question. 'We have always got to look after our money and can't compete with Championship and Premier League clubs. It might be a different kettle of fish when we get there, but we have got to work within a League One budget,' Mitchell reminded everyone.

Other names were in the frame initially. Milton Keynes Dons' Karl Robinson was among the favourites along with Gregg Abbot at Carlisle United, and former Bournemouth player Steve Cotterill was the front runner for a while. The list was endless with former Coventry City manager, Andy Thorn believed to have put his name forward, while out of work candidates included Glenn Hoddle and Alan Curbishley, Sean Dyche, Lawrie Sanchez and Gary Waddock.

Eddie Mitchell, of course was centre of attention and while everyone wanted to know who he was talking to, he didn't give much away. 'The strongest indication I can give is that I don't want expectations of me pulling somebody out of the Premier League, because it isn't going to happen. It is more than likely to be from somebody that is between jobs, [that is] not to say they haven't been a Premier League manager,' Mitchell added.

It was a strange period around the home coming of Eddie Howe and JT. Just like when the local hero had left to join Burnley FC back in 2011, there were days of speculation and intrigue. Thoughts immediately turned to wondering if Harry Redknapp would fill the gap, as he was already at the Cherries as an advisor to Paul Groves. The fans didn't automatically expect Eddie Howe to return, as he was not doing that well in the Championship and Burnley were far from keen to lose Eddie at the time. Lee Hoos, the Clarets chief executive, was less than pleased that Bournemouth wanted to make an approach for their former manager. He described the interest as 'unwanted'.

It seemed like a dream to Bournemouth fans that Eddie Howe and Jason Tindall might return. Could this be happening? The circumstances were extremely sad, as Eddie had lost his mother, Annie, in March 2012. She was his biggest supporter and cheerleader in chief. He needed security and to be around people who he could lean on – there was only one place he wanted to be.

Eddie Howe spoke on the matter a few years later in March 2015. 'There were two totally different sides to coming back – the football part and the family side. They are totally different and there were more reasons to me coming back than I could ever talk about publicly,' said Howe. Being in exile in Burnley was not where he was going to find the kind of stability to feel fired up enough to motivate a team and to manage with enthusiasm. Eddie Howe is not the kind of person who would want to let anyone down either and so something had to give.

The thought of another job probably hadn't even occurred to him. He was dealing with grief and trying to understand things. Whether the Bournemouth vacancy came as a shock to him in October 2012 or as an escape didn't really matter. What it does show about Eddie Howe is that he was keen to take a risk to find happiness. He will have felt loyalty to Burnley in what he had started there. Yet, he must also have looked at the League One table and been worried that what he had created at Bournemouth was quickly disappearing.

'It came very much as a surprise,' said Howe. 'It wasn't something, two-three weeks before hand that had really been on the horizon, so it came a little bit out of the blue. It was very much a case of me having to make a quick decision for the future of my career and obviously for my family and once I'd sort of got my head around it, I knew that it was something I really wanted to do and that I wanted to make happen. And I don't think anyone envisaged quite what would happen after that and how well it would go, but certainly the time around making the decision was an incredibly stressful period,' Eddie confessed.

Events may have been unexpected, but Eddie Mitchell had no doubts who he wanted as the club's next manager. Whether we believe it was down to his dog or his wife's recommendation, or his own volition that Eddie Howe should come back, the call went into Burnley that Bournemouth wanted to talk to Eddie Howe. The Burnley honeymoon would be cut short. Eddie was extremely thankful for Burnley for their understanding and obvious respect, despite being extremely anxious that they wouldn't be able to retain his services.

Howe spoke openly to *Sky Sports* about his appreciation for how the Lancashire club had given him a great opportunity and that he was finding it a really difficult time in his life. 'I can't speak highly enough of Burnley Football Club, the people who work for the club, the players and the supporters, who have all been brilliant to us since we walked through the door, and I would like to thank them for that. To leave is incredibly difficult, but I feel it's a decision I have to make for my family and for personal reasons, which I can't go into detail on.'

It was lucky timing for Bournemouth, or perhaps just crazy circumstances that had opened the door to Howe and Tindall coming back, but it seemed right for Eddie Howe. He had made his mind up, he was returning to AFC Bournemouth. 'There is only one club I would contemplate leaving Burnley for and that is Bournemouth and that is the situation we found ourselves in,' said Howe. It was left to Burnley's joint chairman John Banaszkiewicz and Mike Garlick to make a statement to the Burnley fans that Eddie Howe had left for personal reasons and would return to the south coast to drop back down a division. Tinged with disappointment in losing one of England's youngest managers, Burnley's top brass just had to accept that Howe's heart was no longer in it at Burnley. 'We understand that his decision reflects his personal circumstances rather than any matters at Burnley Football Club, be that supporters, the players or the board,' said Banaszkiewicz and Garlick. 'We wish Eddie well in his future career and thank him for the hard work he has done at Burnley over the past 20 months.'

Eddie left Burnley sitting in 16th place in the Championship and 11 points behind leaders Cardiff City. But if that was a club not hitting the heights, then the Cherries were in a dire situation having won just one their first 11 matches of the 2012-13 season.

Eddie Howe and Jason Tindall strode out onto the pitch at Dean Court in their immaculate suits and thin black and navy-blue ties to rapturous applause. It must have been strange for the Leyton Orient away supporters looking on at the scenes. My feelings were just full of delight to see the managerial team smiling and waving in the sunshine, knowing that they would do their best for the club. It was a new beginning. I also believed that the players that were still at the club from when Howe and JT first managed at Bournemouth would be telling the newer players that they could achieve something special. Winning games was not guaranteed but everyone was in it together. The mood felt good and work would be fun, if hard for the players. But as fans we knew what we were getting – a man who would do everything he could to get some wins.

They couldn't have got off to a better start, although Dennis Rofe was still the caretaker manager and had picked the team. It was appropriate that one of Eddie Howe's signings from his previous reign, Marc Pugh, scored the second goal to beat Leyton Orient. Lewis Grabban had scored the opener and Bournemouth were on their way, up the league!

Eddie Howe had inherited a very different Bournemouth to the club that had been fighting relegation in League Two in 2009. There was investment with Maxim Demin and belief with Eddie Mitchell that Eddie Howe had something special. The fans also felt it, too. Howe could see it was a great time to manage Bournemouth again, as everything was in place to succeed. 'When you look back at the two previous jobs that I've had, they were tough in their own right. I couldn't have had a tougher assignment as my first job – there's no doubt about that. I said at the time that I would never face a bigger challenge than the one I walked in to that day. I don't think anyone could put me in a scenario that is more difficult than that – trying to stay in the Football League with the financial restraints.

'The job at Burnley was difficult. They were trying to cut the wage bill, bring in transfer fees and still be competitive in what is a really difficult division. The expectations were huge there as Burnley had been in the Premier League. Supporters expected promotion, but the resources didn't back that up, so it was an incredibly difficult job. Coming back here, the expectations to do well are high, but the resources are in place. It is a different challenge to any that I have had so far and one I can't wait to start,' said Eddie Howe.

The challenges would come straight away with the visit of table-toppers Tranmere Rovers in the very next game. 'It is a big challenge today for the players, as we face league-leaders Tranmere Rovers. They are unbeaten this season and Ronnie Moore has done a fantastic job,' said Eddie Howe in his programme notes. It should have been the game that Howe would least want at this time, but he clearly managed to get enough positivity into the players that they performed as if they were the top of the table team. A 3-1 home victory catapulted expectations.

One of Eddie Howe's former signings again shined in the win over Tranmere, as Bournemouth came from behind with goals from Harry Arter and Simon Francis. Harry Arter was particularly pleased to have scored the second goal and had a message for the fans: 'The fans love Eddie and so do the lads. He creates that atmosphere very quickly and you could see it on the pitch. I don't want to be disrespectful to the previous management, but he has got his ways of creating a very good team spirit and bringing together the lads as one.'

Another view of how the players were feeling at the managerial change was given by Simon Francis in the Tranmere *Match Day programme*. 'I haven't worked with them before, but I'm excited about them being here,' said Francis. 'All the lads who were here when they were before have raved about them [Eddie Howe and JT]. That goes for all the staff off the pitch and you can tell by the supporters' reaction how good the job was that they did here.'

Eddie Howe was capable of ruffling a few people as well. Wes Thomas, for instance had been out on loan at Portsmouth and Michael Appleton, Pompey's manager was keen to keep hold of the striker, but Howe has other ideas. 'I want to call back Wes to look at him and to see if he is, potentially, better than what I have in the striking department. I think that is our right as a football club. Portsmouth have benefitted from having him for 28 days and now we have called him back. He is our player and we are doing what is best for Bournemouth. I am not going to do what is best for Portsmouth – I am not Portsmouth manager,' said Howe.

Eddie was certainly displeased with suggestions that he hadn't helped his former club. 'To say that I haven't helped out Portsmouth, I gave them Kevin Long for two months when I was at Burnley, and I didn't receive one phone call thanking me for that,' he recalled. 'Because of my time at Portsmouth, I recommended Portsmouth highly and steered him that way ahead of other clubs, so those comments rankle with me.'

As it turned out, Wes Thomas soon asked to leave Bournemouth and Eddie Howe allowed him to join Blackpool on loan for the rest of the season. Michael Appleton had made a managerial change too though and had become Blackpool's new Championship manager!

There was a genuine excitement about the rest of the season. The belief that 'together, anything is possible' was starting to take shape. The main aim at the start though was just to pull away from the relegation zone. The shock 3-1 comeback win over Tranmere took Bournemouth up to 18th. Eddie Howe was delighted to get off to a winning start. 'In the second half, I thought we really got going as did the crowd, and it was a really good half in the end. Huge credit must go to the players. We were 1-0 down at home against the league leaders and the second half was a really good comeback.'

Howe wanted to create a style of play that would see more energy and drive to the Cherries' game and he already felt that his influence was starting to resonate with the players. 'They had a style of football previously and, definitely at home, I want to get more balls into the box, try to create more goal scoring chances and play with a quicker tempo. It was something we worked on in the week and it will take time for the players to get used to that, but I thought we did it really well.'

The honeymoon period seemed to be over quickly, when Bournemouth went 2-0 down against perennial rivals Notts County in the next match. But there was a fight back in the second half with Josh McQuoid and Harry Arter netting, before Jamal-Campbell Rice put County ahead again from the penalty spot. Luckily, within a minute, Matt Tubbs found an equaliser to gain a valuable away point. By beating Carlisle away 2-4 at the end of October, Howe had gathered seven points out of nine on his return. Howe made three changes for the FA Cup match against Dagenham and Redbridge, but the outcome was even more emphatic, a 4-0 win!

Bournemouth continued to pick up wins against Shrewsbury, Doncaster and a big 4-1 win over Oldham. Beating Dean Saunders' Doncaster Rovers 0-1 was perhaps fortunate, in that Harry Arter's one goal could have been only worth a point, when Charlie Daniels took down David Syres in the box. But that was the luck that Bournemouth were having. By the end of November, Eddie Howe was still unbeaten since his return and a 2-2 away draw against Bury saw Bournemouth up to 10th. After the wins against Shrewsbury and Doncaster, Eddie Howe was impressed with the run. 'The run has continued and we want it to go on for as long as possible. We have momentum and are delighted with the start we have had,' said Howe.

There was no reason to take the FA Cup that seriously, apart the extra revenue. Being drawn away to Carlisle United was not an attractive draw.

Still, Bournemouth made short work of Carlisle winning 1-3 to book a place in the third round.

November was significant for the return of Brett Pitman from Championship side Bristol City. The move was a loan at first, but Eddie Howe knew exactly what he could get from Pitman. Brett jumped at the chance to team up with Howe and Tindall again. Bournemouth had the finance with Maxim Demin as well to pay out in the region of £600,000 for Pitman's permanent return in the following January. Howe was equally pleased to get hold of his striker who was affectionately known as 'chicken' for his running style. 'When you get the chance to sign someone of Brett's quality and calibre, it's not an easy one to turn down. We know him and we go back a long way. He did fantastically in his first spell here. Hopefully, he will come in and continue where he left off. He is still a good age [24] and it's a great deal for the football club. It's a statement of intent to show that the club means business. You can't argue with Brett's finishing ability and what he will bring to the team,' added Howe.

Howe was awarded manager of the month for November. As always, he was more pleased for the players than for himself. 'This is all down to the team,' he said. 'Ever since I have come back in, the players have been excellent as has the staff around me, and the supporters have also more than played their part on the run we have been on.'

December was a crucial month to keep the winning run going and the Cherries did just that by beating Scunthorpe 1-2 away, with David James saving a penalty. Three home wins followed including a narrow 1-0 win over Colchester United, and two 3-0 wins over Yeovil and Crawley. That left the Cherries in fifth at the end of the year and chasing promotion. It had been a remarkable turnaround in fortunes and Howe was unbeaten in 15 league and cup games since his return.

With the window soon to open, the Cherries needed to keep hold of Lewis Grabban, who had scored 10 times in the 18 appearances. Grabban's pace to get in behind defences is what helped Bournemouth make teams defend and allowed the rest of the team to get up the pitch. While Charlie Sheringham was still recovering from a foot operation, having gone a year without playing, Matt Tubbs was on the side lines since Pitman had returned.

Positivity was in abundance, so much so that Eddie Mitchell revised plans for a new 2500-seat South Stand, but without the previously planned spa and hotel. The aim was to build the stand in the next pre-season, if Bournemouth were promoted to the Championship.

Following the win against Scunthorpe on 8 December, Howe said, 'I still think we can get better and that is what we must strive to do. You are

looking at perfection all the time. I am looking for
total dominance. Whether we have the finances
behind us or not, that is what we are after and I
don't think we are there yet.'

Finances were a subject that other League One
managers were more than happy to talk about when
it came to AFC Bournemouth. Brentford were
Bournemouth's first opponents of the New Year and
Uwe Rösler was keen to point out the depths of
Bournemouth's finances compared to the rest in the
league, which Steve Cook replied to. 'It doesn't
bother us. What happens off the pitch is not really
down to us, we have got to do the business on the
pitch. Clubs and teams that say that just try to take
our mind off the game but we are a strong side,' said
Cook. 'We thrive on it. We see what managers say in
the papers, the gaffer shows us, and that just
encourages us more. We want to show the league
that we deserve to be up there.'

It was an ominous warning to those still
tantalisingly sitting above the Cherries in the league.
But as the Cherries neared the summit of League
One things suddenly became tricky. Bournemouth
were held by Brentford 0-0 and then by Paulo Di
Canio's Swindon. Bournemouth had been in control
of the promotion chasing game against Swindon
with Arter's 26-minute goal, but in the last five
minutes Bournemouth threw the win away, when
David James came out to clear a ball from Chris

Martin and made a poor goal kick in the heavy rain. The ball sped away from Wes Fogden and into Andy Williams path who grabbed the late equaliser.

Bournemouth then received a boost with an excellent 1-1 draw in the FA Cup away at Premier League Wigan Athletic. Bournemouth had almost landed the shock of the third round when Eunan O'Kane scored in the 41st minute at the DW Stadium, but a 70 minute by Jordi Gómez took the tie to a replay. Little did we know, at that stage, that Wigan would be the eventual winners of the cup that year.

With Wigan knocking Bournemouth out of the FA Cup 0-1 in front of 8890 supporters at the Goldsands Stadium, as it had been called since July 2012, it was Howe's first defeat since returning to Bournemouth. More disappointingly, the game was followed by a league defeat against Walsall 3-1. Eddie Howe knew the unbeaten record had to end at some point, but was surprised that the team just hadn't turned up at Walsall.

'There were a lot of talking points,' Howe said after the game. 'We didn't really show our true colours and it was a disappointing performance. In saying that, it was a strange game and could easily have been different. We had enough chances to have scored three or four goals but it wasn't to be and the penalties were disappointing. If we had defended better, I think we would have won. We

lost our way after they had gone down to 10 men
and I thought our management of the game was
very poor. It was difficult watching because we are a
lot better than that and have shown we are a lot
better. For whatever reason, we were below
standard.'

Bournemouth still had the motivation of stand-in
captain Tommy Elphick to get them back on course.
Eddie Howe was impressed that Tommy Elphick had
made 27 league starts and was inspiring the other
lads in the dressing room. 'He [Elphick] is a real
motivator in the changing room and a real winner,'
said Howe. 'He trains every day at a top level.'

While Frank Demouge had found it hard to get
back in the team, he went out on loan to Roda JC for
the rest of the season. Eddie Howe had also
strengthened in the January window by signing
young keeper Ryan Allsop, Ryan Fraser from
Aberdeen for £400,000 and by making a stunning
coup to land Matt Ritchie, 23, for £500,000 from
Swindon Town. The Wiltshire club had run into some
financial problems and were up for sale. The
excitement from the fans was equally felt by Howe.
'I have known Matt a number of years and was first
made aware of him when he came on trial. Matt is a
talented player and very good technically. He did
well during a loan spell at Dagenham and ended up
getting a move to Swindon. From there, he has really
flourished and done ever so well. He is regarded as

one of the best players in League One and his signing is a real coup for the club. It is also another statement of intent,' said Howe.

'He is a goalscorer and has scored nine times this season. He is also a goal creator and a set piece-specialist. He can play a number of positions, including all across midfield, and can also cover at left-back in an emergency, which is another string to his bow and something we need. For various reasons, his age is very important to us and he will only get better with us. His attitude is probably his stand-out quality. He wants to do well, he is very conscientious and keep to learn and improve. Those are all the hallmarks we look for in a player.'

Bournemouth had dropped to eighth in the table following defeat against Walsall and there were murmurings that perhaps the magic had run out. The wins returned though with a 1-2 away win over struggling Hartlepool United and a 3-1 win over Crewe Alexandra, courtesy of a Brett Pitman hat-trick!

Milton Keynes, Portsmouth and Crewe Alexandra were all swept aside as the promotion push went in to full swing for the Cherries. Bournemouth received their biggest crowd of the season of 9135 when they overcame Portsmouth 2-0 with Grabban taking his season goal total to 13.

The 1-2 away win at Crewe sent Bournemouth top. Howe told his players to 'relish it and enjoy it'.

'A lot of people talk about pressure at the top but, for me, you won't find any more pressure than when you are at the bottom and scrapping for points,' Howe added.

By mid-February Bournemouth were not only top of the division but looked like they would cruise to promotion. But reaching the summit had brought its own pressures and the players couldn't get over the line in games, losing five in a row. The rot started away at Preston North End's Deepdale Stadium. The Cherries failed to respond to two first half goals from their hosts. The defeat was a shock, but Howe did his best to try and get players to focus on where they were at this point of the season. 'We weren't at our best – there is no doubting that. We were second best which is really difficult for me to say because it hadn't happened yet. This was the first time,' Howe commented. 'We have to retain our long-term vision, see where we are in the table and collect all the positives from that and look forward because looking back is going to do us no good now.'

A small crisis was unfolding just at the wrong time. Losing at home to Sheffield United 0-1 was followed by a 2-0 away defeat at Coventry. The goals had dried up for Lewis Grabban and worst still Bournemouth were conceding regularly.

One problem that Howe could correct was the injury list in defence. Captain Miles Addison had been a spectator for much of January and February, while Tommy Elphick also had time out after a horror tackle from Milton Keynes' Ryan Lowes. Meanwhile, Charlie Daniels had played despite a persistent ankle problem. So, Dan Seaborne was signed on loan as a centre-back from Southampton. Marcus Painter was also brought in to cover Daniels at left-back, which should have released Matt Ritchie to play further up field as he had been filling in for Daniels. But Howe liked Ritchie paying at left-back and Painter spent most of his time on the bench.

Following the 0-3 away win at Milton Keynes Dons in February, when Ritchie had played at left-back for the first time for Bournemouth, Howe had commented: 'He is technically excellent so, with the ball, I have absolutely no worries. In fact, he did very well there, technically, going forward. The changes certainly hadn't helped results though as February had progressed. 'It has been untimely for us to shuffle our back four at such a key stage of the season,' said Howe.

Leyton Orient swept passed the Cherries 3-1 with Ritchie unable to deal with Orient's wing play and Jalal and Francis getting in a mix up for one of the goals. Bournemouth needed a rallying call and Eddie Howe delivered it in his programme notes before the Doncaster game. 'We're not going to make excuses for our recent form,' said Howe. 'Nor are we going to allow our heads to drop. We are of course missing some key players, but at the same time we know the ones who have stepped in are more than good enough to win matches, as they've already shown. We are still in contact with the top six and can still achieve our goals. The next 10 games will define our season.'

Despite the brave words, by the time Doncaster Rovers had sneaked a 1-2 win at Dean Court in March, Bournemouth had slipped to seventh. The form was just one aspect of what was going on as David James called time on his association with the club, while some 'restructuring' was required with the wage bill had being further trimmed with Lorenzo Davids, Mark Molesley, Steven Gregory and Gary Bowles having left.

The changes seemed to do the trick. Ryan Allsop now had his big chance in goal and he didn't disappoint. Stevenage and Oldham were both beaten by a single goal as the defence kept consecutive clean sheets. Eddie Howe was gaining confidence that his side now had what it took to get over the final few games, in the position they wanted to be in. Speaking about the Stevenage and Oldham matches, before the Bury game, Eddie said: 'If neither match showcased the attractive football we know we can play, both certainly proved we can stay strong, resilient, and dig in to get the points which are vital at this stage of the season.'

Wes Fogden played at left-back for the first time at Oldham, even though Daniels had recovered from his injury. 'It was great to have both Charlie Daniels and Tommy Elphick involved against Oldham,' said Howe. 'Having them back in the dressing room was a boost for everybody.'

Bury found the Cherries in scintillating form suffering a heavy 4-1 defeat, when they came to Dean Court Bournemouth were up to third and had their eyes on the prize of promotion again. Brett Pitman was in a rich vein of form and notched another 0-1 win at Colchester United at the end of March to move the Cherries up to second. Pitman was doing all he could to make winning become a habit by getting among the goals again for the 1-0 win over Scunthorpe United and the 3-1 home win over Notts County. The win against County was the sixth straight win.

With five games to go Eddie Howe stood on the edge of being only the second manager to guide Bournemouth to the second tier of English football. The immediate task though was just to keep the winning sequence going. 'The record is seven and we are on six, so it just goes to show how difficult it will be to win nine. It has happened though in the 90 years this club has been in the Football League. We need to try and break the record and that is what we are aiming for,' said an eager Eddie Howe.

Better still, a brace of Pitman goals against Shrewsbury helped the Cherries to a 0-3 win. 'The result equalled a club record seventh consecutive victory, and was our fourth consecutive clean sheet on the road,' said a delighted Eddie Howe.

With just two games to go, Bournemouth were on the brink of promotion. The 20 April 2013 would be a day of celebrations, but not immediately after the final whistle for Eddie Howe. Tommy Elphick gave his first programme notes as captain having won the prestigious fans' player of the year award to beat Brett Pitman and Simon Francis. Carlisle United fans were in end of season mood too with many of them travelling down to the game dressed as smurfs, which added to the fun element of the day. But Bournemouth fans knew that with the right result they could win promotion to the Championship. Steve Cook got the party started with a goal in 25th minute before the nerves came back on 50 minutes, when Lee Miller equalised. A stunning goal by Harry Arter put Bournemouth back in front, six minutes later before Brett Pitman celebrated a 90th minute goal to make it 3-1 (incidentally, Robert and Stephen were among AFC Bournemouth's mascots for the match).

Bournemouth still had to wait for the late game to be played between Brentford and Hartlepool, even though Brentford needed a good goal difference to prevent the Cherries securing promotion. Howe was delighted to see that Brentford could only draw and promotion was guaranteed for Bournemouth with one game to play.

Scenes at Dean Court after beating Carlisle United. The Cherries were in touching distance of promotion to the Championship

The final game of the season came at Tranmere Rovers who had been the early league leaders. The boys and I travelled up to Prenton Park for the 3pm kick off. It was a carnival affair for Bournemouth fans. We had brought inflatables and were going to celebrate Bournemouth's season, no matter what the Tranmere hierarchy said. The concourses were full of fans singing 'We're on our way!' The balloons were released and we settled down to see the team try and win the game.

Bournemouth wanted to finish as champions and were in first place before kick-off, but the sandy pitch didn't help their passing game and Tranmere did well to hold out for a 0-0 draw. It meant that Doncaster Rovers would clinch the title with their last game to finish on 84 points one ahead of Eddie

Howe's men having beaten Brentford 1-0. Brentford had won a penalty in the last minute, but Marcello Trotta's spot kick had been saved and, from the resulting break, Doncaster fashioned a winner by James Coppinger to send them up and Brentford into the play-offs. 'The ups and downs are unbelievable. One minute you are up, the next you are down. But we are hardly down because of what we have achieved. We are going to play in the Championship next season, said Eddie Howe.

Talking further about missing out on the League One title Howe added: 'It was the cruellest way to have it snatched away but it was out of our control. We did everything but win the game, we were excellent and Tranmere didn't have any real chances. We bombarded their goal in the second half but just didn't get the break we needed.'

So, Bournemouth could celebrate, but it also felt that they had been cheated out of the League One title in the final seconds of the season. When I say celebrate, the football authorities had already banned any celebrations at Prenton Park. Somehow the bus tour wouldn't seem quite the same with the League One Runners Up trophy. But the club laid on a bus tour from Dean Court and through the town centre which was attended by thousands of fans. The players got their reward too with an all-expenses four-day trip to Las Vegas. The disappointment of Doncaster pinching the title would soon be forgotten as preparations for the Championship would begin right away.

One consolation that Eddie Howe could personally take was in picking up the League One Manager of the Month award for May 2013. 'I am delighted with the award and it is recognition of the run the team went on,' said Howe. 'When the pressure was really on and we knew we had to win games, the players came through when they needed to and that was the pleasing aspect from my perspective. There was a lot at stake during the final two months of the season and it is a hallmark of a good team that you deliver when the pressure is on. The lads certainly did that.'

The task for AFC Bournemouth now was to keep hold of their manager who was soon linked with the managerial vacancy at Everton, as well as fellow Championship sides Millwall and Brighton & Hove Albion.

Eddie Mitchell though was not going to lose his manager again in a hurry. 'I am hardly surprised that, because of his record, he [Eddie Howe] is linked with Premier League jobs. I couldn't see Eddie going to another Championship club, to be quite honest, because his heart and desire to do well with us is very strong. It's paramount I do everything I can to keep him and I will do so.'

It was rather breezy when Dean Court only had
three stands, but all that was about to change

11. CHAMPIONSHIP HIGHS (2013-15)

Visiting grounds that used to be in the
Premier League would soon hold no fear for AFC Bournemouth

Life in the Championship would start with the club
revealing a new golden edge to the club's crest and a
slight colour change to the stripes, while keeping the
popular Dickie Dowset head silhouette. A bigger
statement that the club had arrived in a new division
was the sight of a new temporary stand in the South
End. The facility, opened by Ted MacDougall, added
2000 fans to the overall league capacity which rose

to 11,450.

Still, not everything was new. At least Eddie Howe and JT had experienced the Championship at Burnley for the best part of two seasons. It gave everyone a calm approach to the season knowing what lay ahead. But Bournemouth hadn't been in the Championship since 1990. The excitement in town was fever pitch. 'We are going to be playing clubs with bigger squads, bigger resources and bigger stadiums, so we are really going to have to be smart. We are going to have to try to compete in different ways and be different with our playing style. We are going to need an edge and that is where we need to try to get it because it is going to be difficult trying to go toe-to-toe financially with these clubs,' Howe explained. 'There are a number of clubs with long histories and huge traditions behind them, institutions of English football. It is a great division, but a very competitive one as well. It is a really big step for us but, hopefully, one we can bridge. We have to look to get our edge in terms of team spirit, preparation, training, sports science and the medical department – all areas where money is not the governing factor and it is more about how you operate. It is going to be up to me, Jason and all our staff to make sure we are as well prepared and organised as we can be and that is what we will be looking to do over the next few weeks,' admitted Howe.

Bournemouth knew it was a big challenge ahead and the pre-season in Switzerland gave them the chance to play strong opposition, like FC Zurich, through Maxim Demin's contacts and they would also face West Ham United at Dean Court in a testimonial for Stephen Purches. What the club kept under wraps though until the last minutes was that there would be a pre-season friendly at Dean Court with Real Madrid on 21 July 2013. The excitement on the south coast was enormous with local and national media eagerly anticipating the arrival of the Spanish giants. Scarfs adorned with the two teams emblazoned on them were snapped up on a hot sunny evening as fans walked to the stadium. While we all looked forward to watching the likes of Ronaldo, Kaka, Ozil and Benzema, Eddie Howe had his own concerns about the Real Madrid game.

'It's going to be a big fitness exercise, and I am not sure how much of the ball we will see, but that will be good as our shape and organisation will certainly be tested,' said Howe.

The omens for AFC Bournemouth resilience against a team of superstars led by Carlo Ancelotti didn't seem that good, considering the day before the game a mixed Bournemouth side had lost 2-1 away to non-league Woking. But the result wouldn't really matter. It was a special occasion and a reward for the players who would step on the pitch and, of course, it was for the fans. It was an extraordinary experience to be there. Ticket prices for the game would be in the £60 region for adults with £5 off for season ticket holders, but nobody wanted to miss this game and the pavements outside the ground were packed, with the club squeezing in 11,772 highly-excited fans. Yet, Eddie Mitchell was making no excuses for the ticket prices as the club had landed one of the most eagerly awaited pre-season friendlies for an English club and he saw it as a great marketing opportunity. 'It is really about the opportunity for local people and people from further afield to come and watch one of the best football teams in the world. It is an opportunity which was too good to pass up. It will showcase our club and that is priceless to us,' claimed Eddie Mitchell. 'It is a match of celebration to celebrate us getting into the Championship.'

The game came about because Tom Mitchell, the director of football at Bournemouth chatted to a mutual friend who worked with the Spanish club and who said he could get them to play a friendly game to celebrate Bournemouth's rise to the Championship. 'Tom put it to me,' said Eddie Mitchell. 'I put it to the chief executive [Neill Blake] and we put it to my business partner [Maxim Demin]. We decided that it would be great for the fans and us to pull off something like this.'

The Real Madrid match was a thank you from
AFC Bournemouth to the fans, and it really put
the Cherries on the map

*It would also be the first time that Zinedine
Zidane would be seen next to Ancelotti as first team
coach of Real Madrid. The scene was set. While
Ronaldo astounded everyone just in the warm-up
with his skills and tricks, the match took things to
another level again. While the crowd had to wait 22-
minutes before Ronaldo's opener, it was a special
free kick that beat Darryl Flahavan from 30 yards,
Ronaldo then added a second before Khedira made it
0-3 by half-time. Ancelotti was enjoying the
spectacle by getting as close to the action as he
could, sitting on the advertising hoardings. But
Bournemouth fans were wondering if their side could
just score once!*

*The goals kept coming straight after half-time as
Gonzalo Higuain made it four, before Kaka hit the*

bar and di Maria struck a fifth goal from 25 yards.
Casemiro ended the goal-scoring with a sixth. The
game was not about the score line, but rather the
fact that AFC Bournemouth had attracted some of
the world's best players to play on their ground and
every minute was savoured.

Eddie Howe made sure as many players as
possible had time on the pitch so the substitutions
were like a revolving door. The Bournemouth team
included 11 substitutions.

AFC Bournemouth
Flahavan (Jalal, 84), Francis (Stockley, 84), Cook
(Hughes, 61), Elphick (Addison, 74), Daniels (Thomas,
84), Coulibaly (Harte, 66), Arter (Purches, 84),
MacDonald (Wakefield, 84), Fraser (Matthews, 74),
Pitman (Ward, 27), Grabban (Chiedozie, 66).

Real Madrid first half: Lopez, Carvajal, Nacho,
Coentrão, Modric, Khedira, Ronaldo, Isco, Ozil,
Benzema.

Real Madrid second half: Jesus, Nacho (Quini, 67),
Carvajal (Casado, 67), Morata, di Maria, Higuain,
Casemiro, Illarramendi, Kaka, Cheryshev, Mateos.

Who would have thought that AFC Bournemouth would be entertaining the likes of Real Madrid at Dean Court?

Real Madrid was but a fleeting, glamorous, moment in the history books. Other memories are forged by some players over many years of playing at Dean Court. Steve Fletcher had hung his boots up after 723 appearances for the Cherries and began scouting for the club. While one experienced player, or perhaps the club, felt the Championship was a step too far, at the end of Steve's playing career, Bournemouth signed the experienced Ian Harte on a free transfer to help the defence. Ian explained why he had decided to join Bournemouth and he knew exactly what he'd signed up for. 'I met Eddie Howe on Saturday and just having an hour's chat with him pretty much convinced me to sign. He is a good manager and a young manager and, like me, he is hungry. We both want to push on and do the best we can. This club has a great deal of ambition and it was a great achievement to get promotion I am just looking forward to the challenge ahead. The club is going places and I just wanted to be a part of it,' said Ian Hart.

Elliot Ward, 28, would also join as back up in central defence. He was lured to Bournemouth by Howe's special attraction device – a DVD of how Bournemouth play. Eddie Howe was particularly happy on signing such an experienced Championship player. 'To get an established Championship player to come here is a great thing for the club and, hopefully, it means we are building and trying to be competitive in what will be a very difficult division,' said Howe.

There had also been plenty of summer rumours that Howe wanted to bring Danny Ings back to the club, but the deal just didn't materialise. Attention then started to drift towards Malmo's striker Tokelo Rantie.

My own interest was in a winger called Mohammed Coulibaly, who Howe had spotted while the team had been in pre-season in Switzerland. Cherry Chimes sponsored Coulibaly's shirt for the season when he signed from Grasshoppers, but he only ever played seven times for Bournemouth during his injury-laden time on the south coast. Andrew Surman was a bigger signing in July 2013, even if at the time it was just a loan deal for the season, he and the club would soon decide to turn it into a longer contract.

Cherry Chimes makes a signing as well,
sponsoring Mohamed Coulibaly

For the moment Howe would start with Wes Thomas and Lewis Grabban upfront for the opening game, but Brett Pitman would soon force his way back into the side, playing just behind Grabban in a position that really suited him. A 2-1 win over Charlton Athletic was a great start. Lewis Grabban scored twice in the game and his goals were divided by a spectacular goal from Yann Kermorgant who would soon play more games at Dean Court, but next time in a red and black shirt.

Progression in the League Cup was also gained with a single Eunan O'Kane goal to beat Portsmouth 1-0. All seemed to be going to plan at the start of the new season, but then Bournemouth played their first away game at Watford. It turned out to be a horror show and one of Eddie Howe's biggest defeats. While the Cherries had gone in all-square at 1-1 at the break, with Lewis Grabban on target again, the Hornets overran the Cherries in the second half. They hit five more goals to make it 6-1 by the end, as Troy Deeney bagged a hat-trick.

Eddie Howe ventured that it was the first half against Watford that the players and fans had to remember, while he thanked the supporters for sticking with the team. 'The match at Vicarage Road demonstrated that in this division, we can get punished for any mistakes we make. We were delighted with our first half performance and having conceded an early goal, we worked extremely hard to get back into the match, showed a great deal of bravery, and fully deserved our equaliser. 'While we can take huge encouragement from how we performed in that opening 45 minutes, we equally need to learn quickly from the second half.' commented Howe.

Resilient Bournemouth put the defeat behind them to scrape a 1-0 win over Wigan Athletic in their second home game. It was a big win as Wigan had won the FA Cup the season before and had been relegated from the Premier League in the same season.

Yet, all the doubters started again when the

Cherries were humbled 5-1 in their next away match to Huddersfield Town. 'We were well in the game to start with and I don't think either side was dominant,' said Howe after the defeat at the John Smith's Stadium. 'But they carved us open a couple of times and that can't happen. For the majority of the game and when you analyse who had possession, we had an equal amount but just weren't as clinical with it. But it is a learning experience for a lot of our guys and it will do them the world of good, although it is certainly painful at the moment.'

The start of the season had been really unpredictable for the Cherries. 'We have certainly had our ups and downs, said Howe. 'It has been difficult to take because, in the two games when we have been heavily beaten, we have actually performed quite well for long spells. I know people will disbelieve that due to the score lines, but we have given away some needless goals and that has been our Achilles heel. We have certainly more than matched our opponents, but have been ruthlessly exposed for any mistakes defensively. That is the nature of the division and we have come up against two in-form strikers who have punished us heavily. It is something we will definitely try to address. Results are in the lap of the gods but performances, in the main, have been okay. I know the score lines tell a different story and they are what you are judged on. We will continue to try to react positively.'

It was just Howe's luck that Bournemouth had drawn Watford again in the League Cup at Vicarage Road, but this time it wasn't a rout, even if Bournemouth were disappointed to go out of the competition 2-0. Better news came with the club announcing that the much sought after South African striker Tokelo Rantie had joined the club to become its record signing at £2.5m. 'Jason and I were really delighted to be able to strengthen the squad with the signing of Tokelo Rantie. He is a player we have watched over a long period of time and have been very impressed with. We had to work very hard to bring him here as a number of other clubs were chasing him.' said Howe. 'Such a signing shows just how far this club has come in a short space of time, something which would never have been possible without the huge contribution made by Eddie Mitchell and Maxim Demin.'

The away day hoodoo was eventually beaten by Pitman's goal at Doncaster Rovers at the end of August and the 0-1 win left the Cherries in a healthy sixth place at the end of the first month. Paul Dickov, Doncaster's manager had taken many of the headlines after he had a swipe at Eddie Howe and Bournemouth's staff after they'd criticised David Coterill's foul on Harry Arter. When Howe was asked if Dickov had tried to headbutt him in the ensuring fracas, Howe said 'If he had tried to heat-butt me, I would be on the floor now!'

Bournemouth ended August on nine points, just four points behind leaders Blackpool and yet they had a goal difference that would not have looked out of place in the bottom three. It was as high a position as the Cherries had got to since Harry Redknapp had taken the club into the Championship.

September brought a big change in the running of the club. Maxim Demin took the opportunity to buy out Eddie Mitchell, and his wife Brenda. Eddie Howe gave his views on the departure of Eddie Mitchell to the *Bournemouth Echo*. 'I was surprised at his decision, as everyone else was,' said Howe. 'Eddie [Mitchell] deserves huge credit for the job he has done and for how far the club has progressed under his stewardship. Together with Max, they have transformed it. Eddie is a very driven man and passionate about the football club. That is shown with all his decisions and how hard he has worked. The most important thing for the leader of a football club is the infrastructure and that has been the biggest change. A lot goes on behind the scenes that people don't see. We have had a lot of success on the pitch but the transformation off the pitch has been enormous.'

Demin would now have total ownership of the club as it planned its assault to the top of the Championship. Eddie Howe only had good words to say about Maxim holding such power in the club, although to fans he remained an unknown quantity. 'All I can say to the Bournemouth supporters is that he is a very shrewd operator. He has got the club's best interest at heart, he is ambitious and he wants to move the club forward. He is investing a lot of time and a lot of money in the club and we have a good working relationship, so I am very excited about the future prospects for the club,' said Howe. 'He is very clear on what he wants and he has a good team with him as well. I am very keen and looking forward to working with his team of people.'

While Eddie Howe was the very public face of AFC Bournemouth, the owner was much more mysterious and yet obviously extremely generous with his funding. But Eddie would be helped by the return of Jeff Mostyn as chairman for the second time. I'm absolutely thrilled,' said Mostyn. 'I'm surprised and this came completely out of the blue.'

A home defeat 1-2 to Blackpool and a home win 1-0 over Barnsley enabled the Cherries to settle into the Championship a little, before a highly-entertaining 3-3 at the Riverside Stadium against Middlesbrough. Bournemouth had started well with Pitman sticking two penalties away in the first 12 minutes of the game, before Boro took the lead when Grant Leadbitter scored with 16 minutes to go. But Howe thought it was pretty good for his players to comeback, manage the game, and get an away

point against a promotion contender, thanks to
Jonathan Woodgate's late own goal.

Bournemouth were finally getting to grips with
game management. 'It doesn't mean time-wasting,'
said Howe. 'It can mean just very clever with the
situation you are faced with and making sure you
don't make decisions that make things easier for the
opposition. I think the lads have done that really well
in different ways. I don't think we have overstepped
the mark in any way.'

The mood was a little less cheery after defeats to
Blackburn Rovers and Leeds United saw
Bournemouth slip to 13th in the table. Bournemouth
went down to 10-men in both games. Richard
Hughes was sent off against Blackburn and Ryan
Allsop was given his marching orders in the evening
game at Leeds United. Darryl Flahavan's first job in
the Leeds game was to save a penalty that he
managed to do, but the team still lost 2-1.
Bournemouth had also signed Jack Collinson on loan
for a month from West Ham before the Leeds game.
When asked about the penalty decision, Howe said,
'I have only seen a replay of the penalty decision
once and that was at match speed, so it was a
difficult one. I feared the worst when I saw the
challenge.'

Things would improve dramatically in
Bournemouth's next home game with a stunning 5-2
win over Millwall when Bournemouth had somehow

come back from being 0-2 down in the first 10 minutes. Stephen Henderson played in goal having signed on loan from West Ham United, covering for the suspended Ryan Allsop.

After goals from Ryan Fraser, Steve Cook, Harry Arter and penalties from Lewis Grabban and Brett Pitman Bournemouth completed a stunning comeback. Howe was particularly keen to thank the supporters. 'What pleased me most in winning the game was the character shown, not just by the players, but by the crowd. It would have been easy for them to show their displeasure at what they were seeing when we went 0-2 down at home after 10 minutes and on the back of two defeats. But they really stuck with us and that was absolutely pivotal to the win,' said a thankful Eddie Howe. 'Full credit to them for that because I think they understand.'

Steve Cook revealed that Howe hadn't been so pleased with the way Bournemouth had started against Millwall. 'We had a rollicking from the manager at half-time. It was the first time this season he ripped into us and we deserved it,' said Cook.

Taking the long journey north to Nottingham Forest was one of the matches I had particularly looked forward to and while Forest fans thought they would be far too good for the Bournemouth minnows, with an article in the Nottingham Post that derided the thought that the Cherries should even be

on the same pitch as Forest, they would be in for a
shock. It would be Marc Pugh that made the trip an
extremely rewarding one, as he equalised deep into
added time for a 1-1 draw. However, the sad note of
the day was seeing new keeper Stephen Henderson
stretchered off having dislocated his shoulder when
colliding with Simon Cox.

Defeats were something AFC Bournemouth fans
had to accept in the Championship. It was a step up
and Leicester City and Bolton Wanderers made it
two defeats in a row. Howe was not dismayed
though by the odd defeat. 'I think we have come
through games reflecting that we should have more
points, but that we are not far away from being
competitive in the division. When you get
promotion, there is always that thought of how
strong are you going to be and I don't think we are
that far away from being able to mix it with the
teams at the top end of the table,' said Howe. 'I
always knew it was going to be an incredibly difficult
transition and it has been. The step up is huge and
the quality of every team is very high. I don't think
there is much of a gap between the top and bottom
clubs and that is rare in most other leagues.'

Some of the players were out of their comfort
zone. Keeper Ryan Allsop was certainly feeling the
pressure after his mistake led to Jamie Vardy
sneaking the winner for Leicester. However, Eddie
Howe would reassure his keeper. 'He [Ryan] made a

mistake for the goal but that is the life of a goalkeeper. He will pick himself up from that,' said Eddie Howe. 'It was a soft goal and there were a couple of incidents before it when we could have done better. Ryan had a very good game apart from that. The pleasing thing from his perspective is the mistake is an easy-fix.'

Perhaps Howe was just getting ready for bigger tests? The Cherries bounced back with a somewhat surprising 1-1 draw away at leaders Burnley. Tokelo Rantie had blasted an equaliser from well outside of the box to announce his arrival. The day had been an emotional journey for Howe being the first time he had returned to the Lancashire club since he had left them as manager. 'It was a strange one for me. It was a difficult game because I hadn't wanted to build it up to my players,' said Howe. 'It meant a lot to me to try and get a performance out of the team, to try to put on a display and, more importantly, to get some points. It was quite an emotional day. I was really pleased with the reception from the Burnley supporters and thankful for that. Hopefully, they saw I did my best while I was here and there's no bitterness on either side.'

Eddie Howe was pleased enough with a league position of 13th after the international break. 'I think we can look back positively on the start we have made to life in the Championship. The players are developing all the time, and despite missing key players at times and not always having the points to show for our performances. I believe we're acquitting ourselves well, with more to come,' Howe said.

Still the defeats hit hard with a narrow 0-1 home defeat to Derby County in November before a 1-1 draw with Brighton. Eddie Howe signed Nicholas Yennaris from Arsenal on loan as defensive cover after Elliot Ward was injured, but Yennaris never played for Bournemouth. More important was the contract extension for Lewis Grabban that was extended to 2016. Howe was pleased to have given Grabban his opportunity in the Championship. 'I think he has grown to the level. There are question marks when you gain promotion over how certain individuals will perform and on-one can ever predict that. But he is someone who has really made the most of the opportunity and, hopefully, he can continue to do that,' said Howe.

Losing 3-0 away at QPR though meant Bournemouth hadn't won a game in their last seven games. December would be better. 'Our challenge is trying to find that consistency, because I think we have shown we can perform in one-off games. I thought we were unfortunate at QPR, where we played very well without getting our rewards,' said Howe.

No teams were spanking five or six goals against the Cherries anymore. Part of that might well have been down to Lee Camp who signed a loan extension to the start of January. Howe was starting to bring more experience and professionalism into the squad and Camp was a great man to have in goal. That meant Shawn Jalal would be allowed to leave the club in January, having been at the club since 2008. 'He [Lee] played very well at Burnley and he played really well against Derby. His kicking has been excellent and with how we play, that is so important,' said Howe.

Reading were beaten 1-2 away and, despite another 0-2 home defeat against Birmingham, the Cherries began to string some results together as Christmas approached. Sheffield United were beaten 1-2 with goals from Grabban and Ritchie, while Yeovil were dismissed with a 3-0 home win on Boxing Day, thanks to a double from Ritchie and a marvellous meandering run from Eunan O'Kane that ended with a smart finish.

Bournemouth were still 10 points above the bottom three after Boxing Day. The team would finish 2013 by taking on Ipswich Town who were in seventh place at Dean Court and the 1-1 draw was a welcome point. The New Years' Day match was a south coast derby with Brighton & Hove Albion, where Lewis Grabban scored in another 1-1 draw.

There were a few exits in January as Wes Fogden joined Pompey and Wes Thomas went to join Rotherham United. Meanwhile, Lee Camp signed a two-and-a-half year contract with Bournemouth and Adam Smith would return to the Cherries from Tottenham, having been at the club on loan in 2010-11, but this time he signed a permanent deal. This delighted Eddie Howe as Bournemouth had fended off competition for the highly-rated England U21 player. 'We know Adam from our first spell here and I think that is really important. When you get to work with players, you get to know their strengths and we certainly know what Adam can bring us. He fits the right age profile and is someone we can really enjoy working with for the long term,' said Howe. 'He is going to be a good addition to the squad.'

It had looked like Lewis Grabban would also be on his way to joining Brighton & Hove Albion as the two clubs reached an agreement for the fee, and Grabban went to Brighton to agree personal terms. However, the striker turned the Seagulls down to sign a new three-and-a-half year, improved, contract with the Cherries. While some Bournemouth fans were pleased that he would return, and he was player of the season in 2013-14, others never really came to terms with his ambitions to leave Dean Court.

Only 272 fans travelled away to Wigan Athletic for a crushing 3-0 defeat. Eddie Howe was apologetic for the performance. 'At Wigan we dropped below the high standards we've achieved recently and didn't pass the ball anywhere as near as we can,' he commented.

A bit of squad rotation was implemented for the third round FA Cup tie with Burton Albion with Pitman scoring twice, and Elphick and Fraser adding the goals in a 4-1 win to put Bournemouth up against Liverpool in the next round. Bournemouth fans had helped raise around £3000 for Burton supporters to have coaches to attend the rearranged fixture. Before the Liverpool match, there was the mental test of taking on Watford again who had beaten Bournemouth twice already in the season. A bit of pride was regained with a 1-1 draw with the Hornets with Grabban again finding the net.

The FA Cup fourth-round tie with Liverpool attracted a capacity crowd of 11,475. The game was televised and Eddie Howe took on Brendan Rodgers knowing that a win for Bournemouth would be a huge upset. Liverpool played a strong side though and didn't have much trouble in getting a 0-2 win with the Cherries unable to find much confidence in front of goal. Brendan Rodgers brought the experience of Steven Gerrard, Daniel Sturridge and Luis Suarez to Dean Court to ensure Liverpool were not going to slip up. At least Rodgers was sincere in his respect for what Howe and AFC Bournemouth. 'It is easy to coach a team sit back, not want the ball and defend and then just wait for a hump up the pitch,' said Rodgers. 'The courage that the

Bournemouth players showed today was fantastic –
they have got better, I have watched them as the
season has gone on.'

Howe was more focused on what Liverpool had
showed. 'Everyone says goals change games and
they do because with their first real attack they have
scored and showed the cutting edge that we didn't
unfortunately,' Howe reflected.

League form was now something to concentrate
on and Tokelo Rantie scored a rare winner in a 1-2
away match at Huddersfield Town to complete the
January fixtures. While keeping hold of Lewis
Grabban had been a bonus, Eddie Howe would look
to bring in a new striker in January and he selected
Yann Kermorgant of Charlton Athletic as a player
that would offer something different to the Cherries'
attack. With Kermorgant Bournemouth could hold
the ball up and start putting more balls in the air into
the box. Meanwhile, Josh McQuoid was sent out on
loan to Peterborough United.

Bournemouth would need to find something
special when leaders Leicester City came to Dean
Court. They were well clear at the top of the table
and scored late on to take a narrow 0-1 win back to
Leicester. But when the team fell 2-0 down against
Bolton, Howe was pleased that they found a way
back to get a 2-2 draw, especially as Bolton were
below Bournemouth on the table. 'We took some
heavy beatings early in the season and didn't

respond but we have learned from those games and once we started to believe how good we could be, we saw a good Bournemouth performance today,' commented Howe after the Bolton draw.

While Tokelo Rantie had been finding goals hard to come by, he clearly liked playing against Burnley where he picked up another goal and helped Bournemouth to a point. The last game in February was at Derby County where the Cherries fell to a 1-0 defeat, leaving them in 17th place nine points ahead of the bottom three. Eddie Howe thought the team had been unfortunate to lose. 'To concede a world class goal from a disputable free kick was particularly difficult to take,' said Howe.

Yann Kermorgant had been waiting patiently to start a game and his moment came in the home game against Doncaster Rovers at the start of March. It was a grudge match as Rovers had snatched the League One title from Bournemouth in the previous season in the very last game. Bournemouth had their incentive and Kermorgant started his blitz on the Rovers' goal powering in a header on 26 minutes and completing his hat-trick on 73 minutes. Meanwhile, Harry Arter also slotted a brace of goals to make it a thumping 5-0 win for Eddie Howe. The only disappointment was that Rantie had to come on for an injured Kermorgant in the last 15 minutes. It was only Bournemouth's second win of the year and it relieved the pressure on Howe who now had another top-quality Championship striker. 'Yann took his goals very well and I think you can see the technique of his first goal, he did a few of them on training yesterday and he's outstanding with his feet for a big man and then the really important thing from my perspective was his aerial presence from crosses. I think that's something we've been lacking this season, his two headed goals were high quality,' said Howe.

Moving 12 points clear of the relegation zone was also something Howe could smile about. 'It's important, we don't want to get sucked into a relegation scrap so it's important we get the points as early as we can and results like this against the teams in and around us are very important, so hopefully that gives us more confidence going forward,' added Howe.

Two 0-1 away wins against Blackpool and Blackburn Rovers settled the nerves even further and took Bournemouth up to 12th. Grabban scored his 15th goal of the season at Doncaster. The trio of wins against Doncaster, Blackpool and Blackburn equalled the 1988-89 record for consecutive results in the second tier. 'The side have certainly proven their Championship credentials over the last 14 days,' said Eddie Howe.

With Kermorgant still injured, Coulibaly had a rare start in the goalless home match against Middlesbrough. Bournemouth then conceded a 90th minute goal against Charlton at the Valley, as Dorian Dervite gave struggling Charlton all three points. The Charlton defeat engendered a reaction for sure. Bournemouth were to go on a five-game winning streak starting with a 0-1 away win at Barnsley. Kermorgant was back in the team, but it was Steve Cook who punished Barnsley with a 90th minute goal, which was an extremely satisfying way to get over the Charlton result.

March was also significant as it saw Eddie Howe and JT sign a contract extension of two-years to take them up to 2018. It was an easy decision for Howe and the bond with Max Demin was clearly expressed. 'When I was approached by the club, I had no doubts about extending my contract. I have established a great relationship with the people here and I can't speak highly enough of Max Demin, Neill Blake and Jeff Mostyn. We form a really good team and share the same vision on a lot of things which is so important,' said Howe. 'Max wants us to play entertaining and attractive football and, hopefully, we are providing that. He is very ambitious and wants to move the club forward. We want to do likewise and feel we have a good understanding. When he came to us about the extension, we had no hesitation in signing.'

This was a moment when Eddie Howe and Jason could see that they were close to achieving more than just a winning team. The club was part of them and they were a central part of it. Things were different with AFC Bournemouth. The people, the struggle, the debts, the bricks around the ground – it all mattered.

'The contract doesn't change anything but it is nice to know we are going to have a chance to build and plan something long term. I haven't stayed in a job long enough to leave a lasting legacy and that is what I would like to do here, if I get the results to remain in the job. That's going to be key from my perspective,' said Howe. 'Pressure is something you cannot escape in this profession. I don't want to be here and just tick a box and do okay. I am here to try to win,' said Eddie Howe.

One player that Eddie Howe had not managed to turnaround was Donal McDermott. The talented winger left AFC Bournemouth by mutual consent in March 2014, after a turbulent 26 months at the club since signing under Lee Bradbury. He hadn't played since Boxing Day. It was one of the rare disappointments for Howe, but the club had moved on.

Kermorgant and Grabban scored two each in the 4-1 evening drubbing of Leeds United, which took the Cherries up to 10th. Eddie Howe explained he had used the 1990 match against Leeds United motivate his players. On that day Bournemouth were relegated and the town was barricaded as Leeds fans ran riot, rampaging through the streets.

'It was a dark day for the town and a lot of people still speak about it, even to this day,' said Howe. 'I knew it was a big game for our supporters because of the history and we were keen to put on a good performance for them knowing how much it meant. We tried to live up to the occasion and the players certainly did. It has gone and is history. It was a good to be able to give something back, because they have been excellent for us and it was great to get the result for them.'

Taking on Birmingham City had happier memories. Another 2-4 score line was recorded with Ian Harte enjoying the spotlight having netted one of the Bournemouth goals. Bournemouth knew that QPR would be a much harder game and the challenge of trying to beat the former Premier League side was something that made it easy for the crowd to get behind the Cherries.

Former Cherries managers Harry Redknapp and Kevin Bond were in charge at Loftus Road and were in third place chasing promotion. Bournemouth would triumph 2-1 with Elphick and Grabban getting the goals while Brett Pitman came on as a sub in the 90th minute to head a goal-bound clearance off the line from a QPR corner right at the death. Bournemouth also achieved the win with 10-men, having seen Harry Arter sent off for a challenge on Junior Hoilett with 20 minutes to go. Howe made a tactical change to sub Yann Kermorgant and put on

Eunan O'Kane. 'I was pleased with how the lads carried out the game plan and how they adapted to the different challenges put in front of them. They blocked holes, dropped off and were hard to beat and hard to play through. They carried it out brilliantly. We were up against a top side and the players adapted to every demand placed on them,' said Eddie Howe.

It looked a huge task to try and make the play-offs with six games to go, but a 3-1 win over Reading on 8 April took the Cherries up to ninth in the table. Matt Ritchie was becoming one of the Championship's best players and was adding goals to the team from the right wing, while Grabban had already beaten Luther Blisset's club record of goals scored in the second tier, after scoring against QPR to give him a total of 20 goals.

Drawing 1-1 away at Yeovil pretty much ended the Cherries late challenge to make the play-offs, before a 2-4 home defeat against Sheffield Wednesday proved there was still plenty to learn about in the Championship. 'Having got ourselves back in the game for a second time, we didn't respond well enough to Wednesday being reduced to 10-men, and in our desire to go for the win, we were punished,' recalled Howe. 'We did everything to try to win the game. We weren't at our best, there is no denying that, and I didn't think we managed the last part of the game very well when we had the one-man advantage. The biggest disappointment was that we didn't take full advantage of the situation.

Eddie Howe had to concede that the play-offs had gone after the defeat to Sheffield Wednesday. 'From my perspective, I felt we had to win all four games, so I think it is going to be very difficult but we will try and win the remaining three. With three games left and goal difference which isn't too clever, I think it will be difficult.'

Mid-table looked guaranteed after a 2-2 draw against a physical Ipswich Town, even if Steve Cook's bicycle kick goal was worthy of winning any game. Bournemouth followed it up with a 4-1 demolition of Nottingham Forest after Kermorgant and Grabban weighed in with a brace a piece. Going into the final game, Millwall needed points to avoid being relegated. The Cherries found themselves chasing the ball for much of the game when Martyn Woodford scored on 29 minutes to give Millwall the points to stay up. So, Bournemouth finished 10th in their first season under Eddie Howe in the Championship.

The 2014-15 season would be another historic one for the Cherries under Eddie Howe in the Championship. Maxim Demin had splashed out

£750,000 on a new pitch and matching fibre-sand
training pitches with 3G edging for the new season.
Pre-season saw Bournemouth draw 2-2 with FC
Copenhagen and play more local friendlies against
Eastleigh, Dorchester, Portsmouth, Southampton,
Swansea City and Oxford United.

There had been some changes among the staff
with Richard Hughes retiring from his playing days
and joining the backroom staff. Bournemouth also
had to fight off a couple of bids from Derby for
Simon Francis. The new players coming in generated
great excitement with midfielder Dan Gosling signing
from Newcastle United and Callum Wilson joining
from Coventry City. Lewis Grabban was sold to
Norwich City for a record club fee at the time,
thought to be around £3m, while Junior Stanislas
joined up with Eddie Howe again, this time at
Bournemouth.

'Having worked before with the manager, I have
always liked what he has done. I always felt
confident playing for him so wanted to take the
opportunity to come here,' said Stanislas. 'For me
individually, working for Eddie Howe and speaking to
him about the ambition of this club has, I wanted to
be part of it going forward. Howe made me choose
this club. He understands me and the way I work,'
Stanislas told *BBC Radio Solent*. 'He also gives you a
lot of one-on-one time and attention, which is good
to help develop my game. It was a really difficult

choice because Burnley are obviously offering Premier League football. Once I found out that Eddie Howe was interested in signing me, there was only one place I wanted to go.'

Bournemouth got off to a great start by winning away with a 0-4 result against Huddersfield Town, which was a bit of a welcome surprise. Stanislas only came on in the 90th minute, but Callum Wilson scored twice and Pugh and Kermorgant also scored. 'I've been really pleased with how we've begun our second season in the Championship. At Huddersfield we made the best possible start by scoring in the first minute, which really set the tone for the rest of the performance,' said a delighted Howe.

Progress to the second round of the League Cup was gained with a 2-0 home win over Exeter City with youth product Baily Cargill making his debut, before Bournemouth welcomed newly-promoted Brentford to Dean Court. It needed a substitute appearance by Ryan Fraser and goal scorer Junior Stanislas to keep Bournemouth's winning run going 1-0. 'It was really good to see two substitutes come on and have a positive impact, underlying the point I make about the need for our whole squad to be ready when called upon,' said Howe.

The unbeaten run and clean sheets came to an abrupt halt with a 1-2 home defeat to Nottingham Forest. Blackburn Rovers added more discomfort with a 3-2 win against the Cherries. Bournemouth had gone 3-0 down in the first 25 minutes and while Brett Pitman penalty on 81 minutes and a Steve Cook headed goal led to a grandstand finish, before Bournemouth ultimately ran out of time.

August ended with Bournemouth putting three past Northampton in the League Cup second round and holding Norwich City to a 1-1 draw at Carrow Road with a Callum Wilson equaliser. Wilson's goal was a highly celebrated one as it enshrined the kind of football Howe was so keen to desire. The goal came after a move that contained 31 passes. 'I knew it was a very special goal and knew we had kept possession for a long time. The final part of the move was top class with Junior's pass, Simon's movement and cross and Callum Wilson's finish,' enthused Howe. 'It was great to see us rewarded for keeping the ball and it is not often you see a goal with that many passes so the players should be credited for their bravery.'

Howe was busy in the transfer market securing Andrew Surman on a permanent deal from Norwich City in September. It looked like it would be another tough season to keep in the Championship with new boys Rotherham United getting a draw at Dean Court and Leeds United taking a 1-3 win with them back to Yorkshire.

Harry Arter did his best to get Bournemouth moving up the table again when he scored a screamer from 25 yards out against Watford at

Vicarage Road. However, the Hornets still managed to claw a goal back by Craig Cathcart to share the points. That was after Ian Harte had missed a penalty in the fourth minute of the game!

Artur Boruc had been brought in on loan from Southampton and was made the number one keeper, displacing Lee Camp for the match against Watford. The draw took Bournemouth's winless run to six games. 'It was another game we were bitterly disappointed not to have taken three points from and it has been the story of our season so far,' voiced a frustrated Howe. 'The encouraging thing from our point of view is that our performances have been excellent, but we seem to be on a run where we are getting punished for every mistake.'

Eddie Howe was playing almost a completely different team in the League Cup. The squad spirit was kept high though with seven changes for the match against Cardiff and the Welsh team were well-beaten 3-0 to see Bournemouth go through to the fourth round. Howe had always taken criticism for such cup games where he had rotated the players, but he had something to say after this win about his squad depth. 'The quality of our football was great and the players were excellent. We beat a very good side comprehensively and that will give us a real confidence boost. I felt that the players that had an opportunity took it really well. If anyone doubted the strength of our squad, I think we answered that tonight.'

Wigan, who had provided such stiff competition in the previous season were beaten 0-2 by goals from Simon Francis and Yann Kermorgant. 'They are a former Premier League team and were FA Cup winners not so long ago, so it's a big scalp. To do it in the manner we did was very pleasing,' Howe said. 'It could have been more. We were knocking on the door and thankfully we scored a goal.'

But Howe still didn't have the consistency and the team lost 2-0 away at Derby County with Lee Camp being sent off. He could see that the team was competing better though when they could keep 11 players on the pitch. 'With the home crowd getting frustrated and just 23 minutes remaining, the game turned on its head with Lee Camp's red card,' said Howe. 'Despite the disappointing result, I felt we could take positives from the match, and the way we had contained a team who I'd expect to be near the top of the table in May.'

October would be a full month of seven games that would put the Cherries right in the promotion picture as they leaped from 11th to the play-off positions. The month would also include one of the club's most emphatic wins. Before that, it seemed Howe's players had gotten used to playing with 10-men, as Kermorgant was red carded at Bolton. Wilson's goals were enough to win the game 1-2, but

Pitman was needed now for the next few games. Pitman didn't score in the 1-0 win over Charlton, but he scored two of the three goals that carried Bournemouth to a 3-0 win over Reading in the Tuesday evening game on the 21 October.

Howe was just pleased the Cherries were finally getting their rewards, which hadn't happened in earlier games. 'Earlier in the season, we were close to winning games as comfortably as we did against Reading but, for whatever reason, we didn't quite put teams to bed. I am thinking of the Nottingham Forest, Rotherham and Leeds games which we should have won comfortably,' added Howe. 'People may try to find magic formulas but they don't really exist. It is about the hard work and the fundamentals all the time, even during your indifferent runs.'

The Cherries travelled to Birmingham City knowing that they were starting to score freely and were keeping clean sheets. Birmingham had just changed their manager and Eddie Howe expected a reaction from their side who hadn't been winning at home. But Bournemouth just played some sublime football and notched up an 8-0 win. Marc Pugh scored a hat-trick and Rantie scored twice in the rout. Artur Boruc even saved a penalty in the 53rd minute from Paul Caddis on a day when everything worked well for Bournemouth.

Howe almost sounded a tad apologetic in his next programme notes as he reflected on Bournemouth's biggest win in the Championship. 'Their red card was a big moment in the match and it gave a numerical advantage that we would use to devastating effect. This is not always easy as we proved with our recent away win at Bolton where we overcame the same setback,' said Howe. 'The players were clinical in front of goal all afternoon in a match that will live in the memory for a long time to come.'

A 2-1 win over Premier League quality in the shape of WBA, in the League Cup (known then as the Capital One Cup) fourth round, brought October to a close and saw a clean sweep of wins for Eddie Howe's team. The fans had cause to be excited now about what this season could bring and Howe would have to start keeping a lid on expectations, even though he wanted to enjoy the moment for a while. 'Beating West Brom was a memorable night for the club as it takes us to the quarter-finals of a major cup competition, but more than that it underlines what a strong, united dressing room we have here,' said Howe.

Bournemouth had almost thrown the match away in the 85th minute when Tommy Elphick had inadvertently headed past Lee Camp to wipe out Eunan O'Kane's opener. But Callum Wilson grabbed an 86th minute winner to send the home crowd absolutely wild. 'We hoped one goal would be enough. We defended really well and our goalkeeper made a couple of good saves when called upon and we were unfortunate with the own goal. The mentality of the group is such that we were able to make the changes, but they didn't affect our performance,' added Howe. 'The equaliser was like a dagger through the heart because we didn't want extra-time. Our players had given so much that we feared, had gone to extra-time would have had a few who would have struggled physically. The club has had some dark days and has never before been in this position. To be in the quarter-final of a major cup competition is an incredible journey. It is a very satisfying feeling to bring so much joy to all our supporters, not just for me but for the staff and all players as well.

'We try to play a style of football which we stick to whether that is against West Brom or anybody else. To deviate from those principles wouldn't work for the players. We have those types of players with those types of qualities so wanted to play our normal game. If we had lost like that, we would have been okay with it as long as the players had stuck to our principles. They did and I thought we were very brave and showed a lot of quality.'

The Bournemouth manager also revealed to the local *Echo* that Maxim Demin was missing games because he didn't want to jinx the team. 'He is very superstitious,' said Eddie Howe. 'I had to text him at a certain time before the game against West Brom on Tuesday. I won't say what the message was but he asks me to do certain things to follow his superstitions. He rarely watches our games because he thinks he is bad luck. I try to convince him to come but he prefers not to. He has invested a lot of money in the club and he isn't here to enjoy it. But whatever he is, I know he is a very proud man because he is a huge supporter of the club and wants to know everything that's going on.'

October ended with Eddie Howe winning manager of the month and Callum Wilson picking up player of the month, and in November he received an England U21 call up, the first Bournemouth player to do so since Eddie Howe in 1998. The league programme in November continued with a 3-2 home win against Brighton, when a Yann Kermorgant penalty decided the match. It was six wins out of seven and the Cherries had become real promotion candidates.

Winning away 0-2 at Sheffield United gave the Cherries a brief moment of being top of the Championship. But Bournemouth had to play Middlesbrough and Ipswich next, who were also vying for the top of the league, and drawing both matches saw Bournemouth lose a bit of momentum. Having also drawn 2-2 with Millwall, Bournemouth went into December in fourth place.

The away game at Wolves was an inspiring performance. Bournemouth fell behind to a Danny Graham goal in the first half, but goals from Harry

Arter and Matt Ritchie saw Bournemouth come storming back to take the three points. The game had turned on 59 minutes when Rajiv Van la Parra was sent off for violent conduct but it was wrongful dismissal that was later overturned, while Matt Doherty was also red carded in added time. 'We put them under pressure because we knew they hadn't won for a while. The first sending off was a key moment in the game but I was a lot happier with how we started the second half and our intent,' said Howe.

Bournemouth were in a hurry to get back to the top of the division and Matt Ritchie gave them a 38 second goal against Cardiff City, while in a crazy couple of minutes before half-time, Harry Arter and Marc Pugh extended the lead to 3-1. Despite Sean Morrison scoring twice for Cardiff, Bournemouth ran out 5-3 winners.

It was a great time to take on Liverpool in the League Cup quarter-final with so many goals flying about. Liverpool were having a bad period having gone out of the Champions League and there were mutterings that this could be an upset. Asked whether Bournemouth were a better side than when they faced Liverpool in the previous season in the FA Cup, Howe was as eager as anyone to find out. 'I'd like to think so,' said Howe. 'I think the proof will be when we play them. I'd say we are a better side now than we were then. I think we have progressed with

11 months' work and the players have improved so looking at that side of it, I would say yes.'

Howe knew though that taking on Liverpool was no easy game. 'I think the whole reaction to Liverpool's form makes this game harder for us in a sense that peoples' expectations of us have risen and I think it is my job to bring some perspective to that,' he added.

Liverpool were not about to see Eddie Howe's team get to their first cup semi-final and Raheem Sterling and Lazar Markovic had Liverpool 0-2 up in the first half hour. Raheem Sterling would make it 3-0 before Dan Gosling scored a consolation goal for the Cherries.

If the Cherries were expected to find it hard to get the defeat to Liverpool out of their system, they didn't seem to have any problem in delighting their fans that travelled to a sandy pitch at Blackpool. Bournemouth went on the rampage with five different scorers. The 1-6 away win ensured the Cherries would be top of the Championship at Christmas.

Boxing Day saw Kit Symons' Fulham visit Dean Court. Pitman and Arter eased Bournemouth to a 2-0 win which was followed up by a 0-2 away win at Millwall. Eddie Howe was not getting carried away with the moment. 'I have said before that this is uncharted territory for us as a club and I don't want to put any more pressure on the players than there already is,' said Howe 'This was not expected of us so let's just enjoy the moment and see where it can take us.'

The New Year would start with the FA Cup third round match against Rotherham United. Bournemouth rested players but even those that came in made an impression with a 1-5 away win.

Still, Bournemouth didn't have to wait long in 2015 to feel the despair of a defeat. Alex Neil's first game in charge of Norwich City saw them beat the Cherries 1-2 at Dean Court, on 10 January, despite Johnny Howson being sent off.

Having to go back up to Yorkshire again to play Rotherham United was not ideal but at least the team was rotated. It was never going to be as easy as the FA Cup match and a repeat performance of the big win was unlikely, but Tommy Elphick and Callum Wilson both scored in the 0-2 league win.

January was turning into a real test of Bournemouth's metal. Leeds United dented confidence with a 1-0 win at Elland Road. Bournemouth would have another chance to face Premier League opposition in the FA Cup fourth round against Aston Villa. Despite holding Villa to 0-0 in the first half, Bournemouth fell two goals behind before Wilson scored a late consolation goal.

A Friday night home game against Watford was just what was required to improve the mood and a 2-0 victory kept the Cherries ahead in the table going into February. The win was all the more special with Watford reduced to 10-men in the first minute, after Gabriele Angella had an early bath. For once, things had really gone Bournemouth's way.

Bournemouth were warming to their task and a 1-3 away win at Wigan Athletic was a statement to say how far the club had come from the season before. Yann Kermorgant and Callum Wilson were hitting form just when they needed to. It came as a disappointment to lose top spot with a 2-2 home draw with Derby County on 10 February, but the run-in hadn't really started yet.

Kermorgant's goal against Huddersfield earned a 1-1 draw, but the jitters started to be felt with successive away defeats to Brentford and Nottingham Forest. Andrew Surman had put Bournemouth ahead against Forest with a rare strike from the central-midfielder, so it was hard to explain how the points all disappeared. 'Despite losing, we probably created enough chances to win two games and take encouragement from the fact that on another day the outcome would have been very different.

'Success never comes in a straight line,' added Howe. 'So, at this time, we need to believe in ourselves and what we do and not to deviate from the plan. We know that outside of our club there will be plenty of people who will be writing us off after recent results. This isn't a problem for us, and we'll be further motivated by proving people wrong.'

Bournemouth would win 2-1 against Wolves in their next match and sat in fourth place in a congested table near the top. With 11 games to go it was all about who could turn draws into wins and take maximum points.

One of the most memorable nights of the Championship for Bournemouth fans would come at the start of March in the evening Fulham away game. I remember the match well as I had a merry time with many Bournemouth fans in the Eight Bells Pub before the game. We were high on adrenalin and in good spirits when we entered Craven Cottage, but we didn't expect the Rolls Royce performance that the Cherries were about to put in. The Cherries set about Fulham with their high-paced attacking football and led 0-1 after Brett Pitman quietened the home fans, after a quickly taken free kick. A deflected goal from Matt Ritchie made it 0-2 on 37 minutes, before Pitman went on a glorious solo-run from inside his own half to travel the rest of the pitch and slot a superb shot past Marcus Bettinelli, making it 0-3 on 61 minutes. The goals kept coming with Ritchie grabbing his second 10 minutes later, while Fulham had Fernando Amorebieta sent off. Not to be overshadowed, Steve Cook thought he'd get in on the goal scoring act with a well-taken volley from the right side that picked out the top left corner of

Fulham's goal on 84 minutes. Fulham had managed a single goal on 66 minutes through Matt Smith, but the Cherries had proved again that they were a side full of goals, and they went above Middlesbrough on goal difference to the top of the Championship.

Eddie Howe was astonished by the amount of goals and their quality. 'Thankfully we don't have goal bonuses in the contracts. We took them out. During the five games we didn't win the performance levels were still strong,' said Howe. 'I didn't think there was anything wrong with the team and I think we have proved that. The lead [at the top of the table] has changed so many times it's almost become the tag no-one wants. That's been the nature of it and it may stay that way until the end of the season, so back-to-back wins are so important.'

If Eddie was feeling that he hadn't done the best job that he could have at Burnley, the outside world wasn't seeing it that way now with Bournemouth. In April 2015, Eddie Howe was named manager of the Football League's decade. It was the first time the award had been given, but it was recognition of the progress Eddie had made and it underlined the wave that Bournemouth were on as they got closer to the Premier League. When Eddie picked up his award his league record as a manger read, 295 games, 142 wins, 65 draws and 88 defeats. His teams had scored 471 goals and conceded 339 with a win percentage of 48.14.

Lining up against bottom of the table Blackpool the home crowd were willing another goal fest and the Cherries duly delivered with a 4-0 pounding of the Tangerines. Pitman went one better than his goals at Fulham and scored a first-half hat-trick, while Callum Wilson added to the score with a 49th minute penalty. Pitman was irresistible form having notched-up his 99th, 100th and 101st goal in Bournemouth colours and he was thinking of his team-mate when he didn't make it 102 on the night. Eddie Howe reported that 'the unselfishness he [Pitman] showed in letting Callum Wilson take the penalty was great to see. The designated penalty-taker was Brett but Callum showed a real desire to take it. Brett more than played his part with the goals and was considerate enough to let him take it.'

With Bournemouth, Watford and Middlesbrough all on 67 points from 37 games and Derby and Norwich just two and three points behind, the Championship was becoming a must watch division. Mid-placed Cardiff managed to halt Bournemouth's high-scoring wins with a 1-1 draw. The big talking point was Lee Mason's decision to disallow Callum Wilson's goal, which had come about by the striker blocking goalkeeper Simon Moore's kick, which then rebounded to hit the crossbar, before Wilson tapped the ball into the empty net. All Wilson got though was a yellow card and Bournemouth had to be content with a point which dropped them down to third.

The dropped points could be made up in the following game when Middlesbrough would come to Dean Court on another afternoon in front of the Sky cameras. On a windy afternoon Simon Thomas, Sky Sports presenter lost his notes but carried on the pre-match interviews just in front of us at the corner of the Main Stand and the North Stand. It was the must not lose game as two of the Championship favourites for promotion met. Bournemouth bounced back from the Cardiff result with a 3-0 win after goals from Yann Kermorgant, Harry Arter and Brett Pitman. Arter's goal was the only one not from the penalty spot and it was a stunner, Arter picking out the top left corner from the edge of the box, as he took the ball off of Marc Pugh's toes.

Eddie Howe was now looking for mental strength and hoped the Middlesbrough result would help the team. 'Psychologically it gives us a boost knowing we've beaten one of the best sides in the division and it should serve is well hopefully in the remaining games,' said Howe. 'It is incredibly tight at the top of the Championship and there's everything to play for, for a number of teams,' Howe said in his Matchday programme notes. 'Nobody expected us to be in this position, and having come this far we are enjoying the pressure that is associated with it.'

After the Middlesbrough match the team, minus

a few players – Matt Ritchie and Harry Arter, who were on international duty – the players flew out to Dubai for five days thanks to Maxim Demin's generosity. It was a way of Howe composing the players for the last few games away from English shores and media attention.

To add more firepower to the Cherries seemed a luxury, but Kenwyne Jones joined Bournemouth on loan for the run-in from Cardiff City and his debut against Ipswich was crucial for heading in a late, 82nd minute goal, from a corner to get a share of the points.

Bournemouth fell behind to Birmingham when Clayton Donaldson scored on 18 minutes in the first game of April. The lead was made 0-2 when Dave Cotterill scored. Suddenly Bournemouth were looking shaky again. However, Steve Cook scored six minutes before half-time and Wilson made it 2-2 on 45 minutes. A penalty calmly struck by Yann Kermorgant put the Cherries ahead, three minutes into the second half, and Charlie Daniels completed a sensational comeback win with a goal on 74 minutes to make it 4-2.

There were just five games to go and Bournemouth fans were starting to believe they had the team that could hold their nerve. That was exactly what the Cherries had to do at Brighton where they failed to find a goal in the first half. It needed a special free-kick by Yann Kermorgant to

*break the deadlock in the 70th minute.
Bournemouth's players swamped the French striker.
Having taken the lead, we were jumping up and
down in the away end behind the goal and marvelled
at Kermorgant's free kick. Brighton had not held out
and Callum Wilson made it 0-2 on 81 minutes. Surely,
Bournemouth were heading to the Premier League
now!*

*Playing Reading would be just as difficult a job.
Bournemouth scored early through a Callum Wilson
goal. But it didn't look like it would be enough.
Bournemouth were out played for much of the
match, as Reading did everything they could to ruin
Bournemouth's push for promotion. The Cherries had
to show the defence was strong enough to withstand
a battering, and with the help of their fans they
managed to cling on to the 0-1 win and remained
top of the Championship. Almost there, 80 points
with three games to go – the nervous anguish was
excruciating – it was hard to sleep at night!*

Norwich City and Watford were only four points
behind with a game in hand, while Middlesbrough
were a further place back on 75 points. Howe knew
that his players had struggled against Reading, but
they had held out. 'When questions were asked of
the team against Reading, I thought the players
answered them superbly. It was a gritty display full
of hard work, character and the determination you
need to have a chance of success,' said Howe, on the

brink of making history. 'The scenes at the final whistle where the whole squad and staff celebrated with the supporters was a unique moment. At that moment we were as one enjoying the feeling that winning brings. Moments like that are rare in football, and made all the better when you remember where we have all come from in such a short space of time. For every person who helped save this club and have since helped to rebuild it, we will do everything we can to reward your loyalty with the success you deserve.'

Sheffield Wednesday would make Bournemouth fight just as hard as Reading did just four days earlier. Kieran Lee headed the Owls into a goal lead on 36 minutes to lead at the break. Yann Kermorgant would again come up with a goal that kept Bournemouth on track on 69 minutes, before the game would turn against Bournemouth when Simon Francis was sent off for a second yellow card on 79 minutes. But Matt Ritchie made it 2-1 with six minutes to go. It looked like Bournemouth would get the three points, until Adam Smith mistimed a tackle on Atdhe Nuhiu in the box and Chris Maguire would score from the spot in the 95th minute to make it 2-2.

Bournemouth fans and the team were distraught, but Eddie Howe was adamant that we didn't know how important that point could be. The point kept Bournemouth a point behind Watford on 84 points with just two games to go and Middlesbrough clung to third place also on 84 points, with Norwich still in the automatic promotion picture in fourth on 82 points. Bournemouth's goal difference was superior to all the other teams though on +47, which meant the Cherries could clinch promotion by winning their last two matches no matter what any other teams did.

'That really is tough to take. That is the reason why we love the game, with its drama and twists and turns even in one game. It was a heartbreaking end to the game for us,' said Howe on the Sheffield Wednesday late equaliser. 'In the end we didn't manage to take all three points, but as ever it's important to look at the bigger picture. We find ourselves in a position which we would have given everything for at the start of the season and we still control our destiny, which is so important at this stage.'

I remember driving down the A3 in the early evening on my way to the game with Bolton Wanderers that could just possibly take AFC Bournemouth into a new era. The 'promised land' as the Premier League has been called would bring its hazards as well as its tremendous wealth, but it was somewhere that this AFC Bournemouth had been growing towards for a number of years and thousands of fans like me had their fingers crossed that it just might come true on this night. The stakes were high, but what are we all fans for unless it is to live by the tension and fear of pre-match excitement and the possibility of success or failure? Listening to the radio, I switched over to BBC Radio Solent. Steve Fletcher was about to be interviewed by the ever-young and excited Kelly Somers and I wasn't about to miss what Big' Un had to say about the match against Bolton Wanderers.

I pulled into the services just before heading to Winchester on the A272 road from Petersfield. There were a few people about in the car park and while I was dying to get a drink and to use the facilities, Supa Fletch's voice boomed over the airwaves. He seemed tense, no excited, or was he just nervous? He immediately made the hairs on the back of my neck stand up. There was something comforting and yet exhilarating about hearing him speak. AFCB fans knew exactly how he felt. He was one of us and was petrified and yet extremely proud that the lads had managed to put the club in this tantalising position, just three points away from a date with history.

Kelly Somers was loving the tension and the chance to get over to the fans what the whole thing meant to club ambassador Steve Fletcher. His story was as big as anyone's at the club having saved it from extinction with his most famous goal against Grimsby Town back on 25 April 2009. While the stadium was still proud to bear his name on the North Stand, this was a new team and yet it *mattered – oh it mattered! Steve was bristling with excitement and was even honest enough to say that he did not know what to do with himself in the hours before the game. He had been able to see preparations for the game being played out before him. Jeff Mostyn had been into the ground and done his interviews and had gone back home, before getting ready for the evening game. The TV cameras had been set up quickly as the tree-house like platform made of scaffolding and planks of wood that was carefully positioned, between the Main Stand and Steve Fletcher Stand, having been left in place from the dramatic 3-0 win over Middlesbrough. Now it was all about tonight's game. An evening match in front of a capacity crowd of 11,000. The calmest man of all of course was Eddie Howe.*

The task was simple. Win the game and claim your spot in the Premier League, if other results go your way. But this had not been like the build-up for just any match. The previous game had seen the Cherries suffer a devastating blow to their promotion and title chase. The desperation and frustration from that game still hung close in the air this night at Dean Court, and while everyone was smiling and in expectant mood, there was also more than a hint of apprehension that AFCB might just fail at this final hurdle.

So why did I feel confident that the Cherries

would succeed, I kept asking myself? It never happens for the Cherries. There's always something that prevents a small club like AFC Bournemouth from realising its dreams. Would Bolton Wanderers spoil the party? They had a new manager who spoke confidently on his team's prospects for the game. While the opponents had players that had already made their names in the top tier, Bolton weren't in the kind of form that should hold any fear for the Bournemouth player. But it was surely not going to be easy.

By the time I arrived at the game with my two sons in tow, the crowd was already assembling. I had to park a long way from the ground just to find a space. Faces were a mixture of smiles and worried expressions. I headed straight for the away end where I wanted to see how the Bolton fans felt about the game. There were not so many of them as the game had been moved for TV purposes to be scheduled on a Monday evening rather than the Saturday, when all the other games were played. I managed to find a group of them though who were just enjoying the occasion and speaking to them and hearing their concerns gave me a little more optimism that this would be a night of celebration for the mass of home fans.

Bournemouth started the game well and soon had control of the match when Marc Pugh rifled in a goal from a tight angle in the top corner after 29 minutes. Matt Ritchie doubled the lead just before half-time to really calm everyone's nerves. The second-half was more of a celebration as Bournemouth won a penalty. Yann Kermorgant was confident he would score, but surprisingly ballooned his shot over the bar! It didn't matter. Bolton were down to 10-men and Bournemouth soon scored a third on 78 minutes when Callum Wilson turned sharply in the box to add another goal. Bournemouth's supporters were already singing the theme tune to Match of the Day – they knew where the club was going! At the end of the game I just remember Marc Pugh wearing a sombrero, and the players lining up just before the half-way line before they ran towards the North End and dived on the ground in celebration. Harry Arter and Simon Francis were carried up high on the fans' shoulders and the pitch was just a mass of red and black when the game ended with jubilant faces all around.

The after-game scenes in the changing room were even more wild with Jeff Mostyn getting a good spanking as Bournemouth players held him a loft and Jeff cried 'I love these boys!' Eddie Howe was just a bit more controlled, and yet even he couldn't see Charlton Athletic in the next game securing a 19-0 win to overturn Bournemouth's goal difference to help Middlesbrough catch the Cherries. Second place had been guaranteed and it was on to the Valley to see if Bournemouth could win the title.

But the night against Bolton had to be enjoyed first. Eddie Howe led the applause on a very emotional night for all those involved with the club. 'This club was on its knees six years ago,' Howe told *BBC 5 Live.* 'We had nothing. A group of supporters put their money in their pockets to keep the club alive and they are reaping the rewards. It is the club I watched as a kid, the club that gave me an opportunity in the game as a player and a manager. It shouldn't be them thanking me, it should be me thanking them. It is a family club and deserves its moment in the sun.'

It was a strange feeling traveling up to Charlton on the train for the final game of the Cherries' season. Bournemouth were not in pole position to win the Championship, as Watford sat on top of the table one point ahead on 88 points. They just had to beat Sheffield Wednesday at Vicarage Road to secure the title and the Hornets already knew they were promoted. The only puzzlement I had was what if the trophy was at one ground and the result suddenly changed? The trophy could be needed at the other ground. I imagined there were two trophies and, as it turned out, there was indeed a replica at the Valley, which was a good job!

I don't think many Bournemouth fans were really expecting to see the Cherries become Champions. I had put money on them at the start of the season to win the league outright in a mad moment of optimism, but Watford were surely not going to slip up at home. We did expect Bournemouth to win against Charlton though as the players were in such good form. Matt Ritchie got the game off to a great start with a 25-yard shot that went across the goal and in off the far post. That was followed by Harry Arter capitalising on a defensive error and beating former team-mate Stephen Henderson in the Charlton goal to make it 0-2 in the first 12 minutes. While the cheers of 'We are Premier League' ran out the radio's and phones were out checking up on Watford's score. We didn't have long to be disappointed when Matej Vydra scored for the Hornets on 25 minutes. Bournemouth fans just settled into watching their own game unfold as it didn't look like there was any joy going to come from Vicarage Road.

I remember Kenwyne Jones coming on for Yann Kermorgant with just eight minutes to go, before Matt Ritchie made it 0-3 to Bournemouth. The goal had all the fans singing again. We were calling for two more goals as the team was on 98 goals for the season. While we checked for any unlikely news from Watford's game, there was just a great feeling that Bournemouth's players had done all they could and had played well on the day to round off a fantastic season. Then we suddenly heard a bit of a commotion. What's happening? Something's happened in Watford's game. Sheffield Wednesday have scored! It's 1-1 in that game and that means Bournemouth can be Champions. It was hard to keep calm. The news slowly filtered round, through the crowd, and even down on to the Bournemouth bench where players and staff stood up in preparation for a pitch invasion at the end of the game. Atdhe Nuhiu who had spoiled Bournemouth's fans' hopes, only a week or so ago at Dean Court, by going down from Adam Smith's tackle in the box, had now denied Watford not only a win, but also the title. Bournemouth fans could sing 'Championi! Championi!' as the final whistle went.

Somehow the whole experience seemed so unexpected. Watford were supposed to win their game but they hadn't done it. AFC Bournemouth would be crowned champions and they were going to do it right in front of the away fans at the Valley. We all hugged each other in absolute delight. It was such a contrast to when Tranmere had not let us celebrate promotion to the Championship at their ground only a couple of seasons ago. Many of the Charlton fans even stayed behind to applaud AFC Bournemouth's efforts over the season. Charlton fans were superb in their respect and appreciation, which is something I'll never forget.

The presentation was going to take some time to set up with the stand being carefully assembled piece by piece with the SkyBet sponsored logo for the Championship slowly taking shape and the trophy proudly brought in by Jeff Mostyn, as if he was carrying a newly born child. The team gathered round and one by one they were awarded their medals. Captain Tommy Elphick was first to get his hands on the trophy and the fans belted out another round of 'Championi!' with the TV cameras trying to capture the moment as the trophy was passed around the players. Eventually Jeff Mostyn had the trophy and passed it to Eddie Howe, who had a beaming smile on his face as he held it up and walked towards the fans. This is what we had been waiting for. King Eddie had the trophy and we could go crazy! Being a Bournemouth fan couldn't get better than this we thought. Match of the Day – here we come!

Bournemouth players can finally enjoy themselves after winning promotion to the Premier League

Tommy Elphick can't hold back his excitement

Jeff Mostyn brings out the Championship
Trophy for the presentation

The champagne is out and Simon and Francis
and Yann Kermorgant hold their children aloft,
while the party pictures are taken

Eddie Howe is captured by the media as he
holds the Championship trophy aloft

Yann Kermorgant was a great signing for
AFC Bournemouth who accelerated the club's progression to
the Championship title

AFC Bournemouth's players celebrate their promotion
to the Championship with an open top bus ride between
Boscombe and Bournemouth piers

12. WE ARE PREMIER LEAGUE! (2015-19)

The opening game of the 2015-16 season saw columns of flames greet the players for AFC Bournemouth v Aston Villa

The Cherries had reached the top flight and they had a crucial period over the summer months to prepare for it. At the start of the summer, Eddie Howe had visited Maurizio Sarri at Empoli in Italy's Serie A to see how they had managed to prepare for playing big teams in Italy's top flight. The club chose to go to USA to play Philadelphia Union in pre-season. The MLS was a standard a little below what Bournemouth had to offer though and the Cherries ran out 1-4 winners against the US team. While Bournemouth also played Exeter City, FC Nantes and Cardiff City in pre-season, much of the build-up to the new season was concern over whether the fans would get their replica shirts in time. TSG 1899 Hoffenheim were one of the more uniquely-named teams that Bournemouth warmed up against in August, but the game we wanted to see was the Cherries walking out for the first time in the Premier League against Aston Villa.

Arriving in the Premier League for the first time was like Christmas had come early. Bournemouth was getting prepared for the big time. I drove down to the Lansdowne area of town, where I past a roundabout with an enormous banner with a howling wolf saying 'Bournemouth are bringing goals, goals, goals to the Premier!' It was a Virgin Media and SkySports' campaign banner depicting that Bournemouth were now dining at the top table having scored 98 goals in the Championship. This wasn't my main destination. I was headed a bit further on to see a giant mural of captain Tommy Elphick on the side of a building, which had been painted by graffiti artist Rick Walker, to celebrate Bournemouth's creatives, with Tommy captaining the scene at the centre. It was hard to take it all in.

The glitz of England's highest league was given the full fanfare for the first game of the season against Aston Villa with huge 20ft fire flares greeting the players as they walked out on to the pitch at Dean Court to get the campaign underway.

Bournemouth were on the big stage. What more

proof did we need than to see Ray Wilkins walking out on the pitch to check on Aston Villa's players before kick-off? The game would be a nervy affair. Aston Villa had a new manager in Tim Sherwood, and the TV cameras were watching to see if the Premier League new boys would get a result against one of the oldest names in English football.

The SkySports and Virgin poster promising goals, goals, goals!

When it got down to the football the teams found it hard to live up to all the pre-match hype. It was a goalless first-half, although Marc Pugh had come close by testing Brad Guzan at the end of the half. Rudy Gestede would break Bournemouth hearts when he came on as a substitute and headed in the only goal of the game on 72 minutes. It was disappointing, but Bournemouth had played their first Premier League game. Eddie Howe was not complaining about the result. 'I felt we dominated, especially possession and chances in the first half. If you're not clinical enough in their box and a player like Gestede comes on, you're in trouble,' said Howe. 'It was a great day for the football club regardless of the result.'

Bournemouth's double promotion winning captain Tommy Elphick is immortalised on the side of a building in Bournemouth

Bournemouth had brought in a few players over the summer. Artur Boruc signed a permanent deal, Josh King signed from Blackburn Rovers and Max Gradel arrived from Saint Etienne in France, Sylvain Distin was brought in from Everton to add some experience of top-flight football as well as Christian Atsu on loan from Chelsea. Howe was also being loyal to the players that had won promotion while also signing Lee Tomlin from Middlesbrough, and

Tyrone Mings, the record £8m signing from Ipswich Town. Ryan Fraser went out on loan to Ipswich Town, while Brett Pitman signed a permanent deal with Ipswich Town after finishing a stunning second spell at AFC Bournemouth.

The transition from coaching Bournemouth in League One to the Championship, and then the Premier League saw Howe pick up on what he hated as a defender himself – pace. 'Coming into the Premier League, it was something we identified we needed more of given the number of transitions and the number of moments which are dictated by the pace in the team. We weren't a counter-attacking threat in the Championship. We were solely a possession team and that was something we needed to change,' said Howe.

Going up to Anfield so early in the season was a bit worrying, but Bournemouth put in a great performance. Tommy Elphick thought he had scored with a header in the first few minutes, but it was ruled out and the Cherries lost 1-0 on a night when they'd given their all.

A second away match at West Ham's Upton Park was to have an altogether different outcome. Bournemouth attacked with speed and confidence from the start. It was Callum Wilson's day as he scored a hat-trick. Bournemouth had gone 0-2 up through Wilson's early goals and a penalty by Mark Noble made it a game in the second half. Kouyaté had levelled on 53 minutes and it looked like Bournemouth might not get anything from the game. But Marc Pugh got Bournemouth back in front with his trademark chop and finish across the keeper. Jenkinson's foul on Max Gradel then enabled Wilson to complete his hat-trick from the penalty spot and put the Cherries 2-4 up! Even then, Bournemouth didn't defend well from a throw in and Modibo Maïga ran straight at Bournemouth's defence before making it 3-4. Bournemouth had a very nervy last few minutes, but they got over the line. Perhaps Bournemouth were encouraged by the sight of Darren Randolph in West Ham's goal? He had conceded 20 goals in his last four appearances against Bournemouth, including that famous 0-8 result at Birmingham in the previous season.

Eddie Howe tried to explain the game and Bournemouth's first ever Premier League win. 'It was a really strange game. We were in cruise control in the first half, but that seemed to go out the window after half-time when we made some strange decisions. We have been really heartened by the two previous games, but when you don't win then naturally the players will question whether we are doing the right things.'

The team was changed for the Hartlepool Capital One Cup match and Bournemouth won through 4-0 at home to give them another encouraging result. However, Bournemouth were about to have a devastating blow which would really test the squad depth. Against Leicester City, Bournemouth not only saw Charlie Daniels injured, but Tyrone Mings would suffer a long-term knee injury and Max Gradel sustained a cruciate ligament injury. Gradel was ruled out for most of the season. Chief executive, Neill Blake acted quickly to bring in Glenn Murray and Joe Bennett, while Lee Camp left for Rotherham United.

A point with Leicester City for a 1-1 draw did mean the Cherries got something from the game, but a 3-1 defeat at Norwich City caused concern for Howe. 'Our performances have been consistently high so far this season, so it was a reminder of what happens in this league when we drop below those high standards,' said Howe. Bournemouth had fallen 3-0 down before Steve Cook scored his first Premier League goal in the 81st minute. Tommy Elphick also picked up an ankle injury that would add to the injury list.

A packed Dean Court with 11,271 onlookers saw Bournemouth beat Sunderland 2-0 to get the first home win of the season. Matt Ritchie was the star of the game when he hit a spectacular volley from the edge of the box, after a clearance from a corner, that nestled in the top left corner. Callum Wilson had already put the Cherries ahead on four minutes in one of Bournemouth's characteristic quick starts, and after Ritchie's ninth minute wonder strike, there was no way back for the Black Cats.

Progressing the Capital One Cup was much harder after Preston North End held Bournemouth to a 2-2 draw after extra-time at Deepdale. Bournemouth were pleased to win through 2-3 on penalties and had keeper Adam Federici to thank.

Still, more bad luck followed. A 2-1 defeat at the Britannia Stadium was remembered for Callum Wilson going down with a cruciate ligament injury. At first, he picked himself up and tried to carry on, but he was soon down again. It was devastating to lose another player to what a few seasons ago would have been a career-ending injury. Many Bournemouth fans will also remember the Stoke game as a dark day for other reasons, as long-time *Bournemouth Echo* photographer Mick Cunningham sadly died the next day. Bournemouth were now 16th in the league and had their former promotion rivals Watford at home next. Glenn Murray made his home debut worthwhile with the opening goal, a trademark header. But a mistake from Artur Boruc gave Odion Ighalo a gift of a goal on half-time to earn a 1-1 draw.

Eddie Howe and JT gave a boost to everyone though by signing contract extensions to 2020. Eddie had waited some time before signing a new contract as he said he didn't want to distract from the task of planning how to keep the club up in the Premier

League. Sticking together was now the main theme for Eddie Howe to get across to everyone as Bournemouth returned from the Etihad having shipped five goals in a 5-1 defeat. It was a real mauling with Raheem Sterling scoring a hat-trick in the first half with Glenn Murray giving Bournemouth fans a bit of false hope with his breakaway goal on 22 minutes. Wilfred Bony finished the Cherries off in the second half with two more goals on what had been a learning day at the Etihad. Artur Boruc had pulled up in the warm up and Adam Federici had found it a difficult afternoon in spilling one of the shots straight to Raheem Sterling.

Things didn't get easier with the visit of Tottenham. While Boruc was back in goal, he fared little better as Bournemouth fell to a 1-5 home defeat. Pride had taken a hit. If this was what Bournemouth could expect in the Premier League, everyone thought it would be a quick return to the Championship.

Playing away at Liverpool in the Capital One Cup next would have most teams shuddering, but Bournemouth rolled their sleeves up in a tight game that was decided by a 17-minute strike from Nathaniel Clyne.

Defeats just kept coming and a poor first half left Bournemouth trailing 2-0 to Southampton in their next league game. Bournemouth improved in the second half to prevent another big beating and some harsh words were said at half-time. Howe was pleased with the fact that the team didn't buckle at Southampton, 'Last Sunday we travelled up the road to Southampton in what proved to be a proverbial game of two halves. We were disappointed with our first half display, but the players deserve huge credit for their second half response. After the break we dominated possession, passed the ball really well, and looked more like the side we know we can be.'

Bournemouth were expected to rouse themselves at home against Newcastle United who were a place and a point below in the table in 18th place. But Perez shocked the home team with a goal on 27 minutes. Bournemouth had 20 shots compared to Newcastle's two. Still it was a 0-1 defeat and Bournemouth were in the bottom three with just eight points from 12 games. Eddie Howe was as honest as he could be about the result, 'Sometimes football can be a cruel game and it is difficult to understand how we ended up not taking all three points.'

Everything seemed to be going against Bournemouth. They went 0-2 up against Swansea away with Josh King and Dan Gosling scoring but were pegged back for a 2-2 draw. The mood was soon to change. Maxim Demin decided to sell 25 per cent of his ownership in the club to US Peak-6 Investment. Matt Hulsizer, co-founder of Peak 6 and Jay Coppoletta, the US-firm's chief corporate development and legal officer joined AFC Bournemouth's board. It was a financial boost to prepare for investment in January and to make plans for a new training ground and stadium in the future.

The fightback began against Everton. Funes Mori and Lukaku gave Everton a 0-2 lead before Adam Smith and Junior Stanislas scored Bournemouth goals in the 80th and 87th minute. When Ross Barkley stole in to get what he thought was the winner in the 95th minute, Bournemouth didn't give up hope. They had a couple of minutes and Junior Stanislas brought the house down with a breakaway goal in the 97th minute to make it 3-3!

Eddie Howe just wanted the result to lift the players, 'It's unbelievable how football can play with your emotions,' said Howe. 'To score in the manner we did and at the end was one of the biggest highs I've had in football. An incredible day, though this game is no good for your health. I'll be having an early night tonight.'

Pundits were concerned that Bournemouth were too open and needed to change their philosophy rather than keep their attacking style so much. That was not what Eddie Howe was going to teach his players though. 'We are doing a lot of work on the training ground to improve our philosophy and to develop our philosophy and continue to make tweaks to what we believe will deliver a better way of training to the players. Ultimately, the results will define it this season. But with the way we are playing we would want to change it. Our supporters wouldn't want us to change. And we certainly won't go away from our ideals.'

Bournemouth were still sitting 18th on 10 points when they had to face Man Utd and Chelsea in their next two games in December.

The visit to Stamford Bridge would create a result that would resonate up and down the country. Chelsea were blessed with some of the league's greatest talent and Bournemouth's team cost pennies compared to what Jose Mourinho had at his disposal. Bournemouth fans were crowded in at the Shed End and waited for a miracle. The team was given tremendous support with the singing of 'We come from league two' and 'We're only here for one season', but as the game developed there was a sense that Chelsea were not finding it easy to breakdown the Cherries.

By the time we got into the second half and Chelsea still hadn't scored, Bournemouth even tried to make a few attacks of their own. Eddie Howe made a substitution late on to bring on Glenn Murray. Bournemouth were going to have a go. A late corner in the 82nd minute gave Bournemouth their opportunity. Stanislas floated the ball over, and while Courtois punched the ball away, Steve Cook crossed the ball to the far post again, where Glenn Murray just beat Charlie Daniels to the ball and headed in for the winner. Pandemonium broke out in the Shed End, 'We've got the special One!'

This result was never predicted. Bournemouth had created a major shock and now Sunderland, Newcastle United and Aston Villa were below the Cherries in the table.

Unbeknown to a lot of fans before the Man Utd match, there was a major decision taken by Harry Arter whether to play. He and his partner, Rachel, had lost their baby daughter called Renee, who was stillborn the week before the game. The courage of Arter was amazing. His team-mates wanted to win the game for him and with such a big incentive it probably didn't matter what team were put in front of Bournemouth, any team was going to be in for a very hard game. The fact that it was Man United just made it all the more exciting for the fans. Junior Stanislas whipped in a high corner in the second minute that curled over David De Gea and straight into the top right-hand corner of United's goal to give Bournemouth an early lead. Stanislas ran straight to Arter, kissing his black armband and pointing that that goal was for Harry Arter and his family.

Marouane Fellaini stole in to equalise before half-time, but a well-worked corner routine left Josh King free to score the winner and give Bournemouth back-to-back wins against two of the big guns in the Premier League. Bournemouth were up to 14th and we were just starting to believe that survival might be possible in their first Premier League season.

Confidence was suddenly sky-high and with WBA's physical game, Bournemouth came through the test having seen McClean sent off on 34 minutes for a foul on Adam Smith. Second half goals from Adam Smith and a penalty thundered home off the crossbar by Charlie Daniels, after Gareth McAuley had scored one for the Baggies settled the game. Even then, Salomón Rondón was sent off facing up to Dan Gosling. The game had been won by Bournemouth keeping their cool. Eddie Howe said, 'The players kept doing the right things despite having no goals for their first half dominance. We remained patient and disciplined. Consistency is what every team in this league is striving for so to go five games unbeaten and to gain three consecutive wins is a good start for us as we seek to become the best team we can.'

Bournemouth ended their home matches for 2015 with a goalless draw against Crystal Palace. The media wondered if Bournemouth could upset another top six team in their last game of the year, but Bournemouth succumbed to a 2-0 away defeat at the Emirates to close out 2015 in 16th place.

The New Year brought Juan Iturbe to Bournemouth – a talented midfielder signed on loan from AS Roma. Benik Afobe would also sign a permanent deal from Wolves in mid-January and

Lewis Grabban was re-signed from Norwich City. Eddie Howe did his best to reassure fans that it was a sensible signing to bring Grabban back to Dean Court. 'Grabbs did so well in his first spell with us, and is a really popular figure in the dressing room. He understands how we work and our approach, so it's a big boost to have him back with us.'

Artur Boruc saved a point for Bournemouth at Leicester, when Simon Francis was sent off for bringing down Jamie Vardy. The Polish keeper saved a spot kick for a 0-0 draw. It was a battling performance by Bournemouth as Eddie Howe recalls, 'It was a performance which epitomised the character and collective spirit in our squad, which bodes well for the second half of the season.'

Howe made changes for the FA Cup third-round tie with Birmingham City with Lee Tomlin finally getting some game time. Tomlin and Glenn Murray scored, as Bournemouth came from behind to beat Birmingham 1-2.

Having only had one defeat in eight league games, it was an unwelcome 1-3 home defeat to West Ham United on 12 January 2016 that brought a few doubts back. Arter had opened the scoring on 16 minutes with a powerful drive, but Bournemouth conceded three second half goals as Dimitri Payet and Enner Valencia handed Bournemouth their fifth home defeat. At least Benik Afobe and Juan Iturbe had made their home debuts.

Dan Gosling, Charlie Daniels and Benik Afobe struck to see off Norwich City 3-0 at home on 16 January in one of Bournemouth's most dominant displays. Sadly, it was the last we saw of Yann Kermorgant who left to join Reading. Afobe was immediately liked for scoring again against Sunderland in a 1-1 draw, but he was rested for the FA Cup match. The FA Cup fourth round was safely negotiated as Bournemouth beat Portsmouth 2-1 with King and Pugh scoring second half goals in a late comeback.

The evening match against Crystal Palace at the start of February was a memorable game and not just for Bournemouth's pink shirts. Points were vital to ease relegation worries and this was one of only two away games in February. While Bournemouth had gone behind to a Lee Chung-Yung goal, Marc Pugh was in sensational form as he teased the Palace defenders on the edge of the box in the first half, before finding a bottom corner. Afobe then added to his great start at the club by leaping high to strain his muscles and head Bournemouth into a 1-2 lead which they valiantly held on to.

Eddie Howe signed Rhoys Wiggins as the transfer window closed and was more than happy not to have seen any more players leave.

Arsenal still proved too strong for the Cherries at the Emirates and a 2-0 defeat was not unexpected. Howe would never throw he towel in, but the top teams were impressive. 'Last Sunday we faced Arsenal, in what we knew would be a good examination of our progress. We found it tough going early on and found ourselves chasing the game,' summarised Howe.

Losing 1-3 at home to Stoke City had Bournemouth looking over their shoulder again. Just four points above the relegation zone. Eddie Howe had no trouble in explaining why the first goal virtually killed the game. 'We started the game really brightly and then they scored a superb goal, out of nowhere and it just seemed from our perspective that it dented our confidence and we never recaptured our fluency throughout the game,' said Eddie. 'I just think confidence levels slipped, that's the beauty of this game. For us to win games and excel, we need everyone on song.'

Bournemouth had only won three games at home all season in the league, but at least they had reached the fifth round of the FA Cup. Sadly, Everton were to play a full-strength team with the TV cameras in attendance. Howe made seven changes from the team that lost to Stoke, but a 0-2 home defeat saw the Cherries exit the cup with some disappointment that Eddie hadn't named a stronger side.

A 0-0 draw away at Watford left the Cherries in 15th with 11 games to go. Max Gradel had come off the bench to play having been out since August 2015.

March began well with wins over Southampton and Newcastle United. Beating the Saints 2-0 at home, it had seen another fast start from the Cherries. Howe drummed into his players that early goals win games and Bournemouth were the Premier League leaders in goals scored in the first 15 minutes of games. 'I'm pleased for everyone, the players, the supporters. I think we knew how big a game it was for them today. It's such a long time since we have beaten Southampton and to do it in the way that we did is very pleasing. We were on it tonight, you know the crowd were very good. They got behind us and we gave them something to cheer about. We were on the front foot right from the off. We forced several corners in the first few minutes and that gave us the platform.' added Eddie. 'I think it's one of those games we will remember in the future. We have had a few of them down the years, but this is one that I think will be right up there as a game that we haven't won for a long, long time. We are rarely talked about in terms of our supporters being a rival to Southampton and I've always said that I don't think that Southampton consider us a rival, so it's nice to be on top tonight.'

The 1-3 away win at Newcastle United was probably celebrated even more highly as Bournemouth went nine points clear of the relegation zone with nine games to go. An own goal set Bournemouth on their way before Josh King got a second goal on 70 minutes. Even when Pérez got a goal back in the 80th minute, a storming run by Charlie Daniels and a powerful shot ensured all the points were headed south. Eddie Howe believed it was again the early moments of the game that set the tone for the afternoon's events. 'Our early attacking play and tempo were rewarded with the opening goal, and perhaps the only disappointment was that we didn't add to that tally despite our first half dominance.

'In a season of so many highs, it is sometimes too easy to overlook the achievements of this group of players. To be winning away at St James' Park, at the end of a week in which we've beaten our south coast neighbours for the first time since the 1950s, just illustrates how much credit the whole team deserves.'

Another dramatic Bournemouth performance followed as they led twice before finally out scoring Swansea 3-2 at home on 12 March 2016. Max Gradel scored his first goal since overcoming his knee injury at the start of the season and famously ran over to celebrate by embracing his manager in one of the iconic pictures of Bournemouth's season. Josh King had put the Cherries ahead again, but it needed Steve Cook's header on 78 minutes to win the game.

Despite a 3-0 pounding at Spurs, Bournemouth

ended March in 13th place. Spurs brushed
Bournemouth aside with two goals in the first 16
minutes, before Christian Eriksen added another
goal in the second half. Manchester City also found
goals a plenty as they put four past Artur Boruc on 2
April.

Bournemouth were much stronger against Aston
Villa who they beat 1-2 away. Callum Wilson made
his return to play a few minutes having been injured
since September 2015. The win took Bournemouth
over the 40-point mark. Eddie Howe could be
delighted with the points tally and also pleased with
how his players coped with the angry atmosphere
being created by the Villa supporters, who saw their
team rooted to the bottom of the league on 16
points from 33 games. 'It was a difficult game to play
in because of the toxic atmosphere. We made it that
way with the way we started,' said Howe.

Bournemouth would get close to Liverpool with a
1-2 defeat in April. Two first half goals from
Liverpool had put them in the driving seat, but
Bournemouth had a much better second half and
the disappointment was that Josh King's goal had
come rather late in the 93rd minute. At least Callum
Wilson was back to make a second half appearance.
'When we looked at the fixture list at the start of the
season, while we knew there would be no easy
games at this level, it was clear that our run-in was
particularly challenging. It's a huge credit to the

players for getting so many points on the board ahead of this set of fixtures.'

Eddie was of course right. The fixtures in April were horrendous for the Cherries and they would lose their last two games in April 1-4 to Chelsea and 2-1 to Everton, dropping them to 14th in the table. Still, Bournemouth had secured their Premier league status with two games to go. 'When you consider where we have come from, and some of the setbacks we faced early in the season, I honestly feel that remaining in this division is one of the club's finest achievements to date, and one the whole town can feel proud of,' said Howe. 'I think people like the way we had been brave and attacked the league. We hadn't shied away or changed anything from the season before. There's a lot to admire in that.'

Matt Ritchie would get an 82nd minute goal to add another point to the Cherries' points total with a 1-1 draw at home to WBA. Artur Boruc had given the ball away to see Salomon Rondón score early on, before he had saved a penalty from Craig Gardner.

Bournemouth tried to finish the season at Manchester United on 15 May, but the game was abandoned due to a bomb hoax. A dummy bomb had been left in the stands after a training exercise earlier in the week and when the alarm was raised on match day, Bournemouth fans found themselves without a game and out of pocket. The match was

played three days later on a Tuesday night, when
Bournemouth lost 3-1. Bournemouth had finished
16th on 42 points which would have made the
headlines most seasons for a team that had been
given little chance of staying up, but Leicester City
won the title this season by 10 points in what was
easily the most sensational story in the Premier
League's history.

Bournemouth flew to the USA again in pre-season
handing Minnesota United a 4-0 defeat before
returning home to play Portsmouth, Reading, Cardiff
as well as getting a 1-1 draw with Valencia and
beating Angers 0-1 in France.

Second season syndrome was the phase banded
about before Bournemouth kicked a ball in 2016/17.
Bournemouth had strengthened considerably
though with a record £15m spent on Jordan Ibe from
Liverpool on a four-year deal. Brad Smith also signed
from Merseyside, while Lewis Cook from Leeds
strengthened the midfield. Nathan Aké signed on
loan from Chelsea until January. Emerson Hyndman
was bought from Fulham and Lys Mousset was
signed from Le Havre, while defender Marc Wilson
joined from Stoke City. Bournemouth fans were
shocked when Matt Ritchie dropped down a league
to join Newcastle United, while Tommy Elphick

would join Aston Villa and Shaun MacDonald joined
Wigan Athletic. But the late loan signing of Jack
Wilshere from Arsenal would get Bournemouth fans
very excited about the new season with Man Untied
first up.

Getting off to a slow start, Bournemouth only
managed to earn one point in August. They were
beaten 1-3 at home on the opening day by
Manchester United and a goal-hungry Zlatan
Ibrahimovic, who scored a long-range goal from
outside the box. At least Adam Smith scored a
stunner, cutting in from the wing to open
Bournemouth's goal account.

West Ham United beat a 10-man Bournemouth
1-0 in their first match at the London Stadium, when
Harry Arter was sent off. Howe knew where the
problem was. 'It was a tight game with little
goalmouth action. It was going to swing on a
moment of brilliance or a mistake. Unfortunately,
the mistake for us was going down to 10-men.'

A 2-1 win against Morecambe had seen the
Cherries start their Capital One campaign off more
successfully. The first league point came against
Crystal Palace in a 1-1 draw on 27 August, which
moved Bournemouth up to 19th. AC Milan then beat
Bournemouth 1-2 in a testimonial game for Warren
Cummings. In the league, September began better
with a 1-0 win over WBA with Callum Wilson scoring
late on by carefully redirecting a right-wing cross

into the corner of the net. It was his first goal since coming back from his cruciate ligament injury. Jack Wilshere also made his debut in a Bournemouth shirt as a sub. For once Eddie could smile but he admitted it was more relief, 'relief that we have got our first win, first clean sheet. It's a massive day for us,' said Howe.

Visiting the Etihad was another wake-up call with Pep Guardiola's side smashing four goals past Artur Boruc. Being out played by one of the most super star packed teams was no disgrace, but the 2-3 defeat at home to Preston North End in the League Cup highlighted the fact that Bournemouth were struggling to find form. Eddie Howe was grateful for the accuracy of Junior Stanislas who starred in a 1-0 win at Dean Court over Everton to lift Bournemouth to 13th in the table. Bournemouth were starting to play with more confidence and they were involved in a cracking 2-2 draw at Vicarage Road.

Bournemouth fans began to feel more comfortably when they saw the Cherries take Hull City apart in a 6-1 demolition at Dean Court on 15 September 2016. Bournemouth's biggest Premier League win had five different goal scorers with Charlie Daniels opening the scoring on five minutes. The game looked far from decided though when Steve Cook made a poor pass and Ryan Mason equalised on 34 minutes. Cook would score at the other end though and Junior Stanislas put

Bournemouth into a 4-1 lead, before Hull City crumbled in the last 10 minutes as Callum Wilson and Dan Gosling completed the misery for Mike Phelan, Hull City's caretaker manager.

Bournemouth were now 11th and playing Tottenham Hotspur at home. Holding them to a goalless draw would be as pleasing as the huge win over Hull City, especially with Jack Wilshere playing 90 minutes for Bournemouth for the first time. Any feelings of making a step up though were dashed when the Cherries sunk to defeats from Middlesbrough and Sunderland, who were both near the foot of the table. Hopes rose again though when Nathan Aké's first goal for the Cherries was all that was needed to beat Stoke City away with Adam Federici back in goal. But taking points off Arsenal remained elusive as Bournemouth fell to a fourth away defeat 3-1 at the end of November.

It was December that would define the Cherries' season beginning with a sensational 4-3 comeback win against Liverpool that would keep the Sunday headline writers busy. Liverpool had taken what looked to be a decisive 1-3 lead with Emre Cann's stunning strike with 20 minutes to go, but then Bournemouth hit back as substitute Ryan Fraser got to work. Fraser rifled in Bournemouth's second goal and set up Steve Cook for a savagely struck equaliser and in added time, Loris Karius spilled Steve Cook's long range shot that Aké mopped up to make the score line 4-3. 'I don't think I'll ever forget this one,' said Eddie Howe in his post-match conference. 'A real contrast of emotions. It's probably right up there with the Everton game of last year. At half-time we were in real trouble. Liverpool were excellent. Full credit to them for how they played first half. We weren't very good and they showed their quality. So that makes the comeback even more impressive, because the guys never lost their self-belief.'

Riding on the high of the Liverpool result, the Cherries' chief executive, Neill Blake, announced that the club intended to have a new stadium in place for the 2020-21 season.

Bournemouth were finding still they were slow starters as they fell two goals behind against Burnley and this time the comeback was not big enough with Burnley running out 3-2 winners. Points were not far away though as Leicester City, Premier League Champions, would fall to a Marc Pugh goal.

Forging a rivalry with Southampton was proving less easy as the Cherries were hit by two Jay Rodriguez goals in a 1-3 home defeat, despite Nathan Aké's opening sixth minute goal. Smashed 3-0 by Chelsea at Stamford Bridge and Eddie Howe was staggered at just how many goals the team were conceding. 'We were well in the game today. It's a frustrating one for us because elements of the game-plan worked. Of course, when you get beat 3-

0 we can't be too upbeat, but it's fine margins,' said Howe. 'We've got to do better.'

Better they would be, trouncing manager-less Swansea 3-0 in their last game of 2016 to finish the year in 10th place on 24 points from their 19 games. Eddie Howe might have thought that he had started to get his players to more than compete with the big sides after the Liverpool win, and the visit of Arsenal in January seemed to bear that out. The Cherries drove themselves into a 3-0 lead by 58 minutes and saw Alexis Sanchez haul the Gunners back into contention with 20 minutes to go. Luas Pérez scored on 75 minutes to make it 3-2, but the Cherries slumped back into their own half even more when Simon Francis was sent off for a foul on Aaron Ramsey. Sadly, Olivier Giroud then broke Bournemouth hearts with a 92-minute headed equaliser. Eddie Howe found it all hard to believe. 'It's a strange one for us,' said Howe. 'At 3-0 up you hope the game is over but you can't underestimate the quality of Arsenal and as soon as they got the first goal the game changed. Fate conspired against us in several ways. The emotion is one of disappointment but you have to reflect on the manner of the performance and getting 3-0 up, the goals we scored, the way we pressed, how hard the players worked it was really good to see. But we're here to win and that's why it hurts so much.'

If Eddie was proud of his players for taking the

game to Arsenal on that night, he was less than impressed with a 3-0 FA Cup exit to Millwall four days later. Howe had made 11 changes but even with Wilson and Gosling coming off the bench in the second half the game was lost. Heading up to Hull should have restored some confidence after the earlier game on the season, but the Cherries found themselves losing 3-1, despite Junior Stanislas scoring from the penalty spot in the third minute. It was Marco Silva's first game in charge of Hull City. Eddie Howe was left wondering how to stop teams scoring so many goals against the Cherries. 'We are disappointed with all three goals. We're in the middle of the season we have everything to play for at both ends of the table. Our season could still go two ways,' said a concerned Eddie Howe.

Howe knew he already had defensive frailties. Nathan Aké had been recalled by Chelsea and the game against Hull City was Tyrone Mings' first game back in the Premier League for the season. At least Bournemouth managed a 2-2 draw away at Watford. The week ahead could hardly have gone worse, when Callum Wilson picked up the second cruciate ligament injury of his career in training. Now Howe had to deal with losing one of his main goalscorers.

It was the problems in defence that really began to tell. Bournemouth would suffer four defeats in a row starting with a 0-2 defeat at home against Crystal Palace at the end of January. February didn't see Eddie Howe pick up a single point as the Cherries started to plummet down the table. The biggest defeat came against Everton and a red hot Romelu Lukaku, who scored four of Everton's six goals. Bournemouth were 3-0 down at half-time and two goals from Josh King and a goal, tucked in by the post, by Harry Arter gave some respectability to the score in the second half, although Arter's goal was probably scored after the ball had already rolled out of play! James McCarthy had added to Lukaku's goal haul earlier for the Toffees, while Ross Barkley had time to celebrate Everton's sixth goal even before he had scored it. It was a demolition. Bournemouth had slipped to 14th in the table just six points ahead of the relegation zone. 'We tried something different today [a back three of Francis, Cook and Mings], but it didn't work. The injuries to defenders made it difficult,' said Howe.

In such circumstances it was no surprise to lose at home 0-2 to Man City, but the 2-1 defeat at the Hawthorns was not helped by a punching error from Artur Boruc that led to WBA's first goal. 'When you are not winning games there are errors from the team – it's not one person, we need to take collective responsibility,' said Howe.

Boruc was kept in the starting line-up for the next game against Manchester United, where he was man of the match, and Eddie Howe was delighted to get a response from his team. The United game was memorable for one incident above all others and that was the so-called Ibrahimovic-Mings elbow and stamping affair. Andrew Surman was sent off after getting a second yellow card for pushing Ibrahimovic, and Jason Tindall was sent to the stands. It was a game where the Bournemouth players were cheered off the field for a great point in a 1-1 draw, after Josh King had equalised Marcos Rojo's opener. Baily Cargill had also made his debut, having subbed Tyrone Mings in the second half. Mings was subsequently awarded a five-match ban for violent conduct after the alleged stamp on Ibrahimovic, who also received a three-match ban for the elbow incident.

Bournemouth felt that Mings had been unfairly treated in getting such a large ban and no proof of intent in his challenge to which he apologised twice to the Manchester United forward. Still, the ban only galvanised team spirit and Bournemouth put their problems behind them with a 3-2 win over West Ham United. Josh King was Eddie Howe's hero scoring a hat-trick, including a 90th minute winner, having missed a penalty earlier in the game. Benik Afobe had also seen his penalty saved, so it was a big relief when Josh King later netted the last-minute winner. It was Bournemouth's first win of 2017 and it had taken until 11 March to get. Eddie Howe could at least finally reflect on getting over his worst run of

results without a win in the top division – eight
league games without a win. How was Eddie feeling?

'Relief is the overwhelming feeling. It always is in
those circumstances – a mixture of emotions but the
main one is relief,' said Howe.

The Cherries had turned the corner and a 2-0 win
over Swansea with Benik Afobe adding to an Alfie
Mawson own goal for Bournemouth's first clean
sheet of 2017. A south coast derby with
Southampton should have provided another win, but
Harry Arter's standing foot slipped when he took a
late penalty and shot over. The 0-0 draw at
Southampton at least kept the points ticking over
but the 2-2 draw at Liverpool was more rewarding.
Afobe had given Bournemouth a shock 17th minute
lead, before Coutinho and Origi hit back with two
goals before the hour. Josh King then rescued the
Cherries a point with three minutes to go. That took
Josh King's goals to nine in the last 10 games.

Eddie Howe was revelling in the team's ability to
finally challenge the big clubs. 'It took the win at
Chelsea last year to really get the players to believe
we could win anywhere in the division, but I think
this season the big results against those teams that
have reinforced that belief,' said Howe.

With Chelsea and Tottenham up next, these
words would be tested. Chelsea won 1-3 at Dean
Court. Howe was respectful of Chelsea's class in
defeat. 'I have to compliment Chelsea, they're an

outstanding team and their system works well for them. But I compliment my boys as well because they played very well. In the end Chelsea were too strong,' said Howe.

Bournemouth were hit with a Spurs' whirlwind at White Hart Lane seven days later. Tottenham went 2-0 up between the 16-19 minutes and Bournemouth never recovered with Kane and Janssen completing the 4-0 beating. Spurs were simply quicker in every aspect of their game. Eddie Howe admitted as much. 'They made it very difficult for us to get the ball and they put us under a lot of pressure,' said Howe. 'I'm really disappointed with the goals we conceded because we had two from corners that were really of our own doing and for the second goal we had good possession, so disappointing in that regard.'

Howe was well aware that Bournemouth were not yet safe. 'We know we need more. We've known all along. The danger is if everyone says, 'You're safe'. 'We've got to focus the players' minds that we're not,' he added.

Bournemouth had dropped to 16th in the table, but were still seven points ahead of Swansea City who were in 18th with five games to go. The good news was the next two games would be against two of the strugglers. Marc Pugh enjoyed his 250th appearance for the Cherries against Middlesbrough with an assist for Josh King's opener, while he scored

Bournemouth's third. Gaston Ramirez was sent off on 21 minutes for a second yellow card on Pugh, and Afobe had made it 2-0 before half-time, while Daniels added to Pugh's second half goal to make it 4-0. Bournemouth were up to 12th, seven points above the relegation zone.

Josh King then relegated Sunderland with an 88th minute goal and took Bournemouth over the 40-point mark when the Cherries beat the Black Cats 0-1. Safety was assured with a 2-2 draw at Stoke City, Bournemouth coming from behind twice to get the draw. That took the Cherries to 42 points, exactly what they had ended their first Premier League season on. Talking about the second season, Howe was just pleased to have got the club safe. 'The second season is harder, having gone through it. The first season is a novelty, in the second there is expectation,' concluded Howe.

The last two games gave the Cherries the chance to set a record points total and in the penultimate game they beat Burnley at home 2-1 to move them to 10th in the table on 45 points. Junior Stanislas had scored early in the 25th minute, before Sam Vokes looked to have stolen a point with seven minutes to go. But Josh King got the winner two minutes later. Lewis Cook was now featuring in the games alongside Harry Arter, while King had taken his goals up to 16 for the season. 'Josh King has been excellent. Every team needs a goalscorer and someone to lead the line, there is more to come from him too,' said a satisfied Eddie Howe.

A 1-1 draw with Leicester City rounded off Bournemouth's second season in the Premier League, Junior Stanislas' first minute goal cancelled out by a Jamie Vardy strike on 51 minutes. Bournemouth had finished ninth in the table on 46 points – the standard had been set. Howe said, 'I think we've become more streetwise in the Premier League. It's a challenge for us to improve.'

While the summer seemed to be filled with top players being linked to the club, the most pleasing news we heard from the club was that any new stadium would remain in Kings Park. The team went to Marbella in Spain to start their pre-season against GD Estoril Praia and would play Portsmouth, QPR and Valencia again (having drawn 1-1 with the Spanish side a year earlier), as well as Yeovil Town and Napoli. The summer of 2017 saw the club sign a trio of former Bournemouth players. The biggest of these was Nathan Aké who re-joined permanently from Chelsea for club record £20m transfer fee. Asmir Begovic also signed for the Cherries for a second time from Chelsea for £10m, while the promise of plenty of goals came from the return of Jermaine Defoe, who signed from Sunderland.

Bournemouth also signed Connor Mahoney a young winger from Blackburn Rovers after a tribunal that agreed the fee. Meanwhile, Max Gradel joined Toulouse for the season on loan, Baily Cargill joined Fleetwood Town on loan and Lewis Grabban joined Sunderland on loan.

This season could be labelled Bournemouth's comeback year, but it didn't start well. A narrow 1-0 away defeat to WBA didn't raise too many worries in the first game as Bournemouth had dominated possession. However, a 0-2 defeat to Watford at home was met with real disappointment with Bournemouth only managing two shots on target. 'I thought we were very disappointing and I'm scratching my head as to why,' said Howe. 'I'm concerned generally and we haven't looked like scoring, so there is plenty of work to do.'

Better news followed when Bournemouth beat former managers Harry Redknapp and Kevin Bond in the Carabao Cup at St Andrew's 1-2. Ryan Fraser and Marc Pugh got the goals for Bournemouth's first comeback of the season.

There was a plucky display for the next home match against Manchester City. Charlie Daniels scored with an absolute belter of a volley that was a goal of the season contender. Bournemouth held on to their lead from the 13th minute, until Jesus equalised on 21 minutes. The game seemed destined for Bournemouth gaining a creditable draw, but Raheem Sterling scored in the 97th minute to win the game, even if Bournemouth fans could celebrate Sterling being sent off for celebrating with the away fans. Bournemouth had scored their first league goal of the season and had come close to holding City. 'We thought we had hung on for a point.' said Eddie Howe. 'We had chances to win it too, I am disappointed for the players and the supporters.'

With no points and only Crystal Palace and West Ham below them in the table, Bournemouth headed to Arsenal where they were again beaten 3-0. Eddie Howe was already under pressure. 'It has proved to be a very tough start to the season so far. I take the full responsibility for everything that has happened so far, but I believe now is the time for the whole club to group together and come back fighting stronger than ever,' he said. Bournemouth were 19th in the table and only above Crystal Palace, as the Cherries had at least scored one goal. Spirits rose with a 2-1 win over Premier League new boys Brighton & Hove Albion. A rare goal from Andrew Surman and a winner form Jermain Defoe brought Bournemouth's first three points. In a fixturing quirk, Bournemouth had to play Brighton again in the Carabao Cup, just four days later, when a substitute appearance from Josh King won the tie.

Bournemouth looked like they had control of the game at Everton with Josh King's 49th minute goal, but late substitutions changed the game for Everton and Niasse scored twice late on to win the game 2-1. Howe remained in positive mood. 'I am confident the results will follow. We know what we need to do, and we believe on our approach,' he said.

A 0-0 draw with Leicester City at home was the best Bournemouth could do at the end of September. In two months of football, Bournemouth had only accumulated four points from seven games. Having lost 1-0 away to Spurs, there was delight at picking up a second win of the season at Stoke City. Early goals from Andrew Surman and a penalty from Junior Stanislas put the Cherries 0-2 up in the first 18 minutes. El Hadji Diouf pinched a goal back for Stoke in the second half, but Bournemouth still recorded their first away win. Surman was now Bournemouth's unlikely top-scorer and with seven points on the board the Cherries were only a point from being out of the relegation zone.

Beating Middlesbrough 3-1 in the Carabao Cup put Bournemouth into the quarter-final. Callum Wilson, Lys Mousset and Benik Afobe had all scored on a night that really felt like Bournemouth's season was up and running. Impressive too was Jack Simpson's debut for the Cherries' senior squad.

The last match in October was a home game against the champions, Chelsea. Eden Hazard scored the only goal of the game just after half-time. The defeat left the Cherries in 19th place with just seven points form their first 10 games. Jermain Defoe hadn't had the start to his second Cherries career that he had wanted and the striker only touched the ball eight times in the first 45 minutes of the Chelsea game. But it was the whole team that that wasn't quite at it. 'These games hurt you – we need to find a way to draw or even win these games. It's a challenge as we've gone from being a free-scoring team,' said Howe. 'I don't see a problem with the creative players we've got, we just need to find the right formula.'

That formula came right at Newcastle United, when Steve Cook had risen highest in the 92nd minute from a corner to give Bournemouth all three points. It was a dramatic winner in a game that had seen Newcastle's Matt Ritchie hit the post and Marc Pugh go so close to scoring, just before Cook's late winner. Bournemouth were now out of the bottom three and Howe was keen to remind everyone of it. 'Being in the bottom three is psychologically difficult,' he said. 'These days in the media, it's rammed down your throat, to a degree, so to lift ourselves out of this position temporarily is a good thing.'

More good news followed for Lewis Cook who was given his first full England call up by Gareth Southgate.

Bournemouth had the momentum now and they ripped Huddersfield Town apart 4-0 in the next

fixture with Callum Wilson bagging his second
Premier League career hat-trick to take the Cherries
up to 13th in the table. Wilson was making only his
second league start since his anterior cruciate
ligament injury in February 2017. 'We realised the
importance of backing up the win we got before the
[international] break,' said Eddie. 'We need as many
points as we can. The fixture list changes in
December and it will be difficult for us.'

Points weren't exactly flowing quickly though
when a 0-0 draw was gained at second-bottom
Swansea City before running into an in-form Burnley
at Dean Court. A 1-2 defeat to Sean Dyche's men
Bournemouth sliding back towards trouble. Howe's
40th birthday didn't seem a time to celebrate with
the tough programme ahead in December.

Adam Smith would be the subject of a yellow
card from referee Jon Moss in the Southampton
derby which would lead to a suspension for diving,
while Moss later apologised for getting the decision
wrong and for not awarding the Cherries a penalty.
The points were shared in a 1-1 draw, but the
suspension was a bigger concern for Howe with the
run of games to come.

Jermain Defoe came good at Crystal Palace with
two goals, the second of which was a spectacular
right-footed lob from an acute angle that would earn
a point in a 2-2 draw. All the goals had come in the
first-half, but the late drama saw Christian Benteke

grab the ball and demand to take an injury-time penalty which Asmir Begovic pushed away to safety. 'For the manager it was very difficult to watch, because the game was on a knife-edge, especially in the last 10 minutes as we rode our luck a bit,' said Howe.

But Eddie was delighted for Jermain Defoe. 'We've seen him [Defoe] do that before for us, but that was in his first spell with us. Not many people would have seen that, I think it was against Oxford, but it was an incredible goal. And that was a great pass by Lewis Cook into Jermain's run, but he still had so much to do and he's capable of those things.'

Facing Man Utd, Bournemouth put a courageous performance in at Old Trafford. Only a Romelu Lukaku header on 25 minutes separated the sides. But if Bournemouth could play well against United and come close to getting something from the game, there was hope before taking on Liverpool. Jurgen Klopp's side though were at a whole other level. They swept Bournemouth aside 0-4 with Mo Salah bewildering everyone to leave Bournemouth a point above the drop zone. Eddie Howe knew that by trying to attack Liverpool, Bournemouth had been picked off. But you have to learn fast in the Premier League. 'We are aware our style can leave us vulnerable and we left ourselves exposed at times. We're in the same position as always with a relegation fight,' added Howe.

With the opportunity to clear the heads and play Chelsea in the quarter-final of the Carabao Cup at Stamford Bridge, Bournemouth tried their hardest to try and make their first semi-final in a domestic cup competition. Chelsea had gone ahead through Willian's 13th minute goal and Bournemouth also lost Jermain Defoe to an ankle injury. Still, Dan Gosling had all the Bournemouth fans jumping for joy in the 90th minute when he blasted in an equaliser. But from the re-start, Chelsea shot up the pitch and Morata bagged a winner to deny the Cherries any extra-time. 'The players gave everything,' said Howe. 'In the second-half we had waves of attack and we scored, but the last part of the game was bitterly disappointing.'

A pre-Christmas Eve 4-0 pounding from Manchester City hardly helped the Christmas spirit as Bournemouth fell back into the bottom three. 'I don't want my players to dwell on it too much,' said Howe. 'I think when you play Man City they are one-off games.'

Good fortune certainly accompanied Bournemouth's comeback 3-3 draw against West Ham at Dean Court with Callum Wilson seeing the ball roll off his arm and into the Hammer's net in the 93rd minutes to delight the home fans. Bournemouth had been 2-1 up after an hour with Dan Gosling and Nathan Aké responding to Collins' seventh minute opener, but Arnautovic had looked

to have won the game with two goals in the last 10
minutes before Wilson's late intervention.

The last game of the year finally brought Eddie
Howe a home win with a 2-1 victory over Everton
and an 88th minute winner from Ryan Fraser who
scored both of Bournemouth's goals. It was
Bournemouth's first win in nine games. The league
was tight and Bournemouth rose to 14th, just two
points above the relegation zone. Getting out of the
bottom three for the New Year was key. 'You don't
want to be there for a second in any season, we've
been there and had to take that but now we have
shown the character to fight back and all our success
in recent years has been down to a really tight team
spirit and a club mentality when everyone gets
behind the team. We've had that in the last two
home games, where the atmosphere has been
electric and I'm delighted to see us get our rewards,'
said Eddie.

Eddie Howe was pleased to come away from
Brighton with a point. Anthony Knockaert and José
Izquierdo given Bournemouth problems out wide
and Steve Cook and Callum Wilson had brought
Bournemouth back into the game twice for a 2-2
draw. Josh King had picked up a hamstring injury and
Defoe was still out with a bad ankle, while Junior
Stanislas and Ryan Fraser were also trying to cope
with injuries.

Comebacks were becoming second nature to the

Cherries and they needed another one to save their third-round FA Cup tie against League One side Wigan Athletic. Bournemouth were 0-2 down in 30 minutes and needed Lys Mousset to fire in as a substitute, 10 minutes into the second-half, and a Steve Cook 92nd minute header to earn a replay. Wigan had a good penalty claim turned down just before Cook's equaliser and they had looked the stronger team.

Bringing back the first team players, Bournemouth had an inspired comeback against Arsenal to beat them for the first time in the Premier League in January 2018. The 2-1 win saw Callum Wilson and Jordan Ibe score second half goals to give the Cherries their first three points of the year. 'That was a famous win for the club,' said Howe.

Any celebrations were soon cut short with an embarrassing 3-0 defeat to Wigan Athletic in the FA Cup replay. While Howe had rested players and brought back Harry Arter, the team was second best everywhere on the pitch. 'When you look at the quality we had on the pitch, no way should we have lost by that score,' said Howe. Visiting the London Stadium didn't offer much more relief for Howe. Things started well when Junior Stanislas slipped a perfectly weighted pass through for Ryan Fraser to open the scoring against West Ham. But Chicharito [Javier Hernández] would equalise straight from the restart, latching on to a pass that went right down the middle of Bournemouth's defence, which parted like the Red Sea.

Howe's anger was turned around though with a spectacular counter-attacking second half at Stamford Bridge, when Bournemouth would strike three times through goals from Wilson, Stanislas and Aké dishing out some revenge for the Capital One Cup defeat. 'That has to be our best result and the best performance in getting the result,' said Howe. 'We were very aggressive and everyone was magnificent. Our aggressiveness, work-rate and endeavour – it all came together.'

Supporters could also feel pretty happy when Deloitte announced that the Cherries had become the 28th richest club in the world in its football money. What a rise since the Minus 17 season!

With the win over Chelsea, Bournemouth jumped up to 10th in the table and were on 28 points from 25 games. They had gone six games unbeaten in the Premier league which equalled the club's best record at that level. Optimism of a top-half finish started to rise with a 2-1 home win over Stoke City at the start of February. While Shaqiri had scored in the first five minutes, Bournemouth had come back again with goals from King and Mousset in the last 20 minutes of the game to send Bournemouth ninth. 'We really had to dig deep and we haven't done that a lot,' said Howe.

Another comeback looked on the cards when Huddersfield's early goal from Alex Prichard was pegged back by Stanislas' exquisitely taken finish into the far corner of the goal just six minutes later. But Huddersfield just got stronger and stronger and ran away with a 4-1 win to pull them out of the bottom three. It was a sudden shock for Bournemouth. 'I apologise to the fans for the performance,' said Howe. 'There's not much else I can say.'

Poor early goals against Bournemouth were becoming regular occurrences and Newcastle United were the next visitors at Dean Court to find themselves 0-2 up with two first-half goals from Dwight Gayle. But Adam Smith and Dan Gosling would peg Newcastle back in a mad last 10 minutes as Bournemouth refused to be beaten.

'We had been flat – Newcastle were dogged and made it difficult for us, but you have to compliment the players for the last 10 minutes – that is what we wanted to be, we showed a lot of quality and character to come back,' commented Howe. 'It's another point that nudges us towards where we want to be – everyone could be vital at the end of the season.'

The tables were turned on the Cherries when they visited Leicester City. A win and Bournemouth could start dreaming about Europa League football. Bournemouth had the game in their pocket with

King's early converted penalty, but a late free kick awarded to Leicester in added time would deny Bournemouth a precious win, when Riyad Mahrez stepped up to bend the shot over the wall and score in the 97th minute. 'It's a difficult one for us to take,' said Howe. 'There were only seconds left. We just had to see it out.'

The gap to the bottom three was now just six points, even though the Cherries were 11th in the table with nine games to go. Bournemouth looked nervy with a 1-4 home defeat to Spurs a week later. Junior Stanislas had scored Bournemouth's single goal and his presence was even more important in the game against WBA, when Jay Rodriguez had put the Baggies 0-1 up on 49 minutes. Bournemouth began another comeback with Ibe levelling on 77 minutes, but it was the inch-perfect free-kick of Junior Stanislas just one minute before the end of the game that won it for the Cherries. This put them up to 10th and on 36 points they were more or less safe, not that Howe would admit it. 'I want as many points as we can get. We knew West Brom would make it tough,' said Howe. 'They've got a lot of experienced Premier League players but we had to find a way to win without playing well – it moves us closer to safety.'

Of course, Bournemouth would add to their comeback credentials at Watford with a 2-2 draw thanks to a 92nd minute goal, put away by substitute Jermain Defoe. 'I'm delighted with Jermain's finish, it could be a huge one at the end of the season,' said Howe. 'Coming back from injury he has looked sharp. I expected him to come on and make a difference and it was a fantastic finish.'

Bournemouth were getting points by doing it the hard way and another comeback against Crystal Palace from 2-1 down was a great way to start April. It was Josh King who had left it until the 89th minute to add to a Lys Mousset goal to give Bournemouth a point. It was another great finish to a game at Dean Court and it was almost becoming expected now. '[There's] never a dull moment. It's not good for my health but I'm sure it's the same for the supporters as well; edge of your seat stuff,' said Howe. 'Two defeats in 14 at this level is incredible.'

There was no cheer from Anfield though where Bournemouth held out for just seven minutes before Liverpool began their scoring. Mané, Salah and Robertson helped themselves to a 3-0 win. Liverpool were great, but Bournemouth were sloppy in their next game losing 0-2 at home to Manchester United. 'We're not quite safe – I'm getting bored of saying it,' Howe reiterated. 'We have three massive games left and we need to get over the line.'

Bournemouth were tip-toeing to the safety line. Playing Southampton who were in a more perilous position should have given Bournemouth the chance to send their near-neighbours down and solve their own concerns, but Dusan Tadic scored twice with just a Josh King goal in between. 'I am disappointed with how we played, it was a game we could and should have won if we play like we can, but we didn't,' said an annoyed Eddie Howe.

Mathematically it was still possible for Southampton and Swansea to escape relegation and even catch Bournemouth, despite the Cherries being in 12th place and six points above the relegation zone. So, the penultimate game of the season for Bournemouth, against Swansea City, was a game Eddie Howe could not afford to lose. Ryan Fraser dispelled any doubts over where Bournemouth would play their 2018-19 season with a wonderful strike from a well-worked free-kick that he slotted in, from the edge of the area, on 37 minutes. It was enough to win the game and Swansea never looked like halting their slide towards the Championship. 'We were professional today, and got the job done,' said a satisfied Eddie Howe. 'To get over the 40-point line is massive. We made it hard for ourselves over the last few matches and each time we didn't win was one step closer to relegation, so we're glad to have got over the line.'

With the shackles off for the last match of the season at Burnley, Eddie Howe made a couple of changes to the team. Emmerson Hyndman was given his first start of the season in midfield, Tyrone Mings came in for Steve Cook, Jordan Ibe replaced Marc

Pugh, Andrew Surman came in for Lewis Cook, while Lys Mousset was given a start ahead of Callum Wilson. Burnley had been magnificent all season and would finish in the European places, but they didn't manage to hold a Bournemouth side who once again showed they were the comeback kings with late goals from Josh King and Callum Wilson wiping out Chris Wood's first-half strike.

The winning goal was made by Jermain Defoe who had come on as a sub to tackle Kevin Long before, unselfishly, setting up Callum Wilson, who steered the ball home. Bournemouth ended the 2017-18 campaign having gained 21 points from losing positions. The Cherries had completed their third Premier League season in 12th on 44 points, two points fewer than the season before. But it had only been goal difference between them and a 10th place finish.

The season had been noteworthy for the emergence of Lewis Cook as a future England international having displaced Harry Arter from the team and he signed a new contract to ward off interest from Liverpool. But all the accolades went to Nathan Aké who had proved that he was a defender of the very highest quality and was bringing the best out of other members of the squad with his enthusiasm and long flowing dreadlocks.

Eddie Howe had wanted a hard pre-season because
of the poor start to the previous campaign and
Bournemouth went to La Manga to get some
summer sun in July 2018. Bournemouth played
Sevilla in a 1-1 draw before beating Levante 4-3.
Championship sides Bristol City and Nottingham
Forest were even more of a test and an extra fixture
against Amiens SC sorted some matters out, before a
0-2 defeat to Real Betis. But there was nothing
wrong in the 5-2 crushing of UEFA Cup finalists
Olympique Marseilles before the first league match.

Out-going players included Bournemouth's Ivory
Coast winger Max Gradel who went to Toulose for
£1.75m and Rhoys Wiggins who retired.

Meanwhile, Bournemouth settled their Financial
Fair Play dispute with the Football League for some
£4.75m for the 2014-15 season when they had won
promotion to the Premier League. It had taken a
long time to reach the settlement, but at least it was
no longer hanging over the club.

At the start of the 2018-19 season, Bournemouth
were regarded as an established team in the top
division, but the newly-promoted sides of Fulham
and Wolves had already spent big in the summer.
The World Cup had robbed clubs of time to
complete transfers and AFC Bournemouth fans had
to be content with three summer signings. David
Brooks from Sheffield United was only 20 and would

be a valuable addition in attack, while Diego Rico would provide cover for Charlie Daniels at left-back after his move from Leganes. The record-breaking signing was the £25m spent on Levante's Jefferson Lerma who had played for Colombia in the World Cup. Bournemouth fans would have to wait for their star midfielder to be selected after his fitness was not quite right to be involved immediately, but it didn't stop Bournemouth getting off to their best ever start in the Premier League.

The Cherries beat newly-promoted Cardiff City 2-0 in their first match, despite Callum Wilson having a penalty saved. Eddie Howe was delighted to win his first game of the season, something he hadn't managed in previous Premier League seasons. 'I was very pleased with today's performance, it was a tough game and I have a lot of respect for Cardiff because they gave everything. It was a really competitive game and I thought we controlled the first half without opening them up as much as we wanted to. In the end two moments of quality won us the game. As much as we're happy today we have to remain level-headed,' said Howe.

Taking on West Ham at the London Stadium was not going to be simple either. Bournemouth had only won four away games in the previous season, and West Ham had been one of the clubs to bring in many new signings, including Jack Wilshere and the Brazilian Felipe Anderson. With Nathan Aké conceding a first half penalty, Bournemouth would need to see a comeback. A marvellous individual goal from Callum Wilson and a header from Steve Cook made it two wins from two for the red and black army.

'We scored the goals at good times and Callum's moment of brilliance swings it for us, it's a great finish at the end of a good run,' remarked Howe.

Six points out of six left Bournemouth in the top six and going into the game with Everton there was much optimism that another win could be secured. That prospect seemed even more likely when Everton's top scorer, Richarlison, was sent off for a headbutt on Adam Smith. Yet, Everton still scored first thanks to Theo Walcott and Bournemouth had Adam Smith sent off, before Michael Keane made it 0-2. But this amazing Bournemouth team fought their way back in the last 20 minutes to get a 2-2 draw to make it three games unbeaten. Eddie Howe knew this had been an important game not to lose.

'I'm very pleased with the ability to come from behind as it always gives you a chance in a game, but it frustrates me that we allow it to happen in the first place. There's plenty to learn from it,' said Howe. 'We didn't really get our rhythm going or have enough of the ball to consider ourselves the dominant team. It was another comeback and we're delighted to achieve it because at 2-0 down and at 10 versus 10, it looked really difficult from a mental perspective.'

A 3-0 win over Milton Keynes Dons was all the more rejoiced for Jefferson Lerma and Diego Rico making their debuts, while former Cherry Baily Cargill had returned to Dean Court for the Dons. Bournemouth's progression would set a third round tie up against Blackburn Rovers.

Taking on Chelsea at Stamford Bridge pitted Howe against Maurizio Sarri, who he had spent time with at Empoli in May 2015. Second half goals from Pedro and Eden Hazard broke Bournemouth's unbeaten record, but Howe was keen to stress Bournemouth had given a good account of themselves and it could have been different if Callum Wilson and Nathan Aké had put away their chances.

'Until the first goal, the game was in the balance. We had the best chances and they were two key moments. We didn't take them and, ultimately, paid the price for that,' said Howe.

Bournemouth played Leicester City after the international break in a fixture that had traditionally ended being a draw more often than not. Bournemouth were on fire though and went 3-0 up by half-time with Ryan Fraser scoring twice and Josh King converting a penalty. With Wes Morgan seeing red for a second yellow card, Adam Smith extended Bournemouth's lead to four goals, before Leicester hit back with just a couple of minutes to go. A penalty and a breakaway goal by substitute Marc Albrighton gave more respectability to the score line for Leicester, but it was still a big 4-2 win for Bournemouth.

Burnley were bottom of the league when the Cherries met them in the sixth game of the Premier League season at Turf Moor. The form book was shattered though as Bournemouth fell to a 4-0 defeat. Bournemouth had 63 per cent of the possession but no goals. 'I don't think it was a 4-0 performance.' said Howe. 'We were well in the game and had chances, but we didn't take them.'

Chances were more forthcoming at home against Blackburn Rovers in the Capital One Cup. The Cherries went two goals to the good with Junior Stanislas volleying an early goal, before Jordan Ibe scored from the penalty spot. But this was far from a routine win as Lerma made a mistake to let Craig Conway peg a goal back. Tyrone Mings then flew in at Ben Brereton, resulting in another penalty kick that Adam Armstrong scored. Only an added time headed winner from Callum Wilson spared the lottery of further penalties.

The Cherries really needed to get their league form back on track after the heavy Burnley defeat and Crystal Palace were the opposition on a Monday evening at the start of October. David Brooks scored his first Bournemouth goal off the underside of the cross bar in a well worked goal with Adam Smith and

Callum Wilson, before Patrick Van Aanholt equalised in the second-half. It needed a penalty for an elbow from Mamdou Sakho on Lerma before Junior Stanislas made it 2-1 from the spot in the 87th minute. Bournemouth were up to seventh and had 13 points on the board from their seven games. Eddie Howe was sure confidence was flowing through the team now. 'We're confident we have a goal in us at any time, and match winners in the team who can turn a tight game in our favour,' he said.

More disappointing was a club statement issued on Thursday 4 October in which the club's board stated that they had been 'overly optimistic' that a new stadium would be completed by the summer of 2020. Eddie Howe was naturally as disappointed as the fans.

Yet, winning games was the primary concern. Watford had started the season even better than the Cherries and were sitting in sixth place when Bournemouth, one place below them, met at Vicarage Road. Bournemouth were to record their biggest away win in the top flight with a 0-4 hammering of the Hornets. David Brooks started the rout, Josh King scored twice and Callum Wilson added to the first half goals at the start of the second half. Eddie was delighted with the result, 'It's an outstanding achievement by the players to win by four here and to get a clean sheet and the incisive goals we scored, I'm really pleased. Even when we don't have the ball we can be a threat and I think that's really important at this level and ultimately that phase of our play decided today's game.'

A goalless draw with Southampton kept Bournemouth in the top six before a visit to Craven Cottage at the end of October where the team showed it could win even with without Josh King. 'They [Fulham] had a lot of ball at times, but our positioning and mentality was good. The second goal was a big moment and I think it was key in the game,' said Eddie Howe. 'We changed the system today, it was a challenge and the players adapted well. It was a blow to miss Joshua King, but Callum Wilson got us two goals today and we needed it.'

Beating Norwich 2-1 in the Carabao Cup fourth round would have normally been highly praised, but Eddie Howe was disappointed at the mentality with which the players approached the game. 'I need to speak to the players who played and get their thoughts. We just looked disjointed," said Howe.

It would be Chelsea in the Carabao Cup next, a repeat of the previous season's fixture at that stage. The draw hadn't done Bournemouth any favours with the lower league opposition Middlesbrough and Burton Albion still in the competition.

Any cup fatigue was quickly brushed aside with Man Utd in town for the early kick-off on 3 November. Callum Wilson scored his seventh of the season before Anthony Martial pulled one back and Marcus Rashford grabbed a 92nd minute winner to give Bournemouth their first home defeat of the season. Howe was naturally despondent after the team had played so well but got nothing from the game. 'It's a tough one for us today. I think a lot of aspects of our game were really good, especially during the opening period. We knew the second half was going to be a different game,' Howe said.

One player who had reason to smile the following week was Callum Wilson who received his first England call up. It was an achievement that the whole club could celebrate knowing how hard Callum had worked to come back from his cruciate ligament injuries. He even scored on his England debut.

Callum didn't add to his goal tally away at Newcastle, before the international break, and Bournemouth lost 2-1 with Salomon Rondón giving the Cherries' defence major problems. 'We gave ourselves a mountain to climb going 2-0 down,' said Eddie Howe. Jefferson Lerma did score his first Bournemouth goal but a knee injury to Adam Smith capped a pretty awful outing at St James' Park.

The tough run of fixtures really got going then with Arsenal beating Bournemouth 1-2. Jefferson Lerma netted a spectacular own goal before Josh King levelled to go in 1-1 at the break, but the Cherries saw more points slip away with

Aubameyang grabbing the second half winner. Eddie Howe knew it was a better performance than at Newcastle, but admitted: 'The second goal was a real kick in the teeth. We didn't really look to be switched on at that moment and it cost us the game.'

December began with Tyrone Mings making his first league start at top of the table Man City. While Callum Wilson scored to make it 1-1 at half-time, City won out 3-1. Eddie Howe was pleased with some elements of the match but felt the goals conceded were scrappy. 'When we've come here before we've faced a barrage of shots but that wasn't the case and we were good value for long periods,' said Howe.

A 2-1 home win over Huddersfield Town put Bournemouth back on track, but Lewis Cook ended the game having sustained an anterior cruciate ligament injury which put him out for the season. Along with Adam Smith and Dan Gosling also having undergone operations on their knees, Bournemouth were running short of midfielders.

The going didn't get any easier with the visit of Liverpool who galloped to a 0-4 win with a Mohamed Salah hat-trick and an own goal by Steve Cook. Callum Wilson had also missed the Liverpool match with a hamstring injury. Howe kept his disappointment for the officials. 'The first goal had a massive bearing on the game, because I thought our shape had been good and Liverpool hadn't opened us up at that point. The first goal shouldn't have stood,' said Eddie Howe.

Going into the match with Wolves, everyone knew that a defeat would drop Bournemouth out of the top 10 and after a misplaced pass from Charlie Daniels Bournemouth found themselves a goal down on 12 minutes. Worse still, Tyrone Mings was helped off with a back injury as Bournemouth slumped to a 2-0 defeat.

Taking on Chelsea in the Carabao Cup quarter-final gave a chance to get over the league form and Bournemouth played particularly well, holding out until the 84th minutes before Eden Hazard won the tie. Artur Boruc and Lys Mousset were the star performers and Eddie Howe felt the players had given everything. 'We gave a very disciplined defensive display, we counter-attacked well at times, used the ball well at times and that result could have been very different,' Howe said.

A win over Brighton & Hove Albion pushed Bournemouth back up to eighth in the table. David Brooks' brace earned Bournemouth the win and put a more positive spin on the December results. Eddie Howe stressed that it was not just the attacking side of Brooks' game that was improving. 'He buys into the team ethic and the defensive component of the game. He's an intelligent player, and he has grasped the tactics very quickly, so full credit to him for that,' commented Howe.

There were less reasons to be happy about much after the Boxing Day 5-0 crushing at Wembley given out by Tottenham. Bournemouth lost their captain Simon Francis to an anterior cruciate ligament injury just on half-time and the game sped away from the Cherries with the sharp finishing of Son Heung-Min. Eddie Howe still felt that the performance wasn't all bad. 'It was a strange game and we had some really good moments at the start,' Eddie said. 'We had a couple of very presentable opportunities which we didn't take.'

Old Trafford was not the venue Howe probably wanted to attend next having seen Ole Gunnar Solskjaer do so well in his first two games in charge of United. Bournemouth were battered 4-1 and Eddie Howe couldn't hide his disappointment. 'Defensively we weren't great, with the ball we weren't great and that's a bad mix coming to Old Trafford,' said Howe.

Bournemouth had ended 2018 with 26 points from 20 games and were sitting in 12th place. The January window saw plenty of early activity from Bournemouth. Dominic Solanke was signed from Liverpool for £19m, even if his hamstring prevented him from playing until February, while Nathaniel Clyne joined on loan also from Liverpool.

The New Year began with a chaotic home game against Watford. Dan Gosling returned from injury

and Junior Stanislas fitted in as a right-back. Troy
Deeney gave the Hornets a 0-2 lead within 27
minutes. A Bournemouth fight back followed with
Nathan Aké and Callum Wilson striking back, before
Ken Sema put Watford 2-3 ahead. But the first half
scoring wasn't over before Ryan Fraser made it 3-3.
The game had seen four goals in a crazy six minutes,
but there were no second half goals.

Bournemouth drew Brighton in the third round of
the FA Cup and while Nathaniel Clyne made his
Bournemouth debut, the Cherries lost 3-1 with Marc
Pugh scoring Bournemouth's only goal. 'We were
fine in the game and then suddenly, with their first
shot on target, Brighton score. We wobbled a bit,
conceded again, and then it was a tough afternoon,'
said Howe.

While interest grew in rumours about Callum
Wilson from Chelsea and West Ham, Eddie Howe
was clear that the forward would not be leaving.
However, Jermain Defoe did depart on loan though
to Rangers. With Everton up next, Bournemouth had
the chance to climb ahead of them in the table. Yet,
two second half goals from Everton sunk
Bournemouth. 'When you don't win, confidence
becomes an issue but you wouldn't have known it
from the performance,' said Howe.

Callum Wilson was back for the match against
West Ham United having recovered from a
hamstring strain. He made the most of the

appearance too, smashing in a volley eight minutes into the second half, before Josh King wrapped up the points in added time.

Bournemouth continued to be active in the January window with Marc Pugh going out on loan to Hull City, while the much-tracked Chris Mepham finally got his move to the Cherries from Brentford for £12m. 'Reducing the average age of our squad was something we prioritised around 18 months ago and it's very important that the squad is well balanced,' said Howe.

There was fear that Mepham's signing might be a prelude to Aké departing with the window still open, but the transfer window passed with only Jermain Defoe (Rangers), Marc Pugh (Hull City) and Tyrone Mings (Aston Villa) being loaned out. Meanwhile, Bournemouth Enterprises took back full control of AFC Bournemouth with Peak 6 Football Holdings, owned by Matt Hulsizer and Jay Coppoletta, selling their 25 per cent holding back to Maxim Demin.

A night of high drama hit Dean Court in midweek on 30 January when Chelsea came to town. Sarri's team dominated the first half and Boruc had to make a superb save from Kovacic's header on to the bar and helped create the goalless half-time score. But David Brooks and Josh King set about the Chelsea defence and King scored a counter-attacking goal on 47 minutes, before Brooks pounced on an error from David Luiz to make it 2-0, quickly followed by a third from King. The scoreboard ticked over to 4-0 in added time, when substitute Charlie Daniels guided a header into the far corner of the net.

Eddie Howe signalled that the win over Chelsea was special. 'It's up there with our special performances in the Premier League. I don't know where it ranks, but I just like to enjoy the brief feeling you get from winning,' he said.

There was a more sombre mood at Cardiff City where their striker Emiliano Sala had died on a private flight from Cardiff, having completed his transfer from Nantes FC. Cardiff had only five wins all season but this was a match they desperately needed to perform and they did. A 2-0 home win gave Eddie Howe plenty to worry about. Howe was still looking for some momentum, 'we thought the Chelsea game could've been a turning point for us and we're really searching for consistency,' he said. 'We can't play like we did on Wednesday then play like we did today – the mental side was a factor today,'

Away form was certainly suffering with no wins in seven and Liverpool made it eight away defeats with a 3-0 masterclass against Bournemouth, but the side played with more fighting spirit than against Cardiff.

It was imperative that home form remained steady in this period. Injuries were not slowing down with Steve Cook sidelined with a groin strain that enabled Chris Mepham to make his first start at home against Wolves. While Mepham was relieved to escape from a clear handball in his own box, Bournemouth's early lead through a King penalty was equalised when Adam Smith fouled Matt Doherty and Raul Jimenez scored from the spot in the 83rd minute. Bournemouth could still have won the game when Ryan Fraser was awarded a penalty just minutes later, but Josh King missed the penalty and the game ended 1-1. Eddie Howe admitted there was doubt over whether Fraser had been fouled in the box, but he added that, 'we should score and win.' Worse still, Jefferson Lerma had reached 10 yellow cards and would be suspended for the games against Arsenal and Manchester City.

Bournemouth were also without Dominic Solanke for the Arsenal match as he picked up a thigh injury, while Eddie Howe was at least pleased to name David Brooks among the substitutes at the Emirates. A 5-1 drubbing did little to enhance Bournemouth's away form as Arsenal ran riot after the Cherries had clawed the game back to 2-1 at half-time. Lys Mousset scored Bournemouth's single goal and Sam Surridge made his Premier League debut, but the defeat felt as big as the loss to Spurs on Boxing Day. Bournemouth had slipped to 12th in the league with 10 games to play. Howe was less than complimentary about the team's performance at Arsenal. 'I don't think we were good in any aspects of the game... We have to analyse ourselves honestly and not kid ourselves that it was acceptable,' said Howe.

So, imagine the delight fans had knowing that Manchester City were next up at home. They were chasing the title just one point behind Liverpool. Eddie Howe set-up with five at the back with Jack Simpson and Chris Mepham looking to stop Sergio Aguero and Raheem Sterling. Bournemouth fell to a second half goal from Riyad Mahrez and came in for criticism for no shots on target and just 18 per cent possession. Bournemouth fans were not so disappointed with a 0-1 defeat and nor was Howe. 'The effort was there and the determination to do everything to try to get the result was there, and that's all we can ask,' said Howe.

The second game in March was away at Huddersfield Town who were still bottom of the league. Bournemouth were desperate to end their away run of defeats and they managed it thanks to a first half goal chested in by Callum Wilson from Ryan Fraser cross, and a second half goal from Ryan Fraser when Callum Wilson had the assist. Eddie Howe regained his smile. 'We were very good today, we had our bounce back and a lot of quality. We could have scored more but the goals we scored were of the highest order,' said a content Eddie Howe.

Howe was not so pleased when Bournemouth dropped two points in the final minutes to Newcastle United in a 2-2 thriller. Solomon Rondón scored from a free kick at the end of the first 45 minutes, but Bournemouth got back into the game right at the start of the second half with a penalty converted by Josh King after Aké had been hauled down in the box. Things got even better when King latched on to a pass from Dominic Solanke and fired Bournemouth ahead, but former Cherry Matt Ritchie scored a screamer of a volley in the last minute of added time to leave Bournemouth two points short of the 40-point mark after 31 games.

The internationals gave Bournemouth time to reflect in the Dubai training camp before the next game against Leicester City. The break did Bournemouth no favours as they fell to a two-nil defeat and started to lose touch with the race for seventh. Eddie Howe couldn't hide his disappointment, 'Our away record is a concern and we are trying to find ways to improve what we do.'

Eddie Howe had drafted in Asmir Begovic in the keeper position for the Leicester match which was a shock to many. Vardy's goal was also seen as a misjudgement by Begovic, but he started the next match against Burnley. Burnley were one place above the relegation zone. Things began well when an own goal from Ashley Barnes gave the Cherries the lead in the fourth minute, but after 20 minutes Bournemouth were 1-2 down. Begovic had misjudged the flight of a ball that Chris Woods headed in at the far post, before Ashley Westwood capitalized on a mistake from Chris Mepham. A third goal came for the visitors when Ashley Barnes fired past Begovic after another keeping fumble on 56 minutes.

The poor form had transferred itself to the home games and Bournemouth were marooned on 38 points. Eddie Howe was wondering what else he could do. 'I don't know how many times I've got to say that were not safe,' he cried. 'I don't consider myself safe and on my holidays – and the players are the same…you can't take liberties in this game,' he added.

Eddie Howe promised his team would have to do better in their away match against Brighton & Hove Albion who were themselves still in a relegation fight. Nobody expected the result that Bournemouth achieved. The rain and hail made it a difficult first half, but Steve Cook was back to lead the side and Boruc was back in goal. Dan Gosling put the Cherries into a lead, scoring his first goal for 14 months, before Ryan Fraser made it 0-2, early in the second half, with a stunning finish that lobbed the keeper. Moreover, once Anthony Knockaert was sent off, Bournemouth went into top gear scoring three more goals from Brooks, Wilson and Stanislas to make it an emphatic 0-5 away win. On 41 points, Bournemouth were now safe and the smiles were back on peoples' faces.

'We've been hesitating and spluttering in recent

weeks so it's good to get back into the groove and
show what we can do,' said Eddie Howe. 'We've
been stretched with injuries and it's halted our
progress but we came through it and we want to
finish the season on a high.'

Eddie would be in charge for his 500th game with
the visit of relegated Fulham. Scott Parker's side
were not to be taken lightly though. A second half
challenge by Jack Simpson on Aleksandar Mitrovic
gave the Fulham striker a chance to beat Boruc from
the spot and Fulham won the game 0-1.

The game just didn't materialise how
Bournemouth wanted it to. 'The effort was there but
the quality wasn't there. From last week it was the
polar opposite, the decision making wasn't quite
where it was,' said Howe. Bournemouth had the
south coast derby to try and get the points back on
track and they had a 3-3 thriller with Southampton
at St Marys.

Bournemouth had come back from being a goal
down to an early Shane Long goal to be 1-2 up at
half-time, after Dan Gosling had scored easily the
best team goal of the season, and Wilson had slotted
in from a rebound off the keeper from a David
Brooks' shot. Southampton were still fighting for
Premier League safety and needed at least a point
from the game. They thought they would get more
than that when James Ward-Prowse and Tarrget put
them 3-2 up. But Callum Wilson ran in

Bournemouth's equaliser with four minutes to go from a Ryan Fraser cross, and he had a chance to win the game when clean through against Angus Gunn. Unfortunately, the keeper made the save to give Southampton a draw.

'I think after 20 minutes we'd have done anything for that point,' said Howe. 'But ask me after 95 minutes. I'm maybe not so happy. We obviously had a big chance at the end when Callum went through, but the fighting characteristics of the team were back.

'We've not come back from losing positions enough this season and to do that was a great sign.'

Mark Travers was a surprise starter in goal for the match against Tottenham Hotspur at home. While Spurs also had their second round Champions League tie to worry about against Ajax, they sent a strong team to Dean Court. Things got interesting though when Son Heung-Min was sent off for pushing over Jefferson Lerma in the first half. Spurs picked up three yellow cards in the first half as well, and when Juan Foyth received a straight red for a foul on Jack Simpson, Bournemouth had just nine players to beat. It wasn't until added time though that a corner from Ryan Fraser was headed in by Nathan Aké to give Bournemouth their first Premier League win over Spurs in their final home match of the season.

It had been an emotional day with the fans

saying goodbye to Marc Pugh after his 274 Bournemouth games and there had been a wonderful goalkeeping display from Mark Travers in the first half, when Dele Alli, Lucas Moura and Christian Eriksen had all tested the 19-year-old keeper in his Bournemouth debut.

To get Bournemouth's first win over Tottenham in the league was a great way to end the season's home games. 'I don't think we did particularly well with the advantage we had,' said Howe. 'We didn't use the ball intelligently enough.'

But Bournemouth had played the game with Aké and Lerma in midfield and Ibe playing just behind Wilson as the injuries to Gosling and Brooks had meant that Howe had to shuffle his players. Howe was pleased that Aké was on hand at the vital moment of the game. 'It was difficult and looked like we were running out of time to win the game, but thankfully we popped up with a great goal,' said Howe.

Ryan Fraser won the Supporters' player of the year award as well as the *Bournemouth Echo*'s Micky Cave trophy and Vice-president's award. The Exiles voted for Nathan Aké and the Juniour Cherries for David Brooks. At half-time we had also seen the U21s parade their Central League Cup trophy.

The final match would be a £4m game against Crystal Palace to see who could finish twelfth. Bournemouth named an unchanged starting 11, but

little went their way in the first half with Batshuayi
scoring twice and Jack Simpson finding his own net
to put Bournemouth 3-0 down after 37 minutes. On
the stroke of half-time Jefferson Lerma blasted
Bournemouth into the game with a 30-yard
thunderbolt that went in off the top of the post and
bar. It was really game on when Jordan Ibe side-
footed Bournemouth another goal. Unfortunately,
Crystal Palace had their counter-attacking game on
song and Patrick van Aanholt made it 4-2, before
Josh King's 73rd minute tap built the game up to a
big finish. More goals looked likely, but the final goal
went to Palace with Andros Townsend giving Mark
Travers a day to forget as the Cherries ended up
losing 5-3.

There was little Eddie Howe could be pleased
about having not reached their target of surpassing
46 points. 'We had a real low in the first half. We
didn't defend well, didn't react well to the first goal.
We wobbled a little bit, maybe due to the
inexperience of our team,' said Howe. The Palace
game was such a contrast to the win against
Tottenham and it's summed up Bournemouth's
inconsistent season.

Bournemouth had ended the season with their
highest number of clean sheets in the Premier
League and yet they had conceded their highest
amount of goals on 70. Yet with 56 goals scored by
AFC Bournemouth, only the top six teams scored

more. It was a season of two unequal halves with 26 points coming from the clubs first 18 games and 19 in the second half of the season when away wins were far harder to come by. But beating Chelsea and Spurs at home were games that made 2019 look more favourable than it might have been.

Eddie Howe could still look back on his managerial record in the Premier League with a fair amount of satisfaction. He had accumulated 47 wins, 36 draws and 69 defeats with a total of 201 goals for and 260 against.

Eddie Howe was adamant that, 'it has to be seen as another season of progression.' Indeed, in the grander scheme of things Bournemouth had blooded many new players in the Premier League and the word relegation hadn't really been spoken of in great depth. Moreover, players like Callum Wilson, Ryan Fraser and David Brooks were far more on the wanted list of other clubs as Bournemouth had started to win more and more admirers for their adventurous play.

13. THE NEXT GAME

When it gets to 20 minutes before kick-off, Eddie lets the players get focused on what they need to do. 'I like to be in the dressing room just as a reassuring figure to know that I'm there with them. That's just my way of doing it,' Eddie explains. 'It's now that you have to see the result of your work. So, the work has gone on and the preparation has happened. There's very little I can do now.

'This is the acid test, this is when you can see if you have been good or not... This is what you do the job for. It's an uncomfortable feeling because so much is at stake and you are judged instantly on the game. There is no hiding place from that. So, it's quite a unique environment but it is why you work and why you want the game. You want to be judged and you hope that it's in a positive way and not a negative one.'

Eddie almost sounds like he is helpless just when the fruition of his work is about to be seen by the gathering crowd. Match day can be a lonely place for a manager, left with his own thoughts, even though he has to be there for everyone to see. It's all about the performance and winning, of course.

Match day is particularly sacred. 'Anything that is not a direct influence on the team's performance I will look at as a little bit of an inconvenience. So, the media is important for the supporters and important for the wider world of football, but is it important for my team? No, not really,' explains Howe.

I get the feeling that being satisfied with what he has achieved will never truly be realised by Eddie Howe while he is a manager. To be content would make him half the man he is. Whether at school, as a player or as a manager, Eddie Howe wanted to be the best and, even then, he'll want more from himself. He admits that he gets frustrated by not coming first.

'The fact that I wasn't winning at everything I did has driven me in my life,' said Howe. 'My playing career was a mixed bag and I felt I was fighting every day to stay in the profession rather than winning cups and getting promotion... As a player I thought, when is the next training session? The next game? I have to prove myself all over again. I feel the same as a manager. I have to prove myself to the players every day... There's no satisfaction in the sense of patting each other on the back it's more: let's try to win the next game.

'I struggle sometimes even during a good result,' Eddie told *TalkSport*. 'I'm always thinking about the next game, and the next challenge, that you don't get a chance to sit back and think that was good, that was good fun!

'It's a job that I must love doing. I must do to give everything I do to it. But the moments of enjoyment are quite rare,' Howe admitted.

The task of winning the next game was hard enough in League Two with all the barriers that Howe faced to find 11 players to put on the pitch. Bringing the club together and having a common goal can put such problems in the background though for 90 minutes. Rising out from League One put the club on a very different course from just survival. It was thriving in the Championship. Rather than being daunted by playing teams with fantastic heritage, Howe made Bournemouth play like it was the underdog. Each mountain that was climbed was another step towards where we all felt Eddie Howe belonged – the Premier League.

I do wonder what might have happened to AFC Bournemouth had Eddie Howe decided not to return to the club in October 2012. The last few years would have been spent probably back in League Two and the Premier League would have remained a distant dream. Eddie Howe could have stayed at Burnley and it might well have become tougher for him there, too. I suspect Eddie Howe would have found his way to a good coaching job, without the stress of management, if things had not worked out well.

The fact that Eddie Howe and JT have not only forged many player's careers in the Premier League, but have also developed as a successful management duo at that level, is a fabulous end to the story. They have not only coached individuals but have made a club grow and prosper. Bournemouth have a football team and club that they can be truly proud of and it has been fantastic as a fan to see how each step has been built.

What have I found out about Eddie Howe, which makes him the manager he is? Well, he is competitive and hates losing. He found he could challenge the very best, by encouraging and working with players. He aims to find as many different ways as he can, to gain small advantages, to help his players win games.

Records and targets really matter, because they are challenges that can bring about improvement. Eddie likes to try different things to see if he can learn something new about himself, or his players. He trusts in the energy and enthusiasm of youth. Rather than worry particularly about the opponent, it was time to focus on what the players, under his control, could achieve. Play to your own strengths and do it your own way. But listen to others that have had success and be proud of who you are and your roots. Add to this a person who is a motivator, who has a work ethic that makes him pay great attention to every detail and a desire to take a club to the very top, and we can start to see some of the ingredients that make Eddie Howe who he is. I can't answer all the reasons why success came to AFC Bournemouth, but clubs need people with a vision. Eddie Howe's dream has simply been to try and be the best at what he does.

Now that Bournemouth have become not only a player but a force in the Premier League, there might be a worry that the club would forget where it came from. Massive TV deals and star signings have transformed this south coast club in a matter of years. I suppose Eddie Howe came along at just the right time for AFC Bournemouth to maximise its presence in this global game. It's not just people in Dorset that are looking to see who the Cherries will play next. The names of Eddie Howe and AFC Bournemouth are on the world stage today.

Our small, idyllic, family club is still considered by many to be a surprise guest at the top table. Transforming it further into a top six club and European competition will be a dream for many of our supporters. But our biggest dream should be to see the club simply continue to grow. There are more stories to be told in future games. I hope they will be games that are managed by Eddie Howe and JT. Even if they are not, there is nothing that can take away from us what the duo have given us already. Be proud of what has been achieved

together – you are an AFC Bournemouth supporter
and part of a great story.

'Eddie had a dream, from minus 17.
We had no money and had to buy
the players on loan.
We play from the back with pace in attack.
He went to Burnley
And then he came back, delullah, dellulah!'

The story continues on Cherry Chimes!

Together, Anything is possible!

14. BIBLIOGRAPHY

Websites
11v11.com
AFC Bournemouth Archive
BBC Sport website
BBC Radio Solent
Beats and Rhythms FC
Bournemouth Echo Archives
Bournemouth.vitalfootball.co.uk
Burnley Football club
Burnley Express
Buzz – Bournemouth University
Checkdirector.co.uk
Clarets-mad.co.uk
Clubelo.com
Daily Mail
Daily Telegraph
Dorset Echo Archives
ESPN.com
Grimsby Town FC
InbedwithMaradonna.com
Irish Times

ITV
Lancashire Telegraph
Manchester Evening News
Mancity.com
Newsatden
Pendle Today
Revolvy.com
Sheffield Telegraph
SkySports
Sport.bt.com
Sports Gazette
Soccerbase.com
Stats.football.co.uk
Talk Sport
The Bolton News
The Daily Express
The Daily Mirror
The Daily Star
The Independent
The Guardian
The Sack Race
Thesetpieces.com
Transfermarkt.co.uk
Thesouthend.co.uk
Tribalfootball
Wikipedia
Worldfootball.net
YouTube

Books

Crook A, *Match of my life: Twenty-Five Cherries relive their greatest games* 2018

AFC Bournemouth, *Together Anything is Possible* (2016)

Edwards L & Trevelen J, *The Definitive AFC Bournemouth* (Tony Brown, 2003).
Meldrum N, *AFC Bournemouth – The fall and rise* (Worthing, Pitch Publishing 2018)

Nash K, *The Cherries – First Hundred Years AFC Bournemouth 1899- 1999* (Bournemouth, Reed Post 1999)

SkySports, *Football Yearbook 2013-14* (Chatham, Headline Publishing 2013)

Printed in Great Britain
by Amazon

44748221R00219